CAN WE ROCK THE GOSPEL?

CAN WE ROCK THE GOSPEL?

Rock music's impact on worship
and evangelism

John Blanchard and Dan Lucarini

EVANGELICAL PRESS

EVANGELICAL PRESS
Faverdale North, Darlington, DL3 0PH, England

e-mail: sales@evangelicalpress.org

Evangelical Press USA
P. O. Box 825, Webster, New York 14580, USA

e-mail: usa.sales@evangelicalpress.org

web: http://www.evangelicalpress.org

First published 2006

British Library Cataloguing in Publication Data available

ISBN-13   978-0-85234-628-0   ISBN 0-85234-628-X

Printed and bound in the United States of America.

CONTENTS

INTRODUCTION

God loves music!

We say this not because either of us has a vested interest in securing God's backing for our ministries nor because we want to get God onside as a help in promoting some kind of musical enterprise. Our claim rests on the solid foundation of Scripture. Simply put, *God says so!*

There is more than a hint of this when we are told that at the dawn of creation, 'the morning stars sang together' (Job 38:7). This is not meant to be a scientific description of origins, but it surely means *something*. If God uses a musical metaphor in telling us of the wonder and glory of his creation, we can be certain that he has music in his heart. What is more, the created elements themselves are commanded to join in God's worship and the Bible tells of times when 'they break forth into singing' (Isaiah 14:7).

With the whole of creation called to unite in a musical tribute to its Maker, we should expect God's people to be under special obligation to express their praise — and this is what we find, on page after page. 'Sing to him a new song; play skilfully with a shout of joy' (Psalm 33:3) and 'Sing out the honour of his name; make his praise glorious' (Psalm 66:2) are just two of many places at which believers are told to sing to God's glory. As these exhortations come from God's chosen spokesmen we can be sure that their words have his endorsement. Israel's King David goes even further and testifies that music is not only *for* God but *from* God: 'He has put a new song in my mouth — Praise to our God' (Psalm 40:3). Moses sees an even closer link between music and his Maker and cries out, 'The LORD is my strength and song' (Exodus 15:2).

New Testament believers also used music to express their faith. Imprisoned at Philippi, the apostle Paul and Silas are found 'praying and singing hymns to God' (Acts 16:25), while Jesus and his disciples made their way to his betrayal in the Garden of Gethsemane 'when they had sung a hymn' (Matthew 26:30). Elsewhere in the New Testament, Christians are told to express their common faith 'in psalms and hymns and spiritual songs, singing with grace in your hearts to the Lord' (Colossians 3:16). Nor does the theme end here on earth, as the apostle John's visions of heaven included one in which all of God's redeemed people 'sang as it were a new song before the throne' (Revelation 14:3). With all of this data, it is small wonder to find the great reformer Martin Luther saying that anyone who does not see music as a gift from God is 'truly a clod'!

Yet an important question needs to be asked. *Does God endorse music of every kind*, regardless of its structure or features? Put another way, is there any music which does *not* get his seal of approval? Tightening this even further, are there musical forms or ways of using music that violate biblical principles and which Christians should therefore reject? We sincerely believe that there are and that the question takes on an even greater urgency in these days as many influential church leaders and popular Christian musicians have recently claimed that God endorses all kinds of music without distinction. This book is an expression of our convictions and concerns.

In writing it we have drawn heavily on research undertaken for *Pop Goes the Gospel*, first published in 1983, and *Why I left the Contemporary Christian Music Movement*, first published in 2002, as well as on our experience in handling the vast amount of feedback that both titles generated. In spite of their wide circulation, it had not been our intention to add to these titles, but our publishers at Evangelical Press have persuaded us that in the present church scene there is an urgent need to revisit the subject and to pool our research and experience in a new book. This is it.

We are aware that it is likely to be praised by some and pilloried by others; we trust that God will give us grace to cope with both responses. Our sole motive in writing is that God himself will be glorified as Christians of every stripe come to a fuller understanding of his 'good and acceptable and perfect will' (Romans 12:2) and commit themselves to it in unqualified obedience.

JOHN BLANCHARD
Banstead, England

DAN LUCARINI
Denver, USA

July 2006

1.

HOW WE GOT TO WHERE WE ARE

Music is a part of us, and either
ennobles or degrades our behaviour.
(Roman philosopher Boethius)[1]

Over twenty years ago, John Blanchard wrote in the preface to *Pop Goes the Gospel*, 'The use of pop music in evangelism has become a very "hot potato" in recent years ... Pop gospel turns some people on; it switches others off. Some see it as a blessing from heaven; others as a curse from hell ... The time has come to take a calm, balanced, thorough and biblical look at the whole subject of what we might call "entertainment evangelism"... Pop gospel is one of the most important issues facing evangelism in large areas of the world today.'[2]

Pop Goes the Gospel was hailed as an important book and the first of its kind to sell in large numbers across the globe. When it was first published in 1983 the big debate was over the use of rock music for evangelism at crusades, concerts and festivals held outside the local church. It refers several times to the huge Greenbelt festival, a music gathering held annually in the UK at outdoor venues far from the church doors. At the time, only a small minority of churches were actually using rock music in their worship services. The future 'worship wars' were more like border patrol actions, limited only to a few skirmishes at the distant frontier.

Perhaps at this point it would be helpful to define what we mean by 'rock music'. It is a notoriously difficult term to pin down, as can be gathered from the fact that the *All Music Guide* lists no fewer than 187 variations of rock music under twelve headings! In some countries the term 'rock music' has a more or less specific connotation, while in others it is a more generic term. In this book it will almost always be obvious what the speaker or author we are quoting had in mind. For ourselves, the term is meant to cover a wide range of contemporary music linked to its original concept. Our tracing of its development over the years will help our readers to get the picture.

In the 1980s, opponents of 'Christian' rock seemed to many to be rather like the politicians and journalists who write and speak about distant battles from the security of their far-removed cities and comfortable offices, in that they could join the fight without the risk of actually seeing combat. At the same time, conscientious objectors — those who were offended by rock music or opposed it for a variety of reasons — could relax in the knowledge that they did not have to face the fight in their conservative home churches. Rock music was the domain of a small group of churches and outreach organizations and posed no threat to the 'homeland' of the average local congregation.

When challenged, pop gospel music promoters reminded their critics that William Booth used the pop music tunes and styles of his day to reach the down-and-out on the mean streets of England, so they were following an honourable tradition. While their example was not historically accurate, one could hardly question the sincerity of their motive. Even those who did not agree with them and had real issues of biblical conscience probably thought it best to shelter behind the apostle Paul: 'Some indeed preach Christ even from envy and strife, and some also from good will... What then? Only that in every way, whether in pretence or in truth, Christ is preached; and in this I rejoice, yes, and will rejoice' (Philippians 1:15, 18).

Crossing the Rubicon

Now fast-forward fifteen years into the late nineteen-nineties, by which time the scene had changed dramatically. The barbarians, as it were, once so distant a threat on the frontier, had crossed the Rubicon[3] and were now at the gates of the city. Rock music was no longer only an evangelistic tool to be used in order to reach those who would never darken the doors of the local church. Nor was it confined to the realm of personal Christian liberty, allowing people to listen to Christian rock in their private time, with like-minded friends, or at concerts intended for the fans only. Nor was it the sole domain of the few churches that used it for their worship services.

Throughout the nineteen-nineties, rock music entered the sanctuary in a huge way; in many churches, organs and hymn-singing were out, while praise bands and worship teams were in. Rock rode in on the coat tails of successful church growth movements like Willow Creek (a megachurch near Chicago, Illinois, USA, with Bill Hybels as the senior pastor),[4] and The Purpose-Driven Church (which has its roots in Saddleback Church, Lake Forest, California, USA, where Rick Warren is the senior pastor). Scott Thumma, a professor of sociology at Hartford Seminary, reports: 'One of the studies we did found that church growth was strongly related to the use of electric guitars. It's not surprising that megachurches have a full worship band with drums, guitars and an electric keyboard.'[5] His study found that over 93% of churches used electric guitars or bass and drums often or always in their services.[6] Rock music also entered through charismatic influences present in ministries like PromiseKeepers in the USA, the Anglican worship renewal project in the UK, and the Integrity worship music company. The best-seller *Why I Left the Contemporary Christian Music Movement* (published in 2002 by Evangelical Press and written by one of this book's authors) exposed the problems related to this nineteen-nineties invasion.

Many conservative churches who had no association with these movements still allowed rock to enter the church building through the youth group, where loud rock music was tolerated by the church leaders as long as it was kept under wraps in the youth precincts and prevented the young people from abandoning the church.

We know what happened next. By 2006, everything seems to have flipped over. What was once outside is now inside. The minority has attained majority status. Here are some examples of rock's current popularity in worship services.

- A religious news article reported, 'On a recent Sunday at Willow Creek Community Church, a Christian rock band joined by dancing children powered up in the cavernous main hall, their images ablaze on several gigantic screens. Thousands of worshippers from the main floor to the balcony and mezzanine levels were on their feet rocking to a powerful sound system.'[7]
- A staff member at Saddleback Church told an interviewer that it now offers various worship venues: 'Whether it's guitar-driven rock ... or a mix of contemporary songs, every weekend thousands of people worship in the style that best fits their God-given shape.'[8]
- A student in Illinois told a local newspaper that the Rock (a local megachurch) offered her a personal freedom that her regular church does not. 'It's good to be able to worship differently,' said the nineteen-year-old. 'You can worship however you're comfortable worshipping. You can dance around if you want.'[9]

- *MTV News Online* reported in 2005 that Brian Welch (a former member of the rock group Korn) plans to launch a solo career with music about his experiences as a new Christian, and then give the money to charities and to Valley Bible Fellowship's plan to *build 'rock and roll churches' across America*[10] (emphasis added).

Worship band seminars and DVDs are now available to help this new generation of church musicians learn to adjust rock music to the needs of church worship. For example, rockworship.com is a resource and discussion site for worship leaders in churches that offer 'alternative' style services/music, claiming, 'It's all about ... how to create, perform, produce, and lead music that will speak to people in a language they understand.' Also, a recent review in a *Worship Music* newsletter highlighted a DVD that goes beyond the basics into the more specific subject of how to play the keyboards in worship. 'Topics such as voicing and voice leading, *vamps*,[11] simplicity vs busyness, creating melodic motion, modern rhythms and much more. Pianists are notorious for hogging up sonic space and tend to overplay when it comes to playing in a worship band.'[12]

Churches have also added special 'rock' services at different times:

'*Sunday Night Live* is our new Solid Rock Worship on Sunday evenings at 5.30. It's geared toward youth and the music for this service is led by a rock band.'[13]

'At Sacred Revolution (a post-modern-emerging-church-worship-gathering-for-creative-artistic-people) you'll find eclectic rock 'n' roll music...'[14]

There are now worship jobs that specifically require rock music talents.

'Worship Ministry Coordinator Job Responsibilities: Put together a rock worship band to lead worship.'[15]

'First Baptist is seeking an Associate Pastor of Outreach and Worship. An immediate responsibility will be the creation of a new modern worship service targeting unchurched young adults. This service will embrace modern music and technology.'[16]

It gets better (or worse!). Churches without talented rock musicians can now hire a band to mix worship and entertainment.

'The Rock Prophets exist to glorify God through skilful musicianship, anointed performance and heartfelt testimony by leading worship, evangelism and entertainment events to an ever-increasing audience. The band plays for churches and other organizations that are seeking Christian entertainers.'[17]

If a church has neither the home-grown talent nor the funds to hire the Rock Prophets, they can buy *iWorship*, the total worship musical and video experience from Integrity Music, featuring songs from the very best Christian rock bands. One of the authors experienced an *iWorship* demonstration at the 2002 Christian Booksellers Association exposition, and when he asked to whom this was targeted, the salesperson listed small churches as a target and commented that now they could have great music just like the megachurches.

In the contemporary worship music movement, much has been made of the diversity of music styles, yet it seems that the vast majority of contemporary worship music used in churches around the globe is one form or another of rock music. In 1995 Rick Warren, one of Christian rock's most influential cheerleaders, wrote: 'For the first time in history, there exists a universal music style that can be heard in every country of the world. It's called contemporary pop/rock.'[18]

Thousands of praise bands have since taken his advice and made rock music the nearly-universal music style in the global church. One of the authors of this book has received over 1,500 e-mails from readers all over the world who report that in most towns or cities in the USA, UK, Canada, Australia, Brazil, New Zealand, Singapore, Korea, Greece, Germany, France and many other countries you might be hard-pressed to find a reasonably-sized evangelical church that does not have a praise band playing rock music songs in at least one service. Countless other churches are experimenting with it because pastors are afraid to be left behind in the 'gold rush' for growth, or are facing pressure from church members. These men feel driven to conform to the success of the megachurches, which according to Thumma 'have responded creatively to the new needs and interests of people in a new cultural reality.'[19]

Yet we need to qualify the impression that rock music completely dominates our churches. Drawing on national surveys among churchgoers, worship leaders and pastors of Protestant churches, George Barna revealed that nearly half of Protestant churches in the USA still offered at least one service with traditional worship music.[20] According to Barna, there would not seem to be much of a problem.

Problem? What problem?

But why should there *be* a problem? Why not learn to accept rock music as just another style with no negative implications? The authors of this book have talked to and corresponded with many Christians including close friends and family members who see no problem with using rock music in God's service, but accept it as part of God's plan for the church to remain relevant. We have also researched hundreds of books, articles and blogs written by Christian rock musicians, fans and apologists, and found the same general attitude. The following comment by an artist using CCM (Contemporary Christian Music, a catch-all phrase for pop music with Christianized lyrics) is typical: 'I have no problem with any style of music or sound as long as the lyrics are clean. We had some teens do a punk song for offertory one Sunday morning and I thought it was great but there was a lot of backlash from the older generation. I feel you have to be all things to all men that you might win some.'[21]

Some sincerely believe the problem is only with a few judgemental, elder or misguided Christians, and that the victims here are actually the rockers. This is characterized in an excerpt from a recent interview with Bill Gaither, the renowned gospel music composer. The interview was conducted by Kim Jones, member of the Christian rock band Road to Revelation and a columnist for a Catholic publication:

Kim: Something that I encounter much more frequently than I'd like to is people that are [so] very bound by the traditionalism that they point fingers, not just at the music itself, but also at the people that perform it. To me that is so sad because God created all music.

Bill: You know what? You're right! Finger pointing is never, I think, of God. Because I know that Scripture, 'Judgement is mine, saith the Lord.' When we get out of the judgement business and just get into the being business, the being what God wants us to be, it will take care of itself. I get weary of the finger pointing also.

Kim: Yes, sir. It's sad and it doesn't reflect well on Christianity as a whole.[22]

John Schlitt, a member of Petra, one of the first commercially successful Christian rock bands, talks about the evolution of rock as an acceptable genre in Christian circles: 'As far as the doubting Thomases are concerned they are always going to hate anything that is contemporary that gets past the church doors. The difference now is there aren't as many of them that are opposed to rock. They have listened to rock music and can see how it is going to work.'[23]

The same rationale lies behind the argument that Christians should come to accept the dance rave, the latest Christian music craze. A rave is an all-night dance party featuring non-stop techno-dance music, psychedelic lighting and what most mothers would still call 'dirty dancing' — as well as, at least in the secular version, the widespread use of a drug called ecstasy. Many Christian parents and pastors alike wonder whether this can actually be used for God, given the fact that it directly mimics the secular culture. D. J. Casey of the Dance Chapel says, 'I think it's the same sort of thing the Christian rock scene went through when it first started. People were asking if there was really a place for Christian rock because of all the negative connotations surrounding rock music. Now Christian rock bands are commonplace.'[24]

The praises of Christian rock's positive impact on the church are being sung widely, on web sites, blogs, magazines, newsletters and elsewhere. Some enthusiasts claim that teenagers and the Generation Next twenty-somethings are excited about worship now because they can relate to the alternative rock music style. Others rejoice that Baby Boomers can use their Sixties and Seventies classic rock talents to bring a worship offering to God. There is talk about the key role that rock music has played in the worship renewal movement, particularly in the UK.

Trusted Bible preachers, evangelists and other respected Christian leaders have also been busy assuring us from the pulpit or from their media platforms that there is nothing wrong with rock music in the church. They do their best to see that their church or ministry has the best top-notch rock, and they like to associate with 'cool' Christian rock musicians. Some of these same leaders once spoke out against rock music, but now they say they have grown and can accept it as a God-given vehicle for worship and evangelism.

Young Christians are by and large oblivious to the issues involved. Few churches, evangelists or parachurch ministries preach or teach any longer that rock music is worldly, evil and something to be avoided. Most Christians under the age of twenty-five were raised to believe that music itself is amoral and neutral, that all music styles are acceptable to God for worship, and that the only thing that matters is the attitude of one's heart. The authors regularly receive letters like these from young people:

'I fail to see the link between the rock beat and the sexuality and other sins that go along with it. Part of this could be due to my experience growing up. I was raised in a Christian household. When I hear a praise song with a rock beat, I don't think about things that secular rock music brings to mind.'

'I am of a generation that has always had "cool Christian music" so rock honestly does not carry a negative stigma with it for me. I love my Matt Redman, Chris Tomlin, Tim Hughes, Casting Crowns, Third Day, Rebecca St James, Kutless, Jars of Clay, David Crowder, MercyMe, Audio Adrenaline, Relient K, Jeremy Camp, etc. Sometimes I even forget that secular music exists!'

Who is teaching this generation about music and worship, and where are they being taught? Ken Steorts, guitarist of the popular Christian rock band Skillet, was asked in an interview how important he thought it was for fans of Christian music to attend Christian concerts. He replied, 'Christian concerts ... are essential to Christians. These are the artists that can affect, change, encourage, and move us, and say all we want to say and *teach us how to worship*'[25] (emphasis added).

Even conservative churchmen who favour sacred hymn-singing traditions have concluded that music style is at best a tertiary issue in the church and not worthy of much discussion.[26] Surely we should all accept that one's choice of music style is purely a matter of personal preference, and learn to be passively tolerant when other Christians make different choices to ours?

Feedback

The evidence points in a very different direction. Rock music is a stumbling block and a scandal to many Christians today and it is dividing the church. Over the past three years, the authors have received literally thousands of e-mails, letters and phone calls from discouraged and offended believers. They tell similar stories to the ones you will encounter over the next few pages. We ask you to read them through carefully and to treat these testimonies with the same integrity with which they are given.

'I was shocked to walk into the sanctuary of my Christian Reformed church one Sunday morning and find the communion table shoved off to the back corner of the platform and replaced by a drum set directly under the cross and a microphone front and centre — all illuminated by coloured stage lights. The problem as I saw it was not the arrangement of the furniture *per se* — but rather what this communicated, intentionally or not, about whom and what the church valued and focused on in worship. In other words, who *was* our god? I feel somewhat like Martin Luther: "Here I stand. I can do no other. So help me God." I do not want to leave the church but I doubt that I can in good conscience continue to worship there long term if changes are not made.'

(A Bible study leader)

'A number of years back we attended an Easter service in a Baptist church. The pastor was quite involved in missions and the theme was "Christ died for all and rose for all". For the end of the service he asked someone from Africa to play the drums. It seemed a bit jolting to me, but it absolutely devastated my Cuban husband and ruined the whole service for him. He immediately recognized it as a rhythm used in Cuba to bring in the spirits in a seance. He remembers nights when this would play in a nearby home for hours on end.'

(A former missionary
who grew up on a Caribbean island)

'We had a 75th anniversary service at our Methodist church led by a "Praise and Worship Team". I was appalled. Members of the praise band looked exactly like the rock musicians my former husband used to record. The seductive dress of the women mimicked the styles worn by contemporary rock stars. There was a lot of prancing and dancing and performing just like at a rock show. This was not a "worship service", but rather a "rock show with somewhat sacred words". The music was deafeningly loud due to the massive sound system. After 15 minutes, I left because my ears were hurting from the high decibel level of the music. Others walked out as well.'

(A classically trained musician with a master's degree and
involved in church music from her very early years)

'I joined a rock band as a drummer in East Texas and played classic rock from the 1970s. I was indulging in all the sins of the flesh. I finally left this lifestyle and like the prodigal son I returned to the Lord. He showed me how the devil was using this music to destroy people. But to my amazement, the same rock music followed me back into the church. I was alarmed but as hard as I tried, I could not seem to convince others of the dangers of "Christianizing" the devil's music. I thought the church had learned from history the danger of mixing pagan music or anything else not pertaining to God.'

(A former rock drummer)

'I attended a service [in a large megachurch] ... last year that made me uncomfortable. There were strobe lights twirling with artificial smoke swirling inside the lights. And many camera close-ups of guitarists and the drummer were projected onto a video screen. I have to say that it left me somewhat cold. It really seemed like a format for the worship leader to show his talent more than anything.'

(A Presbyterian minister)

'I am a member of the Greek Free Evangelical Churches. Before I met Christ as personal Saviour, I was a fan of heavy metal music (AC/DC, Queen, Deep Purple and so on). The first thing that God did in my heart was to set me free from this kind of music. However, it is so sad to see how the devil manages to persuade the believers to use this same music in the Lord's House!'

(A deacon at an evangelical church in Greece)

'Last year I visited a Baptist church where I had once been the organist. I had to leave the service. It was "rock concert" city. The "blended service" consisted of loud, boisterous music with slamming drums and screeching guitars. A few traditional hymns were thrown in for the benefit of the few senior citizens who could stand the rock music.'

(A long-time organist)

'At ... Chapel, the worship was awful. It was like pure noise. The drums were so loud that I couldn't hear the praise team sing. And the bass was really loud too. It was like going to a rock concert. And the songs they picked were not worshipful, to say the least. They troubled my spirit.'

(A thirty-one-year-old who has since left that church)

'I'm in what was until a few years ago a very conservative 200-year-old Presbyterian church. Our new pastor has begun a campaign to break down people's resistance to new worship music by levelling charges in sermons such as "If you care about tradition or traditional worship, you're living in sin." How horribly wrong and hurtful! I am regularly in the cross hairs, and am praying for deliverance from this situation, by God's grace. It is unsustainable over the long haul, without completely compromising what I believe God's Word clearly teaches about how he wants to be worshipped.'

(A Presbyterian church's music minister)

'It is sad that people will say that it is "my way or the highway" when it comes to CCM in our church. Someone this week left a handwritten note in the front of my personal hymnal saying "Ichabod — the glory has departed" because of the traditional form of worship here. How sad. These people are just as closed-minded as they accuse traditionalists of being.'

(Pastor of a 300-year-old American Baptist church)

'The loudness of the music is unjustified. There is an old saying, that when a pastor has nothing to say, he needs to yell louder and pound the pulpit. The noise alienates the older people. Their ears cannot tolerate the sound. I know many people, including my own parents, godly people, who have stopped going to church for the simple reason that the loudness of the music is intolerable to their ears. And the message is: "Young people matter ... you don't."'

(Former president of an international
Christian broadcasting ministry)

'At one Christian camp the programme director got up on stage before all of the campers and started dancing and singing, "Do a little dance, make a little love, get down tonight" [from a hit song in the 1970s by K.C. and the Sunshine Band].' He was oblivious to the fact that this was outrageous. He also played secular rock during activities, unaware that it was even wrong. The songs, all of which I knew from my past, were not all "neutral" in their message — some were just outright ungodly.'

(An evangelist and Christian camp speaker)

'I was the music teacher in the Christian school and was teaching a course on the history of American music that culminated with what's wrong with rock music. I held that there is no such thing as "Christian" rock — because if it's Christian, it's not rock, and if it is rock, it is not Christian. I had to resign and leave my teaching position because the new Music Pastor at the church was teaching music is amoral and all music is good, etc. He called me in and explained that I would have to change my beliefs and teachings, to which I said no and left the school.'

(A long-time school teacher)

'When I went into the youth building for the first time, I was nearly blown back out of the doors by the rock music that they regularly performed. I felt like I was having a cardiac arrest! But, what really struck me was that their worship area (lights dimmed, band up front, techies [technicians] in the back, etc.) was just like the bars in college where I had spent time so long ago. The only exception was that there was no booze or glittering disco ball on the ceiling. Whew. It was the pits.'

(A Sunday school teacher, high school science teacher
and self-professed former party girl)

'I am directing Vacation Bible School. Our motto this year is 1 Corinthians 6:19: "Your body is the temple of the Lord, therefore glorify God with your body." Today was the turn for our ears. I talked about things that go into our ears, and one thing I talked about was rock music. I mentioned the group

KISS. One parent called this evening — very irate. She was most upset that I was voicing my opinions to innocent children. She said I could talk to them about God etc. but not my "opinions" about music.'

(From a Mennonite church in North America)

'It breaks my heart to watch our people cover their ears and walk out, because the music is too loud. I hear people say, "I don't want to go into the sanctuary and hear that rock and roll music." What do we do? We don't want to leave the Nazarene church, but we must.'

(A senior member of a Nazarene church)

'We were beginning to wonder if we were all alone in our frustration with our community's churches. We have been searching for over a year and are appalled at what churches are offering as worship to God. At some churches we had our eardrums shattered; at others we were embarrassed trying to go along with inappropriate congregational music. It appears that worship today has boiled down to singing a group of pop songs. There are no longer any Scripture readings, prayers, quiet meditation, confession of sins, and affirmation of faith ... things that are part of true worship.'

(An elderly church couple)

'The Women's Missionary Union leader showed a video that emphasized that heaven is a big rock party, and she played some loud and chaotic rock music to show the ladies how wonderful heaven will be. One lady came to her afterwards in private and said that she did not think heaven would be a big rock party, and the leader replied, "You have your opinion and I have mine. Do you really think that we would just be angels with wings, flying all around, strumming on harps all the time?" "No," she answered, "I only believe what the Bible says about heaven." The leader said as she walked away, "Well, if you don't like it, then don't watch it!" The movie was shown that Wednesday night to the whole congregation.'

(A member of a Southern Baptist church)

'We are a GARBC church [General Association of Regular Baptist Churches] with an AWANA program [a popular Bible club for children]. Have you seen their new programs? The Bible memory tapes are accompanied by pure rock music and the local annual leader training program is a CCM service complete with video screen and a sound system to shake the walls and blow your eardrums, just like the rock concerts we used to attend.'

(Long-time AWANA leaders in a Baptist church)

'The drums this morning pretty much drowned out the other music. He's behind plexiglas which just means they turn up the volume louder. I have gone to this church just about all my life. I feel so badly that the Assemblies of God have lowered their standards to this type of music. But my husband is with the Gideons and speaks in many different types of churches and I must admit that I dread having to go to any church with him because the music is mostly contemporary there too. I just can't get myself to go to Sunday evening service because it is all contemporary. I went one evening because communion was going to be served in the evening service. But a guitar and the drums were the music for it.'

(A lifelong member of an Assembly of God church)

'We should have known to leave when we saw the stage area with a trap set up there, but I don't know what we were thinking — maybe they wouldn't use it on Sunday morning? When the deafening noise began, I turned to my husband and said I couldn't stay. I had to get out of there, whether anybody else did or not. That put him in a difficult situation because we were visiting with his brother-in-law. He looked over to our teenagers (ages 15, 17 and 19) and he could tell they were visibly disturbed. We made the decision to leave that church, even though it would look like a very judgemental statement and we knew our relatives would take it wrong. As we left the church building, a woman ran after us and asked us what was the matter. My husband, in a very controlled but deliberate way, told her that what was taking place in that building was displeasing to our God.'

(A Christian family visiting relatives)

We could fill hundreds of pages with similar stories from Christians who are genuinely hurting — spiritually, physically and emotionally — because of rock music in the church. The problem is very real and the issue simply cannot be swept under the carpet, whatever the motive for doing so. Rock music is dividing the church.

Love it or leave it?

Then what should Christians do when they find that rock music has taken over? Should they simply walk out? Should pastors simply accept that this will happen? Rick Warren discusses that option in his book *The Purpose-Driven Church*, a training manual on how to do church differently. We must take Warren seriously because his Pastors.com web site boasts that over 20,000 churches, representing eighty different denominations and a dozen countries, have participated in his '40 Days of Purpose' programme. More than 320,000 pastors and church leaders from over 120 countries have attended Purpose-Driven Church seminars in eighteen languages, and tens of thousands of churches have adopted the PDC strategy.[27]

We should note that when Warren talks about music style, his personal preference seems to be classic rock such as Jimi

Hendrix[28] and he enthusiastically exports Saddleback Church rock music around the globe as part of his '40 Days of Purpose' videos. Warren admits that a church will inevitably lose members over music changes — but what does he counsel pastors to do? 'Once you have decided on the style of music you're going to use in worship, you have set the direction of your church in far more ways than you realize. It will determine the kind of people you attract, the kind of people you keep, and *the kind of people you lose*'[29] (emphasis added).

Putting aside for a moment the absurd notion of a Christian shepherd counselling 320,000 other shepherds that it is acceptable to drive some sheep out of the fold over a music style, we need to realize that Warren appears to contradict himself, as he also teaches that God loves all styles of music because he invented them.[30]

This 'love it or leave it' option may have seemed viable some years ago in the United States, and American Christians are historically notorious for their church-hopping ways, often on very slender pretences. Perhaps this can be explained by the freedom of worship rights enshrined in the nation's Constitution and the lack of a strong state church. That freedom tended to paper over disputes on music styles (and other issues) and there was little or no confrontation because it was so easy to leave and find another church. But the situation is vastly different today. Many Christians are finding they have little option but to grit their teeth through rock-saturated services, arrive after the music for the preaching time, or stay home and watch religious television where at least they can mute the sound when they wish.

If you are one of the 'conscientious objectors' to Christian rock music, it is more and more difficult to find a church where you will not be confronted with it. You will know that many churches advertise 'blended' services, but even the blend is often dominated by rock. Other churches hold multiple services, usually including one labelled 'traditional' for the 'golden oldies'. There are also many evangelical churches who would not think of rocking out in the main worship service, yet parents are encouraged to send their teenagers to a Sunday school class or youth group that includes a rock band, and dispatch their small children to a Children's Church that uses beginners' rock music.

Outside church buildings, the ubiquitous Contemporary Christian Music industry is hard at work to promote its message and method in bookstores, on radio and television, and on the Internet. One of the authors recently stayed at a hotel in Minneapolis which had a video kiosk in the lobby showing advertisements for local attractions and facilities such as restaurants, shopping malls, theme parks and churches. One video from a local megachurch featured a praise band playing classic rock music and the pastor boasting, 'We have a rippin' band — I think you'll really like it!' It is becoming increasingly difficult to avoid the sound, or the issues it raises.

Identity parade

In the course of our research this statement on the dust jacket of George Barna's new book *Revolution* caught our attention: 'Millions of committed Christ followers, looking for more of God, have stopped attending churches on Sunday mornings. Why are they leaving? Where are they going? And what does this mean for the future of the church?'

Our first thought was that Barna had in mind Christians leaving their churches because they could no longer cope with the rock, but when we read further into the book we quickly realized we were wrong. He was not talking about Christians who were 'offended out' of their churches by rock music, but about Christians who could not get *enough of* passionate rock worship in their own local church and had to seek it in outside events! Midway through the book he writes, 'Not associated with a specific church or denomination, these [worship] gatherings feature ... Chris Tomlin, David Crowder, Matt Redman ... playing extended sets of worship music for audiences who had no prior connection to each other. The events are designed to help people connect with God through an intense worship experience.'[31]

Be that as it may, we are convinced that Christian rock music's conscientious objectors are to be found in greater numbers than is generally supposed. They fall into two main categories that we could label 'the offended' and 'the prophets'. To the 'offended', rock music in the church is a stumbling block and a scandal, and they often feel powerless and defeated in its presence. The 'prophets', on the other hand, strongly object to rock music in principle, seeing it as a sinful and worldly activity that clashes with biblical principles and therefore believing that such music should be rejected out of hand.

The combined sales of *Pop Goes the Gospel* and *Why I Left the Contemporary Christian Music Movement* give us an indication of the size of the resistance to the rock invasion, and these are backed up by the mountain of correspondence that we have received in the past three years from people dismayed at current trends. In addition, we also know of hundreds of pastors, missionaries and parachurch organization leaders who in turn could well represent literally millions of Christians in many countries. Both authors also speak at numerous conferences, churches and seminars around the globe and are guests on radio and television broadcasts with listeners and viewers who represent many more like-minded Christians. Barna's research may indicate one part of reality, but there are also countless churches all around the world that still use non-rock music styles and together represent untold millions of believers. Yet although the numbers are meaningful and hard to ignore, they should not be seen as the most important indicator, and we have never put much stock in Gallup-style polling when it comes to spiritual matters.

It is also fashionable among some Christians to label the typical Christian rock objector as a mean-spirited fundamentalist. Visit a Christian rock chat room or one of the web sites devoted to Christian rock, and it will not be long before you encounter this stereotype, but it needs to be exploded. The fact is that the objectors are a surprisingly diverse group. We have been encouraged by the volume of support we have received from pastors, musicians and laypeople from within every major Christian religious group, all reporting the same problem with rock music in their circles.

It is true that many objectors are at what has been called 'the metallic age' (silver in their hair, gold in their teeth and lead in their boots!). They belong to churches they have attended for many years but which have now changed music styles. Many of these 'senior saints' would find it very difficult to leave for health reasons, lack of mobility or just a lack of energy to start all over again. So they sit and suffer the music silently, sometimes enduring unkind jokes about being the pillars of the church that 'just hold things up'! But objections to rock music are not confined to the senior age group. The protesters range across all age groups, with a surprising number under forty years of age, a fact that challenges another persistent stereotype painting objection to rock worship as nothing more than a generational 'taste' issue.

There is also diversity among their comments, though as far as rock music in God's service is concerned the following themes seem to be consistent:

- Worldliness
- Irreverence
- Strong association with the deeds of darkness
- Sensuality
- The use of rock as a mystical new worship experience.

These countless conscientious objectors include many who attend contemporary churches featuring rock worship but are now ready to leave and are looking for churches without it. For some, rock worship was their home church's norm when they came to faith, but having grown in Christ they find this fails to meet their needs and are therefore searching for alternatives.

Fuel to the fire?

The authors do not wish to add more fuel to the 'worship wars' fire, but we feel deeply for these brothers and sisters in Christ, who are like wounded refugees from a civil war. The vast majority of them are *not* the flamethrowers and grenade launchers from the anti-rock side; there are actually very few of those. They are simply caught in the crossfire. They are not looking for a fight, and feel unable to mount a strong defence. Yet their voices deserve to be heard, their consciences deserve to be protected, and they deserve to worship in peace without continual offence.

Pop Goes the Gospel exposed and confronted the key issues over the use of rock music in evangelism. Using some of the same research, this book will also confront the use of rock music in the church and show why its adoption into God's service causes painful consequences to Christians all over the world. We want to represent those who feel they are without a voice, those shouted down from the pulpit or stage, or quietly marginalized by church leaders — 'wounded butterflies', as Dan and Judy Lucarini called them in *Why I Left the Contemporary Christian Music Movement.*

We are not the only ones aware of this problem. Some within the contemporary worship movement have also seen the unintended consequences of adopting the rock music style and are working to sensitize their peers to the issues. In a 2004 letter

to one of the authors, an internationally known and widely respected worship leader and musician admitted, 'While I think
there are many ways God has used the worship phenomenon to
bless the church, I have increasing concerns about how elements
of the rock culture affect our understanding of how we worship
God as a church.'[32] We invite other contemporary worship leaders with similar reservations to read this book and understand
more about how the 'other side' thinks. It is our desire to break
that terrible cycle of one side judging the other. But we also understand the biblical principle that there can be no lasting peace
without confession, repentance and attempts at restitution.

The authors make no secret of the fact that we count ourselves
among those who are offended by rock music in God's service
and are truly perplexed that so many other Christians go to
such great lengths to defend their use of it in both worship and
evangelism. We are also concerned at the way in which some
leaders, from their positions of power within the church, have
forced it upon the rest of us.

The stumbling block

Writing about relationships within the Christian church, the
apostle Paul gives this counsel: 'Therefore let us not judge one
another anymore, but rather resolve this, not to put a stumbling
block or a cause to fall in our brother's way' (Romans 14:13).
Our aim in this book is to show how and why for many believers
rock music is a stumbling block, causing many to fall and suffer
pain or feel outrage.

Some who read this book will come from ministry positions
that promote rock music and may not even be aware that they
are offending not only members of their own church but many
others outside through the influence of the Internet. Our hope
is that what they read here will serve as a wake-up call.

We also know from experience that many more ministers and leaders are well aware of this stumbling block, yet are virtually in denial, refusing to take any action and at times even blaming offended Christians for causing the problem. Fully aware that the words also apply to us, we believe that the warning contained in Matthew 5:23-24 may be relevant: 'Therefore if you bring your gift to the altar, and there remember that your brother has something against you, leave your gift there before the altar, and go your way. First be reconciled to your brother, and then come and offer your gift.'

Commenting on this passage, a contemporary Christian teacher points out: 'The altar was a place for burning sacrifices as a sweet savour to God. Reconciliation is putting out the stench of bitter fires so God can enjoy the aroma of our worship. God is so concerned about reconciliation that He wants us to interrupt our worship of Him in order to restore fellowship with an offended brother.'[33]

Albert Barnes, a nineteenth-century Presbyterian minister and theologian, made the implications clear: 'The worship of God will not be acceptable, however well performed externally, until we are at peace with those that we have injured. He that comes to worship his Maker while at war with his brethren is a hypocritical worshipper, and must meet with God's displeasure. It is our duty to seek reconciliation with others when we have injured them. This should be done before we attempt to worship God. This is often the reason why God does not accept our offerings, and we go empty away from our devotions.'[34]

Yet even with this in mind there are those who would ask, 'Why another book on contemporary Christian worship? Are there not enough already? Will you not be adding more fuel to the fires and creating even greater divisions?' These are perfectly fair questions, but we believe that four major problems justify the book you are now reading.

1. *Widespread ignorance in the church about rock music and the problems it has caused.* We receive endless feedback from readers saying they are shocked to realize this is still an issue, one they thought was settled years ago. We also interact with many young Christians who are ignorant of rock music's history and heritage. We will seek to address these issues.

2. *Biblical illiteracy on the subject of worship.* Many Christians are learning how to worship from the teachings of men and women, rather than learning from the Word of God. They are led to believe that mixing the right 'holy words' into a rock music atmosphere can somehow produce the presence of God and that the resultant 'goose-bump' experience equates to worship. They are spoon-fed lumps of questionable worship music theology from the music industry, its rock stars and the preachers who support them. The worship of God is a serious matter, and there simply cannot be enough books written to correct erroneous teaching about it.

3. *New and controversial teachings about rock music are taking hold in the church.* The teaching that music is amoral and neutral was first introduced by the Christian music industry starting in the late nineteen-sixties, when influential music leaders, artists and even some preachers insisted that we can use any music style in our worship. Yet in fact the 'any style' argument was offered to defend the introduction of one style — rock music. Since that time, this teaching has been widely reinforced and expanded by pop preachers, rock musicians and other influential leaders. Christians today are now taught that God himself invented all music styles, so that rock music should not be a problem. This teaching needs to be challenged.

4. *Incorrect assumptions about those who object to rock.* It is common among some to label the Christian rock objector with a negative stereotype. Yet, as we have noted, we have evidence of a wide diversity of ages, denominations, cultures and even musical preferences among those offended by rock music. Incorrect assumptions have also been made about the reasons why some Christians object to it, limiting these to matters of cultural upbringing or personal taste. We will show that this is not the case and will look at the deeper and more serious concerns at play here.

We do not for a moment believe that rock music is the *biggest* problem facing the church today, but who can deny the disproportional importance that it has been given in many churches, or the widespread impact this has had on the lives of countless believers? Nor can there be any doubt that music represents the language and the style of a church, in a non-verbal way speaking volumes about the church's attitude towards pop culture and entertainment values. Music is often the sharp tip of the church growth movement spear and there can be no denying its importance there. When asked what one thing he would do differently if he could start his church all over again, here is what Rick Warren had to say: 'From the first day of the new church I'd put more energy and money into a first-class music ministry that matched our target. In the first years of Saddleback, I made the mistake of underestimating the power of music so I minimized the use of music in our services. I regret that now.'[35]

It is against this background that we believe this book to be relevant. We admit that many Christians who agree with us have not always been gracious in presenting their grievances. Some have laced their criticism with gossip and innuendo, while others have 'played the man instead of the ball', attacking fellow Christians instead of the choices they have made. Still others have not grounded their arguments on biblical foundations, allowing passion to override principle. We will earnestly seek to avoid all of these errors as we explore the roots of rock music, its impact on our secular and Christian cultures, the development of Christian rock, and key concerns about using rock in God's service. Many of the sources we will quote come from the time-slot taking in the nineteen-fifties to the nineteen-eighties, but we ask our readers not to dismiss these particular data as being 'yesterday'. There is now a fifty-year history between rock and the church and close examination shows there is much to learn from the recent past. For all its variety of expression, rock has changed comparatively little. To translate the famous French saying, 'The more things change the more they remain the same!'

In the following pages we will try to present a soundly-based case in a firm but gracious manner, trusting that for all of their weaknesses, God will graciously use our efforts to open the eyes of those who do not understand why rock music in the church offends so many and to encourage faithful and godly believers who are in one way or another offended by its use.

2.
A SLICE OF HISTORY

Rock music really is *the universal language!*

(Rock musician Eddie Van Halen)[1]

We live in a world that is constantly being massaged by music. It seems to be everywhere. Background music fills the air in supermarkets and department stores, warehouses, factories, car showrooms, restaurants — even some dentists' waiting rooms! Travel by ship, and it is piped into every room; go by airplane, and it is available on multi-channel headsets. Escape all of that, get home and settle down to watch television — it is there again, saturating everything from commercials to soap operas. Decide to watch nothing except the news, and you are not allowed to see the headlines until you have heard the music. Spin the tuner on your radio and you will discover channels devoted almost entirely to music of one kind or another. Go online, and web site home pages will automatically load a song into your PC speakers.

Music's penetration into our modern society is nothing short of a phenomenon, something that has a profoundly significant impact on the lives of millions of people around the world. If this is true of music in general, it is especially true of what is loosely called 'rock music' — the term is imprecise as we will see in the next chapter — which has such a staggering impact on the lives of young people in particular.

In the beginning...?

In his book *Summer in the City*, Malcolm Doney said, 'Rock music is not simply another branch of popular culture. It has shown itself to be perhaps the most significant art form to emerge this century.'[2] What is more, he sees its importance as going far beyond music; he calls it 'a gauge of the shifts in young people's attitudes towards sex, authority, taste, their contemporaries and ethics.'[3]

If these statements are even half true, rock music is something of great significance that has 'happened' during the lifetime of everyone in the world who is less than fifty-five years of age. But did it just 'happen'? We cannot begin to understand rock music until we discover something of its beginnings and, as with so many things, that is easier said than done.

Yet some people have no problem doing so. They would say that all rock music stems directly from the devil, and that its journey can be traced very simply — from hell to the African jungle, from the African jungle to America, and then, on twentieth-century airwaves, from America to the rest of the world. But that is neither factual nor fair. Blanket condemnation of the whole of today's rock scene by condensing its history into one searing sentence deadens discussion, but it hardly helps to arrive at the truth.

The fact is that rock draws from several streams. It is a complex Mississippi of music, with many different tributaries flowing into the vast river of sound we are now hearing, and it is very difficult to trace all of those tributaries back to their sources.

Roots

Even if we do not buy the 'All rock is African jungle music' line, there can be no serious doubt that the roots of rock do run back into the West African slave culture of the fifteenth century, which was eventually carried to the West Indies and on to the southern part of what we now know as the United States of America. After his visit to Africa, former Grateful Dead percussionist Mickey Hart recounted his personal epiphany about rock's rhythmic heritage: 'It was my first exposure to the mother rhythms from West Africa that later mutated into my tradition becoming rock 'n' roll.'[4] Best known for fronting the new wave group Talking Heads, David Byrne's world music experiences led him to tell *Rolling Stone* magazine that voodoo[5] sounds 'are a big part of where our popular music comes from... Rock 'n' roll comes from those traditions.'[6]

Music played a very important role in the lives of the slaves, enabling them to express their emotions in terms of their own traditional culture rather than in those dictated by their grim conditions. Yet eventually they began to assimilate some of the other musical values with which they were surrounded — ballads from Elizabethan England, quadrilles from France, traditional Spanish dances which were particularly popular in Louisiana, and, of course, the country music that was already becoming 'American' in its own right. Primitive, home-made instruments were added to the rich a cappella vocal tradition of the 'spirituals', then later replaced by the clarinet, trumpet, cornet and trombone, with the piano, guitar, banjo, double-bass and drums eventually forming the 'rhythm section'.

In the development of all musical forms, there is a mixture of assimilation and innovation and the same was true in the development of rock music. Slowly, distinctive styles began to emerge and to spread, and this continued right through the time

41

of the slaves' emancipation in 1865 and on into the twentieth century itself. Blues (slow, gritty and sad), rhythm and blues (more
heavily accented), rag-time (strongly syncopated), jazz (lots of
improvisation) and gospel (adaptation of hymn tunes) — one
trend led to another. When the Chicago church described as
'the birthplace of gospel music' burned to the ground in January
2006 the media reported that this was where Thomas Dorsey —
considered the father of gospel music and known best today for
his song 'Take My Hand, Precious Lord' — perfected his mixture
of 'the raw soulfulness of the blues with the sacred music of his
youth and that other churches around the country thought his
music was too secular'.[7]

In this historical development nothing was entirely new.
Every emerging style borrowed something from the past and
reflected something of the present, mirroring its moods and
expressing them in popular form. Steve Lawhead summarizes
it by saying that these developing musical styles 'were formed
in the give-and-take of many cultural backgrounds (German,
Czech, French, Irish, English and others) over many years'[8] and
adds, 'Even the music of Africa did not originate spontaneously
on its own. It was shaped by its contact with Europe, Asia and
the Middle East.'[9]

Not that dispersing the roots of rock sanctifies it. The original
blues singers rejected the Christian faith as part of a hostile
white culture, and placed a heavy emphasis on 'the pleasure of
this world, particularly the enjoyment of illicit sex... Heaven, if it
existed, was to be peopled with dancing girls.'[10] Rod Gruver said
that the blues poets insisted that 'no other love can compare
with the love that comes either before or outside marriage.'[11]

These examples alone serve to remind us of one simple fact
— that in all cultures we must expect to find an underlying trend
of values that are not just sub-Christian but anti-Christian. Man
is fallen, and his fallenness comes to the surface in every age,
in every country and in every part of his culture. It is all part of

what the Bible means when it says, 'All have sinned and *fall short* of the glory of God' (Romans 3:23) and our italics emphasize the fact that man's fallenness is a continuing reality.

Haley's Comets

Popular music after the end of World War II was a tired hangover from what went before — romantic, sentimental and predictable. But by the early nineteen-fifties the new generation of American teenager was discovering other sounds — updated versions of rhythm and blues (R&B), in which 'the vocals were rough and uncompromising, the lyrics personal and explicit'.[12] Rock 'n' roll emerged from America in the nineteen-fifties, though elements of it can be heard in rhythm and blues records as far back as the nineteen-twenties. Early rock 'n' roll combined elements of blues, boogie woogie, jazz and R&B, and was also influenced by the honky-tonk wing of country music, traditional Appalachian folk music, and even gospel music.

The music was written and performed primarily by black R&B musicians like Big Joe Turner, but soon white country and western groups began to cover the tunes and create 'rockabilly' music, the fusion of R&B with honky-tonk. Leading the way was a middle-aged band called Bill Haley and the Comets. They would hardly have been typecast as revolutionaries, but by the time they had recorded 'Shake, rattle and roll' (toning down the words), 'Crazy, man, crazy' (the first white rock 'n' roll record to hit the charts) and 'Rock around the clock' (which eventually sold fifteen million copies as a single), popular music had been catapulted into a new era. Big Joe Turner's original 'Shake, rattle and roll' was an indecent tale of adulterous love, but the Comets transformed it into a bouncy teen dance number with ambiguous lyrics — an example that would be repeated over and over again in the early days of rock 'n' roll, and then copied many years later by Christian musicians who thought a change of lyrics was all that was needed to 'tame' rock and roll.

Elvis

What was now needed was the man to match the music, someone young, raw, mean and exciting. He arrived in the form of a one-time choirboy called Elvis Presley. From the moment he hit the headlines Presley was worshipped by some and hated by others. To his millions of fans he was 'the King', to others he was not far short of the personification of everything evil. He appeared arrogant, sensuous and obscene. He was said to consult with a psychic in Colorado, and to be heavily into drugs. One of his bodyguards claimed that the rock 'n' roll idol's buttocks were 'so punctured with needle marks that there was hardly room left for an injection'.[13] When he died in 1977 at the age of forty-two, 'Elvis the Pelvis' had earned 4.3 billion dollars from a career which remains without parallel in the history of popular music.

The lads from Liverpool

Elvis opened the floodgates for hundreds of imitators and followers in the same raw, aggressive, sensual style, yet surprisingly the trend did not last very long. By the end of the nineteen-fifties rock 'n' roll was disconnected and no longer dominant, its place on centre stage taken by something much more generally acceptable — folk music. Folk was almost 'thinking man's music' compared to rock 'n' roll. It spoke about serious political issues and it was the perfect vehicle for the protest songs of people like Joan Baez and the legendary Bob Dylan. It was quieter, with the acoustic guitar taking the place of the electric guitar with its stacks of speakers to amplify the sound. But Dylan's 1963 release of the album *The Times They are A-Changin'* brought the passion and poetry of folk ever closer to rock.

Bands from England soon began to dominate the rock 'n' roll world. They started by covering standard American tunes by artists like Sam Cooke, Chuck Berry, Ray Charles and Bo Diddley, adding their own industrial-class grit to tunes like 'Twist and Shout'. Soon they produced their own songs and the masses loved it. In 1964 the Beatles led the British rock music invasion of America. However tame their music may sound to many people today, the Fabulous Four hit the music scene like a runaway bulldozer. Their sound was described as 'fresh, new and inventive'[14] — but to others it was outrageous, irreverent and dangerous. What is certain is that the Beatles' sound was sensationally popular, leading John Lennon to make his now infamous statement that the Beatles were more popular than Jesus Christ. As Doney commented, 'The Beatles became more than hugely famous, they became cosmic.'[15]

The Beatles' brand of music was generally less abrasive and raw-edged than was usually the case with nineteen-fifties-style rock 'n' roll and they were the major influence in the need to coin a new phrase that would embrace the widening range of Beatles-inspired sound. 'Rock' became the post-Beatle word for all kinds of contemporary popular music — and serves the same purpose today, even though that can be misleading at times.

Perhaps as a reaction to the success of the British invasion and its threat to folk music, Dylan soon began to use amplified instruments and a rock beat, most famously in his performance at the 1965 Newport Jazz Festival and later that summer with the release of the very rocky 'Like a Rolling Stone'. From that time on, he had a powerful influence on all rock music styles, particularly on today's alternative acoustic guitar-driven rock.

The Stones and the darker side

The hippie counterculture, largely a reaction to the Vietnam War in the latter part of the nineteen-sixties, adopted rock 'n' roll as their music. The Beatles' *Sergeant Pepper's Lonely Hearts Club Band* album became 'the anthem of the hip culture'. In the United States, psychedelic rock featuring long jams and distorted electronic sounds emerged out of the drug scene, with Jimi Hendrix, Jefferson Airplane, Iron Butterfly and Grateful Dead among the leading bands. Pink Floyd sprang from British psychedelia, and later became a very successful progressive rock band.

Then came the gigantic outdoor festivals. The mother of them all was Woodstock (New York) which was attended by 500,000 rock fans in August 1969 and has been described as 'three days of dope, sex and music'.[16] Soon afterwards came Altamont, a music festival at a raceway near San Francisco, where the hippie dream turned to ashes. Three fans died of drugs, and one was stabbed and beaten to death in front of the stage by members of the Hell's Angels motorcycle club while the band played on. The band playing on was The Rolling Stones.

The Stones' image was clear, but hardly clean. Nik Cohn said, 'They were mean and nasty ... and they beat out the toughest, crudest, most offensive noise any English band had ever made'.[17] Derek Jewell agreed: 'They projected the harshest, nastiest, sweaty-sexiest and most pointedly offensive musical image yet to frighten all law-abiding Britons with daughters under twenty-one out of their minds'.[18] Drugs, promiscuity and occultism have all been part of the Stones' package — and their influence has been enormous even into a new millennium when they were featured in American football's Super Bowl half-time show in January 2006. As Doney said, 'It is difficult to exaggerate the impact of The Rolling Stones. They brought upon themselves more scorn and adult hysteria than any musicians before or since'.[19]

Following hard after the Rolling Stones' success came another wave of British bands. They were influenced more by American blues music than their predecessors, and the lead guitarist was the key musician in these bands. Cream (featuring Eric Clapton) and Led Zeppelin are early examples of this heavier and grittier blues-rock fusion; they were followed by heavier rock bands with ever darker personas such as Black Sabbath and Deep Purple. Eventually this style of rock would morph into heavy metal music, which placed less emphasis on individual guitar skills and more emphasis on extremely loud guitar chords along with bombastic stage theatrics. Many heavy metal bands followed this path in the nineteen-seventies, including AC/DC, Aerosmith, Alice Cooper and KISS.

Rock music also developed a softer side, marked by the 'bubble gum pop' era of the late nineteen-sixties and early nineteen-seventies that featured such groups as Tommy James and the Shondells, The Monkees, Paul Revere and the Raiders, and the Partridge Family. Solo artists such as Billy Joel and Elton John and groups like America and Bread would later popularize the soft rock format that is today's dominant pop sound.

The nineteen-seventies also saw the rise of Southern rock from out of the American South. Southern rock wanted to revive rock 'n' roll's blues and country roots but also drew from the heavy blues-rock of the late nineteen-sixties, creating a distinctive style. The Allman Brothers Band is generally considered to be the seminal Southern rock band. They were followed by Lynyrd Skynyrd, who played even heavier and louder than the Allman Brothers and set the standard for all the Southern rock bands that followed them. Other well-known Southern rock bands were the Marshall Tucker Band and .38 Special. A fondness for long, drawn-out guitar jams, drinking Jack Daniels whisky and pot-smoking were distinctive characteristics of the Southern rock experience.

In the late nineteen-seventies, punk rock came on the scene. Derek Jewell described their music as 'the latest musical garbage bred by our troubled culture'[20] and the punk rockers as those who loved 'hate, aggression, apathy, lust, alcohol, anarchy'.[21] Punk rock started as a reaction to disco and to the commercialism of mainstream rock. Punk bands did not require expert musicianship; it was and still is three-chord guitar music played extremely loudly and with the lyrics shouted and screamed more than sung. Punk bands also set out purposely to shock society. Led by the Sex Pistols who chose stage names like 'Johnny Rotten' and 'Sid Vicious' and did their best to live up to them, punk bands had an anarchistic, confrontational and often violent stage presence. Punk rock never really became solidly established (although it did inspire some later innovations like today's immensely popular band Green Day) and soon the rock world moved on to the next big thing.

On to the present

In the nineteen-eighties, rock music became even more diverse. Heavy metal bands like Van Halen and Metallica helped to usher in a new era of hard rock music. They were followed by Mötley Crüe and other 'hair-metal' bands that became known more for their degenerate lifestyles and big hair than their musicianship. Their music was overbearing, aggressive and macho, with lyrics focused on sex, drinking, drugs and the occult. During the early part of the decade, Michael Jackson would also reach the peak of his remarkable career with the dark rock-funk album *Thriller*. New Wave bands like Billy Idol, The Cars and The Go-Gos also sprang to fame out of the punk scene.

At about the same time Bruce Springsteen, Bob Seger and his Silver Bullet Band, and John Cougar Mellencamp firmly established the popular American 'heartland rock' sound, with its distinctive guitar-driven anthems. Rock music was also fused with a variety of folk music styles from around the world, a fusion that would come to be known as 'world music'. This movement was led by singer-songwriter Paul Simon and Peter Gabriel, an original member of the British megaband Genesis that also produced rock star Phil Collins. Another important milestone was the arrival of MTV and the proliferation of rock music videos, which brought along with it the perception that a band's image might now be more important than its musical substance.

By the late nineteen-eighties the rock scene was dominated by slick commercial pop-rock, heavy metal bands and ageing rock artists. Most traces of the original rock 'n' roll ethos of rebellion and sexual freedom had disappeared into a corporate-sponsored and mass-marketed musical product. Disaffected by this trend, some younger musicians created crude, sometimes angry music that defined the alternative rock or grunge style that produced bands like Nirvana, Pearl Jam and Stone Temple Pilots. In the late nineteen-nineties, the mix of grunge, metal and hip-hop led to new metal, featuring bands like Korn, Creed and Limp Bizkit.

In the first years of the new millennium, rock music is still very much alive and well and is still morphing and assimilating. Current trends include emo (or 'emotional') rock which draws from alternative rock and punk styles and features bands like Jimmy Eat World and Dashboard Confessional. There is also a revival of techno rock dance music with bands like The Killers who mix post-punk and new wave styles with driving electronic beats.

As has always been the case, yesterday's stars are fading, and tomorrow's are rising in the sky to replace them — and the appetites of those who listen to rock music are apparently insatiable. David Wilkerson goes so far as to say that rock music is 'the biggest mass addiction in the world's history'.[22] Whatever one's personal opinions on the phenomenon, it seems difficult to disagree with Steve Lawhead when he writes, 'For so long as young people feel repressed and awkward, as long as society can indulge one affluent and self-centred generation after another, as long as there is electricity, there will be rock music.'[23]

3.

IDENTITY CRISIS

I know, it's only rock 'n' roll,
but I like it, like it, yes I do!

(Rock singer Mick Jagger)[1]

Before trying to link rock music's past with its present use in Christian circles, we ought to settle on our definitions. What does rock music look and sound like today? Some say, 'I can't describe rock music, but I will know it when I hear it!' Others can easily reel off the names of their favourite rock artists and sing a few of their tunes. Still others will argue that rock music is merely one particular musical style or another. This makes it clear that in any discussion about rock music and the church, it is vital to define our terms.

To begin at the beginning, what do we mean when we use the phrase 'rock music'? After all, there is sweet rock and acid rock, soft rock and hard rock, glam rock and glitter rock, folk rock and punk rock — everything from gay rock to God rock — to say nothing of reggae, heavy metal, new wave, grunge and alternative. No wonder Derek Jewell felt compelled to write, 'No one has satisfactorily defined rock ... you suggest its properties rather than pin it down firmly.'[2] These days 'rock' is a label which loosely covers a wide range of contemporary popular music, though, as we shall see, there is a common musical thread.

The American Heritage Dictionary of the English Language gives this definition of rock 'n' roll: 'A form of popular music arising from and incorporating a variety of musical styles, especially rhythm and blues, country music, and gospel. Originating in the United States in the 1950s, it is characterized by electronically amplified instrumentation, a heavily accented beat, and relatively simple phrase structure.' It then calls rock music 'a generic term for the range of styles that evolved out of rock 'n' roll'.

The music industry is endlessly classifying and reclassifying music styles in order to market its product more effectively and the diversity of styles grouped under the rock music heading is nothing less than staggering. In 2006, the *All Music Guide*[3] listed no less than *187* variations of rock music, grouped under twelve main headings:

1. Alternative/Indie-Rock
2. Hard Rock
3. Rock & Roll/Roots
4. Soft Rock
5. Pop/Rock
6. Psychedelic/Garage
7. Europop
8. Punk/New Wave
9. Foreign Language Rock
10. British Invasion
11. Art-Rock/Experimental
12. Folk/Country Rock

Yet despite this seemingly endless diversity, there are certain characteristics basic to rock music. What are they, and how do they relate to the use of rock as a vehicle for worship or evangelism? Common musical and style denominators come together in rock music. The *All Music Guide* describes it like this:

From the outset, when the early rockers merged country and blues, rock has been defined by its energy, rebellion and catchy hooks. Everything from Chuck Berry's pounding, three-chord rockers and the sweet harmonies of The Beatles to the soulful pleas of Otis Redding and the jarring, atonal white noise of Sonic Youth has been categorized as 'rock'. For most of its life, rock has been fragmented, spinning off new styles and variations every few years, from Brill Building Pop and heavy metal to dance-pop and grunge. And that's only natural for a genre that began its life as a fusion of styles.[4]

On and on and on and on...

One of the basic characteristics of rock music is constant repetition. Listen to any rock song you choose, and one of its major features will be the constant repetition of chord patterns, beat, a narrow range of notes or a rhythmic figure. There is obviously no 'law' about the amount of variety that is needed before a piece of music becomes 'legitimate'; the most we can say is that variety is one of the marks of any good music, regardless of style.

Some people might say that there is considerable repetition in certain classical music, and this is true. But it is typically creative, with subtle variations woven into it. Is there honestly any comparison between, say, the repetition in a Vivaldi concerto movement and that in Led Zeppelin's 'Whole Lotta Love' (widely considered a classic piece of rock)? Quite apart from the erotic elements and simulated orgasms, 'Whole Lotta Love' has little creative variety. This may seem an extreme example from the past but no one can seriously deny that driving repetition is still a staple of rock music styles today.

This insistent repetition immediately raises warning flags about the suitability of rock music in worship or evangelism, because constant repetition has a hypnotic effect. Mickey Hart, formerly of Grateful Dead, has made the study of drumming his life's work. In his book *Drumming at the Edge of Magic* he explores the impact of drumming on people's spiritual lives and writes: 'Drumming is made for trance and for ecstatic states. The basis of percussion is redundancy and redundancy is the basis of trance.'[5]

Professor William Shafer, a non-Christian sociologist, says, 'What is undeniable about rock is its hypnotic power. It has gripped millions of young people around the world and transformed their lives.'[6] Dr Granville Knight agrees: 'There is no question in my mind about the hypnotic effect of these songs.' So does Dr W. J. Bryan: 'Children are being hypnotized without their knowledge, and that is the really insidious part about these records. The more often the hypnotism is repeated the higher the susceptibility of the subject.'

In the course of his specialized study on hypnosis, Andrew Salter indicated that rock music is an ideal vehicle for individual or mass hypnosis.[7] Even more telling is this statement by the late Jimi Hendrix, one of the most dynamic and influential superstars in rock music history: 'Atmospheres are going to come through music, because the music is a spiritual thing of its own. You can hypnotize people with the music and when you get them at their weakest point you can preach into the sub-conscious what you want to say.'[8]

This obviously has very serious implications for the use of rock music in worship or evangelism. Any medium of presentation that induces any loss of self-control or awareness and makes the listener unusually susceptible to whatever suggestions are made by the lyrics is clearly dangerous, and will almost certainly encourage a response that will be largely psychological instead of that which God requires, which is that we should worship him 'in spirit and truth' (John 4:24).

Into the groove

As with constant repetition, a driving beat is an indispensable ingredient of rock. 'The backbeat is one kind of drum groove; it's the *essential* one for rock and roll,' wrote Mickey Hart.[9] This rhythm technique sounds a strong accent on the 2nd and 4th beats (or the backbeats) in a 4/4 time and is usually played on a snare drum. The tension between the normally much stronger first and third beats (the downbeats) and the backbeats creates the interest. This distinctive rhythmic style emerged in the late nineteen-forties in rhythm and blues recordings and is the backbone of rock and roll music, used today in virtually all pop music. In 'soft rock' or 'pop/rock' music, the backbeat is usually in the background and does not normally dominate the other musical components of melody and harmony. That however is the exception rather than the rule; the backbeat dominates in most rock music songs, hard, soft or otherwise.

Since drums are primarily rhythm instruments, '"They affect the body directly," says Don Saliers, a distinguished professor of theology and worship at Emory University in Atlanta. "They are somatic [affecting the body as opposed to the mind or spirit] in that sense. If you ask about rhythms in the human body as a starting point for spirituality, we think immediately of heartbeat, breathing, walking, clapping, stomping, dancing. In other words, the human body is already an instrument that drums speak to, for good or for ill."'[10]

Drum circles, based on Afro-Latin pagan drumming traditions that formed the basis of what became rock's rhythm, have become popular in the West in recent times. What is a drum circle? Simply put, several people sit in a circle or semi-circle and play various percussion instruments in order to reach a certain mind-spirit state of unity through rhythm. According to Mickey Hart, 'The ultimate goal [of the drum circle] is not precise rhythmic articulation or perfection of patterned structure, but the ability to entrain and reach the state of a group mind. It is built on cooperation in the groove, but with little reference to any classic styles.'[11]

One avid drum circle[12] participant explains the attraction: 'Over the years, drumming in various drum circles ... I have become more and more *entranced* with the experience. A composer living outside Toronto, Ontario, started teaching Afro-Latin drumming to small women's groups. Most expressed the feeling that drumming *took them somewhere* that other musical activities did not. One class member summed up why the drumming is so appealing to her. "It's *mesmerizing*. When I play the piano it's all up at the heart level which is wonderful but *drumming gets me lower, at the belly*. It feels heavy, strong"'[13] (emphasis added).

The difference between the constant, hypnotic beat of rock and its ancestral rhythms and genuine musical rhythm has been well put by the distinguished Russian composer Igor Stravinsky: 'Rhythm doesn't really exist [in rock], because no rhythmic proportion or relaxation exists.'[14] There is evidence to suggest that when the beat overrides the other elements in a song the communication level is significantly changed to one which is primarily physical and often specifically sexual. Rock musician Tom McSloy has no doubts about this: 'To get into rock you have to give in to it, let it inside, flow with it to the point where it consumes you, and all you can feel or hear or think about is the music.'[15] Mickey Hart agrees: 'I had heard of the phenomenom of rhythmic entrainment that rock and jazz musicians call the groove. Billy [fellow former Grateful Dead drummer] taught me to trust in it, to let it draw me in like a tractor beam.'[16] Hart also admits he had to be careful not to get too far into a trance state.

These are alarming statements — but they tie in perfectly with some words written by someone who comes at it from a completely different angle, the well-known British preacher, Dr Martyn Lloyd-Jones. In his classic book *Preaching and Preachers* he has a section in which he warns of the dangers of preachers making a direct attack on either the emotions or the will. In it he writes, 'We can become drunk on music — there is no question about that. Music can have the effect of creating an emotional state in which the mind is no longer functioning as it should be, and no longer discriminating. I have known people to sing themselves into a state of intoxication without realizing what they were doing.'[17]

We can take it for granted that he was not writing about a rock concert — so the point we are making here is not part of an 'anti-rock' diatribe. What we are saying is that the element of relentless beat and repetition in rock music increases the danger of a shallow, emotional, unthinking response, made at the wrong level and for the wrong reasons. In his book *New Singer, New Song* David Winter openly admits that 'An incessant beat does erode a sense of responsibility in much the same way as alcohol does... You feel in the grip of a relentless stream of sound to which something very basic and primitive in the human nature responds.'[18]

Surely this is a highly dangerous thing? To quote Lloyd-Jones again, 'The important point is that we should realize that *the effect produced in such a case is not produced by the truth...*'[19] (emphasis added).

Dangerous decibels

As with repetition and beat, we need not waste time proving that volume is an important element in rock music, with huge stacks of equipment often needed to produce the required amount of amplification. This report by Derek Jewell of a sell-out concert in London's Albert Hall by the British group Cream

(Eric Clapton's band, now disbanded but which broke Beatles' attendance records in the United States) tells us the kind of impact that can be made: 'It contained some highly skilled, if perverse, talent — especially the guitarist Clapton. But its Albert Hall show was misconceived, an attempt at a gigantic tour de force, with the accent on force. I have never heard louder music. It destroyed itself in sheer decibels. The juggernaut of sound assaulted the stomach as well as being a danger to the ear-drums. It was mind-fragmenting music, involving one in what the pop avant-garde fashionably calls total experience. I don't want total experience in a concert hall ... I want musical experiences...'[20] Jewell's report is not outdated by any means; if anything, the problem has become worse.

Ever since the dawn of rock 'n' roll, teenagers have scoffed when their mothers warned them, 'You will go deaf listening to that music!' There now seems ample evidence that mother was right all along. Here is an astounding 2006 confession from the legendary Pete Townshend, the lead guitarist for The Who, one of the loudest rock bands in history: 'I have unwittingly helped to invent and refine a type of music that makes its principal [listeners] deaf... Hearing loss is a terrible thing because it cannot be repaired.'[21] Townsend's own hearing was irreversibly damaged by years of rock music and he is now warning music lovers that they could end up with hearing problems as bad as his own if they refuse to turn down the volume of the music to which they are listening. His warning has never been more relevant, not least when we think of the huge popularity of today's portable media players.

Volume for volume's sake is also a trademark of heavy metal, which arrived in the late nineteen-sixties with groups like Deep Purple, Black Sabbath and Led Zeppelin and is still very popular some forty years later. Malcolm Doney describes it as 'horrendous, heavy, mind-deadening music ... blacksmith music ... a battering-ram against the senses.'[22] Lemmy Kilminster of the group Motorhead said his group wanted to see 'blood comin' out of everyone's ears, if possible. Nothing dangerous, just enough to let us know they're having a good time.'[23]

As with repetition and beat, volume can have a hypnotic effect. Doney writes of audiences who 'were only too willing to let themselves be pushed along. They offered themselves up to the music. They went to concerts with the specific intention of being zonked out.'[24] When we think about the young people listening to heavy metal rock music, the word 'malleable' immediately comes to mind. It means 'capable of being altered or controlled by outside forces; easily influenced.'[25] How does something become malleable? By being 'shaped by beating with a hammer or by the pressure of rollers; as applied to metals.'[26] Surely we can apply that meaning to heavy metal rock with its constant audio pounding?

But how loud is loud? Sound level is measured in decibels. In a paper entitled 'Hearing Acuity in Young People exposed to Pop Music and other Noise' Drs David Hanson and Ronald Fearn report that in visits to over thirty youth clubs in England they found average rock music decibel levels of between 84 and 118, with only one rating falling below 90.[27] At rock concerts, similar readings are common and can sometimes be in the 120-130 decibel range. There have even been readings of 138 decibels. (As a working comparison, a vacuum cleaner generates about 80 decibels and a pneumatic hammer 94.)

Yet even these figures do not tell the whole story. Decibels increase logarithmically, not linearly, which means that an increase of only three decibels indicates double the intensity of sound. The standard British work on the subject of the effect of noise is *Hearing and Noise in Industry* by Burns and Robinson, published by Her Majesty's Stationery Office. In this book, they suggest that for an eight-hour working day, the maximum volume level should be 90 decibels, with the exposure duration being halved for every increase of three decibels.[28] This means that at 93 decibels the recommended maximum exposure should be four hours; for 96, two hours; for 99 one hour, and so on. Getting up to rock concert levels, the danger marks would be as follows: at 111 decibels, 3 minutes 45 seconds; at 120 decibels, 28.12 seconds; and at 129 decibels, 3.51 seconds. At the top recorded level we have mentioned (138 decibels) it would only be safe to listen for less than half a second!

With these figures in mind, it is not surprising to find that exposure to loud rock music has had serious effects on the hearing of the listeners. An ear, nose and throat specialist in the United States estimates that about 40% of students entering university have hearing defects caused by listening to rock music; in pre-rock days, the figure was 1%. In a study carried out on 505 British students in higher education, Hanson and Fearn discovered that 'statistically significant hearing losses were found in the group that admitted frequent attendance at pop music entertainment'.[29]

Other studies by Ronald Fearn in the course of his work at Leeds Polytechnic in England during the nineteen-seventies suggested that up to one million young people in Britain suffered some degree of hearing loss caused by listening to loud music and that many have hearing problems normally associated with sixty-five to seventy-year-olds. It is no wonder that Hanson and Fearn conclude their paper by calling overloud amplified music 'a widespread hazard'.[30]

It has been suggested to us that loudness in rock music is a matter of conditioning, but surely this is a highly dangerous philosophy? Should we allow ourselves to be conditioned by something that is potentially so harmful? Hanson and Fearn have the more obvious and sensible solution: 'The main requirement must be the reduction of amplification levels.'[31]

Quite apart from the sheer decibel level, another factor associated with volume calls into question rock music's suitability as a medium for worship or evangelism. Two musicians who are part of the Christian rock scene once put it to us like this: 'The major problem of rock music is the noise level. The words are often inaudible and even if they were audible the degree of truth in them would be negligible. The whole scene has become a mess, with very many people not seeming to know why they are doing what they are doing.' That is a tragic commentary on the contemporary Christian music scene, made by people actively involved in it — and its most telling point is the one that states the music makes the words inaudible.

Yet in both evangelism and worship, *the words are vitally important.* The Bible addresses Christians as those who 'heard *the word* of truth, the gospel of your salvation' (Ephesians 1:13); it says that the gospel is 'the *word* of life' (Philippians 2:16); and that Christians are born again 'by the *word* of truth' (James 1:18). Elsewhere it teaches that we are sanctified, purified, instructed and corrected by the Word of God (Ephesians 5:26; John 17:17; 1 Timothy 4:5; Colossians 3:16; 2 Timothy 4:2). Then how can the work of evangelism be helped by something which makes its message more difficult to hear? How can Christians worship in truth and experience sanctification, instruction and correction when they are unable to hear the words?

In all the reasoning which we seek to bring to bear on our readers in this study of the use of rock music in Christianity, there is nothing on which we are more definite than this: any method or medium (we need not confine ourselves to rock music) which makes the Word of God more difficult to hear, and therefore to be understood, is not serving the cause of God but actually hindering it. The enthusiasm of the performers, the sincerity of their motives and the quality of their work may not be in question, but if at the end of the day the listeners are unable to hear the words clearly all of those qualities count for nothing.

The Christian music myth

If our analysis of rock music is right, using it in God's service is spiritually perilous. *But is it scripturally possible?* Is there such a thing as 'Christian rock music'? The way to begin answering that question is to ask a much more fundamental one, which is this: is there such a thing as 'Christian music' at all? What do we mean by the phrase? Are we describing the music? Take a sheet of music from a 'Christian' song and one from a 'secular' song. Are they essentially different? Is a B flat in a hymn any different from one in a bawdy rock number? Can you tell a Christian vibrato from a non-Christian one? Is it something to do with the instruments? Is there such a thing as a godly guitar, a sanctified saxophone or a born-again bassoon? Nobody is questioning the point that one can have Christian musicians, but the simple fact of the matter is that there is no such thing as 'Christian' music. There are Christians and there is music; there is good music and there is bad music (and that should have nothing to do with taste, style, culture or the age of the performer or listener); there is music that reflects God's glory and music that does not.

We can take this further. There are Christians who write and play bad music, and non-Christians who write and play good music. Music is not 'good' because it is being performed in a religious context, any more than music is 'bad' because it is being performed in a secular context. All these divisions tend to blur the truth. Music must be judged not solely by its context but more by its content. Beautiful flowers can be found in a dusty desert and poisonous plants in a lovely garden.

At this point, we need to differentiate what we are saying from others who seem to be saying similar things. Rick Warren represents the contemporary Christian view when he writes, 'There is no such thing as "Christian music", only Christian lyrics.'[32] We agree with the first part of the statement, but disagree with the second part; by saying 'only' the lyrics count, Warren is subtly setting us up for the 'music is amoral' argument. We know this because a few words later he closes the deal: 'I reject the idea that music styles can be judged as either "good" or "bad" music. Who decides this? The kind of music you like is determined by your background and culture. Music is nothing more than an arrangement of notes and rhythms; it's the words that make a song spiritual.'[33] Warren is obviously a music universalist who believes God invented all music styles.[34] But if we follow his reasoning to its logical end, each person becomes his or her own judge and no one else is permitted to say whether a form of music is appropriate or not for God's service. We strongly disagree with his opinion, which effectively sets up man, not God, as the measure of all things good and righteous. Could it be that Warren's real issue is not really musical, but as with most Baby Boomers he simply rejects anyone else deciding for him what is good or bad?

Then how should we apply the principle we established in the previous paragraph? Man's first and constant duty is to honour his Maker in every area of his life — and that includes the most mundane things: 'Therefore, whether you eat or drink, or whatever you do, do all to the glory of God' (1 Corinthians 10:31). Every part of life is to be seen as one in which God can be glorified by our obedience to his revealed will. But this is not limited to 'religious' activities, let alone to evangelism and worship. It is exactly here that so many people go wrong. Here is a musician who becomes a Christian. In no time at all, he is encouraged to get involved in gospel music — because 'the Lord wants you to use your musical gift as a means of reaching other people with the gospel and leading God's people in worship'. But who says so? Nowhere does the Bible tell the Christian that he or she must use whatever talents or means they have at their disposal (regardless of what they might be) as vehicles for direct evangelism or to aid corporate worship.

Lost property?

It has even been suggested to us that to question the appropriateness of using any particular kind of music in evangelism and worship is to deny the lordship of Christ over part of his creation — but exactly the opposite is true. We deny his lordship when we decide that we can use any means *we* choose, then bring him in at the next stage and ask his blessing on it. The musician's duty is the same as that of any other Christian — to begin with Scripture and discover exactly what methods and means God has authorized. To imagine that by taking any kind of music (or other art form) and using it in God's service we are somehow 'redeeming' or 'reclaiming' it for God is another popular piece of woolly thinking. According to Scripture, only believers' souls (now) and bodies (eventually) are redeemed by the blood of Christ; and God's plan 'to reconcile all things to himself' (Colossians 1:20) is something that he himself will bring to pass in 'new heavens and a new earth in which righteousness dwells' (2 Peter 3:13). The Christian is under no instruction or obligation to reclaim art forms for God as if they were some kind of lost property.

Christians should certainly be active in the arts, including music, but they do not have to drag the gospel into their art to make it biblically legitimate. A musician's first responsibility is to make good music, not 'Christian' music, and God will be glorified by the honesty, beauty and integrity of his work. As Professor H. R. Rookmaaker so perfectly put it, 'Art has its own value'[35], and that value is not tied to worship or evangelism. The Christian artist (musician or other) need not feel trapped or confined to worship or evangelism only as a 'spiritual' expression of his art form. He has liberty to use his gift elsewhere.

As we will see next, 'Christian' rock is now well established as its own genre and has its own identity within the music industry and the church. As a result we shall have to go on using the phrase 'Christian rock' in the course of this book but it will help us to keep our thinking straight if we remember that in fact there is no such thing!

Christian rock?

Historically speaking there has always been a religious element associated with rock music, as demonstrated by the early rockers such as Elvis Presley and Little Richard who came out of gospel music backgrounds. They did not call themselves 'Christian' musicians; they were rock musicians who also happened to be religious or came from a Christian background. There was no such genre as 'Christian rock' (that is, rock music accompanied by Christianized lyrics).

It was not until the late nineteen-sixties that rock music with Christianized lyrics was brought into the church and other settings such as Youth for Christ rallies. Ralph Carmichael's folk-rock Christian church musicals (such as *Tell It Like It Is* and *Natural High*) played a major role in the introduction of rock music styles into evangelistic and worship services. He went on to form his own label, Light Records, in partnership with Word Records and worked with others to create what is now known as the Contemporary Christian Music (CCM) industry.

At around the same time, hippies in Southern California and elsewhere turned to Christianity and became known as the Jesus People. As a result 'Jesus rock' was born, a religious mix of blues-rock, country-rock and folk-rock. Paul Baker of the Jesus rock band Liberation Suite describes the early days:

> The Movement came out of young people's search for spiritual answers that they felt — correctly or not — the establishment and the established church hadn't given

them. To many of them, Christianity meant 'church-ianity' and hypocrisy. Teenagers and college-agers began expressing their newfound faith through what for them was the most natural, most effective of languages: music — especially folk and rock. Much of the mainstream Christian church did not take easily to those popular styles in music of worship and praise, choosing instead to stay with the staid hymns. So in a further effort to distance themselves from what they believed to be the hackneyed term 'Christian', to describe this new music of the faith, the writers and singers and players labelled it 'Jesus music'.[36]

The pop music industry quickly saw the market value of 'Jesus music'. From 1969 to 1973, more than twenty pop songs about Jesus, including 'Amazing Grace' and 'Put Your Hand in the Hand', reached the US music charts Top 20. Norman Greenbaum's 'Spirit in the Sky', a song with the words 'I've got a friend in Jesus' that features a strong rock beat and distorted electric guitars in the psychedelic rock mode, went all the way to No. 3 and sold two million copies. The same album also included 'The Day They Sold Beer In Church', a satirical ditty about hypocritical religious people. Was this another example of the Jesus People mocking the mainstream church? One interviewer asked Greenbaum the big question in a 1996 interview: 'Why did you write a sort of religious song that featured Jesus? Are you now or have you been born-again?' The answer is that Norman Greenbaum wasn't a Christian then, and still isn't a Christian.[37]

The Doobie Brothers scored a top hit in 1973 with 'Jesus is Just Alright', a cover of a gospel song by Art Reynolds that The Byrds had earlier covered in their 1969 album *The Ballad of Easy Rider*. As the first gospel group to record for Capitol Records in the late nineteen-sixties, the Art Reynolds Singers were pioneers in the development of 'gospel rock', something many churchgoers considered too secular for the time.[38] The Doobie Brothers apparently did not record the song for its evangelistic or worship value. When asked about the name of the group, Doobie Brothers' founder Pat Simmons remarked, 'It has been a little embarrassing at times, especially trying to explain it to my kids ... (who) come home from school and say, "Dad, you know what somebody said about you guys? They said your name means marijuana cigarette." I go, "WHAT??!! No it's like Frank Sinatra. Doobie doobie do." That won't work much longer. They are all pretty much wise to it now.'[39]

The Byrds, a rock band from America with top psychedelic rock hits like 'Eight Miles High', recorded other religious-themed songs like 'Turn, Turn, Turn' (based on Ecclesiastes 3), 'I Am a Pilgrim' and 'The Christian Life'. When asked about the motive behind recording them, Roger McGuinn of The Byrds admitted, 'We just recorded those songs for their musical value at the time.' He was converted to Christ about ten years later.[40]

More importantly, the Jesus People were the first to use rock music in their worship services. According to *CCM* magazine, '1971's The Everlastin' Living JESUS Music Concert was the first release from fledgling *Maranatha! Music* — an outreach of Calvary Chapel of Costa Mesa, a mecca for long-haired Jesus people.'[41] *Maranatha! Music* went on to become a highly successful publisher of 'praise and worship' choruses that have been widely adopted by churches of all types.

The same *CCM* magazine article states that the contemporary Christian music revolution 'began in earnest in 1969, when Capitol Records released "Upon This Rock", an album by a scrawny, long-haired, enigmatic singer/songwriter named Larry Norman, an artist *Time* magazine would describe as the Jesus movement's "poet laureate" and the *New York Times* would hail as "Christian rock music's most intelligent writer and greatest asset"'.[42] Norman was also notable for making a clean break with traditional hymns. In 'Why Should the Devil Have All the Good

Music', he sang about the hymns, 'I don't like none of these funeral marches. I ain't dead yet.'[43]

Christian rock was initially considered a very controversial style in the church and was strongly resisted by many, because preachers and churchgoers believed almost universally that rock 'n' roll music was the devil's music style. As we saw earlier in this book, they had good reasons for doing so. The origins of rock, the lifestyles of the songwriters and performers, their stated intention to capture the hearts and bodies of young people, and the sex-drugs connection were enough to keep many thoughtful Christians away from it.

But as time went on others began to see Christian rock as an effective way to reach the unconverted, by wrapping spiritual messages in an attractive musical package. (It was this trend that led to the publishing of *Pop Goes the Gospel* in 1983.) Still others, inspired by the example of the Jesus People, saw Christian rock as the best way to experience God in their worship and decided to promote this 'worship style' to other Christians.

No style left unturned

Today there seems to be a Christian version of every rock music genre listed in the encyclopaedic *All Music Guide*. Christian musicians are quick to mimic the latest and greatest twist on rock, and then claim it for evangelism and worship.

The Christianbook.com web site is a popular place to buy music. Listed under 'Music Genres' are several of the same categories we would find in the secular *All Music Guide*. There is a Metal category with bands like Demon Hunter and Living Sacrifice. The *All Music Guide* describes heavy metal music as relying on 'brutal guitar riffs and pummelling rhythms — from the drums to the guitars, it's about being as loud as possible.'[44] There is Hard Rock, described as 'true to the bluesy rock 'n' roll of the

Stones and with a certain swing in the back beat whose riffs and hooks are played almost as loudly,[45] with bands like Relient K and Pillar listed. There is also a plain Rock category featuring bands like Third Day, David Crowder Band and Jeremy Camp.

The web site also highlights Alternative/Modern with bands like Jars of Clay and Sixpence None the Richer, who owe a lot to alternative pioneers REM and Nirvana. Then there is Punk represented by Superchick and MxPx among others, imitating the same music favoured by the likes of the Sex Pistols and the Ramones, music that is played extremely loudly and with lyrics shouted and screamed more than sung.

On the same web site rock music can also be found hidden under some distinctively Christian labels. Under Modern Worship we find MercyMe, Chris Tomlin and Matt Redman, artists whose CDs are categorized as rock music in *CCM* magazine reviews. The Praise and Worship category includes Third Day (a Lynyrd Skynyrd – Southern Rock clone) and softer rock artists from Hillsong and Integrity. The Contemporary category lists Casting Crowns and Rebecca St James, both of whom perform rock music that once was considered to be 'hard'. Finally, there is the Hymns category, where you can find Jars of Clay rocking out on 'It is Well with My Soul' or Phil Keaggy performing 'Nothing but the Blood of Jesus' by mimicking Jimi Hendrix's 'Hey Joe' style, complete with psychedelic electric guitar distortion.

The U2 thing

No survey of rock music and Christians would be complete without mentioning the incredible impact of the rock band U2 and their Irish frontman Bono (born Paul Hewson). In the course of our research we uncovered an entire 'Christians for U2' subculture, including a Presbyterian church in Iowa offering a four-week course titled 'Spirituality of U2' that asks the burning question 'How is a concert similar or different than worship?' This is answered by paraphrasing a U2 song, 'Church services and rock concerts are one, but not the same.'[46] Yet the idea that rock concerts are like church services did not originate with U2 and their fans, as we shall discover in the next chapter.

Describing U2 as 'a combination of zealous righteousness and post-punk experimentalism', *All Music Guide* goes on to say, 'U2 became one of the most popular rock & roll bands of the '80s. Equally known for their sweeping sound as for their grandiose statements about politics and religion, U2 were rock & roll crusaders during an era of synthesized pop and heavy metal.'[47] What impact has U2 had on Christian rock? *CCM* magazine poses a rhetorical question: 'Can you name a recording artist who has inspired Christian music's top acts as much as Bono and his band U2? Good luck. Think about the Irish group's faith-infused songs — performed by everyone from Michael W. Smith on his Worship DVD to MercyMe on its latest tour. U2 guitarist Dave Evans' (The Edge) trademark sound has been consistently present in the music of The Choir, Sixpence None the Richer and newcomers like MuteMath and Starfield. Bono's distinctive vocal style is one that few can invoke as well as dc Talk's Kevin Max or Martin Smith of Delirious?'[48]

One U2 fan's devotion to the band came crashing down around her at Madison Square Garden in 2005 when 'Bono began to chant "Jesus, Jew, Mohammed — all true. Jesus, Jew, Mohammed — all true." He repeated the words like a mantra. Was Bono, my supposed brother in Christ, preaching some kind of universalism? As I looked around, I saw all the people standing and chanting with him — it was disgusting... When he stated that lie so boldly, it devastated me. It was, without question, the most disturbing experience of my life; I felt like I'd been covered in bile. The reality is that Bono held too high a place in my heart. And I don't think I'm alone there. *I've wrongly held him up as the heroic ideal — the cool representative for Christianity*; he may have been my "Christian idol", but he was my idol nonetheless'[49] (emphasis added). How many other Christians will be jolted out of their U2 worship by this news?

Bono was the keynote speaker at the US National Day of Prayer in February 2006 and was quoted in *CCM* magazine as saying, 'I appreciate the absurdity of being a rock star and quoting the Scriptures. I've never seen why there should be a separation.' He went on to say that for most of his life people have asked, 'Why doesn't your music proclaim Christ? ... It does! Creation has its own proclamation of its Creator.'[50] Perhaps this is all no more than Bono's way of deflecting criticism of the band's music and not really intended as a theological statement on music — but how many Christians will think otherwise and take it to heart?

The clear connection

As evidenced here, there is essentially no difference between the rock music written and performed by secular artists or by Christian artists. Stylistically and musically, they are exactly the same. In this sense Rick Warren is right when he claims: 'There is no such thing as Christian music — only Christian lyrics.'[51] In an April 2005 article about how Christian rock is becoming 'almost good enough' for secular listeners to appreciate, *Los Angeles Times* proclaimed that 'Hawk Nelson and Kutless (Christian bands) are simply a few more inspirational lyrics and a lot fewer expletives removed from Good Charlotte and Bowling for Soup.'[52] By means of explanation, Good Charlotte is described as a punk and post-grunge quartet with thick, distorted grunge guitars and angst-ridden songs, while Bowling for Soup is a punk revival band who released 'Drunk Enough to Dance' in 2002, and nabbed a Grammy nomination for the single 'Girl All the Bad Guys Want'.[53]

Christian rockers labour under the burden of mimicry. They work hard to imitate every style of rock music — indeed they are on a quest to produce 'excellent' rock music because they are criticized by the very secular world they are trying so hard to impress, not with their lyrics but with their musicianship. An article from *GQ Online* frames the credibility problem faced by Christian rockers: 'Rock music used to be a safe haven for degenerates and rebels. Until it found Jesus. Every successful … secular group has its Christian off-brand, and that's proper, because culturally speaking, it's supposed to serve as a stand-in for, not an alternative to or an improvement on, those very groups. It's possible — and indeed seems likely — that Christian rock is a musical genre, the only one I can think of, that has excellence-proofed itself.'[54]

But through years of practice and performance, some Christian rockers have attained musical equality with the world and are now gaining its praise and respect. *Rolling Stone* magazine said this about the latest album from a well-known British rock worship band: 'Known as the galvanizing force that changed the face of worship, Delirious? are an openly religious group whose song craft is good enough to appeal to a much wider audience than their Christian core of fans. As the once rigid divisions between Christian and popular music continue to crumble, Delirious? are leading the charge from amen corner to center stage.'[55]

According to the *Los Angeles Times*, 'Nowhere has the Christian rock crossover been more convincing than in heavy metal. No small irony in that, as metal has for years personified the devil's music for some of the more vocal members of the religious right.'[56] Christian heavy metal bands such as Underoath and Chariot have played to large crowds of metal fans, many of whom are decked out in Slayer or Metallica T-shirts, and they boast about bringing their faith to the foreground whenever possible. "'Underoath is one of the premier hard-core bands in the country," says Tim Taber, a California music promoter and label owner. "They're as heavy as any secular metal band out there right now. And they'll come out and thank Jesus on stage, and these non-religious kids will just be yelling and screaming.'"[57]

Then have 'Christian' rockers changed the nature of rock music or have they simply joined the gospel to it and left rock unchanged? On a *60 Minutes* TV broadcast in December 2004, Cameron Strang, the publisher of *Relevant* magazine (a kind of *Rolling Stone* magazine for Christians) says, 'We can still call it rock music. That's a style.' The CBS reporter responds, 'But when you get down to it, is it really all that different? Isn't it all still just rock 'n' roll?' Strang continues, 'Yeah, and rebellion. There is no greater rebellion than to say sex and drugs and rock 'n' roll isn't the only thing in life. The Christian rock thing is almost rebelling against the rock establishment. Rock 'n' roll is rebellion.'[58]

Given what we have learned so far about rock music and its well-earned 'worldly' reputation, why do worship leaders, evangelists or church musicians work so hard to perfect the use of it? To accommodate this inconsistency, Christian rock apologists have had to construct a new faith system to offer religious cover to those who do so. This system requires adherence to one or more of the following credos:

- God created all music — therefore rock music was inspired by him.
- Although rock may have been corrupted by bad people, we have the power to redeem it for God.
- Music itself is neutral and amoral, and only the lyrics matter. Therefore, there is no such thing as 'evil' or 'good' music.
- The end justifies the means — if it brings someone to Christ, God can use it. If it brings me into God's presence during worship, it must be from God.

The lyrics of Christian rock songs may in and of themselves be respectful to God and Christian principles, but can anyone honestly say that these Christians have created a 'new' song, or that their music compositions are inspired by God rather than by men? The evidence suggests otherwise and leads us to believe that Christian rockers are simply copying and imitating a music style that was created and inspired by men who in their lust for freedom — free sex, freedom to get high on drugs anytime they please, freedom to seek a god of some sort through altered states of consciousness, and freedom from any kind of authority — have rejected the God of the Bible. This is an important distinction to remember in the ongoing debate.

In the next chapters we will turn from our very brief survey of its history, its current state and its Christian imitations, to take a closer look at rock music's content and characteristics. In doing so we will not be short of information. Publicity is the staple diet of most rock performers, and their opinions, convictions, aims and philosophies are often public property. We can therefore get a great deal of help straight from the musical horses' mouths. It may not make pleasant reading, but it will certainly help to fill in the major pieces in the phenomenal musical jigsaw called rock.

4.

STRANGE FIRE

We sold our soul for rock 'n' roll!

(Heavy metal band Black Sabbath)[1]

One of our major concerns about rock music's suitability for Christian worship or evangelism is based on its close connection with the occult and pagan religious practices. It has been said that 'Any fusion of secular methods with sacred intentions is in danger of becoming a truce with the world,' and if rock's connection with the occult and pagan religions can be demonstrated, then its fusion with the Christian faith would be absurd as well as dangerous. It would not merely be a truce with the world but with the underworld; and 'What fellowship has righteousness with lawlessness? And what communion has light with darkness?' (2 Corinthians 6:14).

Dark world

The word 'occult' means 'hidden, secret, supernatural', but we must not let those vague words fool us and hide the fact that the occult world is real and menacing. One of Satan's most successful tactics has been to convince people that he does not exist, that he and his agents are just figments of man's religious imagination. Yet no Christian should fall for that. The Bible teems with references to him, and always as a real and living being. He is brilliantly intelligent and staggeringly powerful; the Bible even goes so far as to call him 'the god of this age' (2 Corinthians 4:4). What is more, he is in vicious and bitter opposition to everything that is good, wholesome, pure and righteous. The very word 'Satan' means 'adversary' or 'opponent', and as biblical scholar Leon Morris says, 'Satan is a malignant reality, always hostile to God and to God's people.'[2]

The Bible is equally clear about the existence of Satan's countless agents, which it refers to as 'demons', 'devils' and 'evil spirits'. We read of them oppressing some people and possessing others. They have the power to bring about physical, mental and spiritual disorder, as well as to cause their victims to be gripped by sin of one kind or another.

One of the greatest powers possessed by Satan and his agents is their ability to appear harmless, benign, or even helpful. The Bible says that there are times when Satan disguises himself as 'an angel of light' (2 Corinthians 11:14) — and this must surely be one of the reasons why this dark, sinister world has so much fascination for many people. The UK-based magazine *Mojo* observed that 'the nineteen-sixties witnessed an occult revival unlike anything seen since Aleister Crowley's *Golden Dawn*',[3] while the Spiritualists' Association of Great Britain has spoken of the greatest upsurge of interest in spiritualism since Victorian days. There are flourishing occult book clubs and large sections of libraries and bookshops in many countries are now devoted to the subject. There are hundreds of thousands of witches operating all over the world, while horoscopes appear in countless newspapers and magazines and are e-mailed to millions of people on a daily basis.

Pastors alert to the situation are alarmed by the growing number of shops selling books and paraphernalia related to new age beliefs (which originated from pagan religion), the gothic lifestyle and the occult. One has written, 'I feel called to challenge and warn the church about witchcraft. Some feel the UK is under judgement and the church needs to rise up and respond.'[4] No wonder the experienced British evangelist Peter Anderson begins the first chapter of his book *Talk about the Devil* by saying, 'One of the biggest challenges facing the Christian Church today is the fact that thousands of people are interested in the supernatural but rarely, if ever, associate it with the ministry of the church!'[5]

Ignorance iceberg

As one should expect, Satan and his forces have deeply invaded man's social and cultural structures — and music has not been left out.

One of the people with whom we discussed the whole subject of rock music is a highly qualified Christian musician who writes, arranges, performs and teaches music from the classics to rock. In a private paper he wrote, 'There is no disputing that satanic and occult connections occur in the rock world ... this is a spiritual minefield and it is right that you should be concerned that many Christians are ignorant of these matters.' In a Christian music magazine article Dave Roberts warned naive readers, 'I'll bet you aren't aware of all the occultic propaganda in your record collections.'[6]

How widespread is the ignorance? We can certainly give many examples from our observation and experience over the years. We have seen young Christians wearing T-shirts advertising groups heavily into occultism. A UK music store owned by Christians once had a large central display promoting Black Sabbath's album *Live Evil*. At an evangelical church we once found the youth leader playing 'Bat out of Hell' by Meat Loaf while preparing the church hall for that night's coffee bar; he was amazed when we told him of the group's occult connections and said that he had been playing the album all afternoon — it was one of his favourites! At another church we had a limited opportunity to speak on rock music and the gospel and when we got back to our host's home he immediately went to his music collection, picked out a fistful of albums and said, 'These will have to go. I had no idea these groups were into the occult.'

In these early days of the twenty-first century, Christian young people are still in serious danger of being affected by occult influences from music. To give one example, today's rave music represents the occult philosophy, providing an experience that one raver calls 'the closest I have ever felt to god'. Raves were primarily an English phenomenon during the late nineteen-eighties and early nineteen-nineties and were conducted in large venues such as abandoned warehouses and open fields. Eventually, the British Government became concerned that raves were a dangerous, antisocial phenomenon that had to be shut down, but rave parties never disappeared completely and within a few years they had become a cult event in the United States.[7] In his book *Rave Culture: An Insider's Overview*, author Jimi Fritz noted that there are probably more ravers today than there were hippies in the nineteen-sixties. He pointed out that this 'life-changing ritualistic, cultural phenomenon is as powerful as any spiritual practice from the past or present'. In fact, many young people who have had no previous interest in religion start to develop an interest in spirituality after attending a few raves. Christian rave DJ Scott Blackwell has participated in enough secular raves to know this is true. In a *Charisma* magazine article he wrote, 'There is something about the repetitiveness and energy of the electronic dance music that causes people to drop barriers and let walls down. It's worship to them — they just don't know who or what they are worshipping.'[8] While rave may be relatively new, techno-trance DJ Goa Gil tells us that its methods are as old as pagan religion: 'Music has undergone a complete cycle. It started in ancient times with tribal drumming and now it's come back to tribal trance techno. I'm basically using this whole party situation as a medium to do magic, to remake the tribal pagan ritual for the 21st century; it's an initiation.'[9]

We are sure that this is just the tip of an 'ignorance iceberg' and that thousands of Christians, including pastors and worship leaders, are unknowingly supporting the work of musicians whose beliefs and practices they would find frightening and revolting. We are aware that the 'shock effect' works only when the occult is blatantly present in rock music, but Satan is the master of subtlety and we will see how he has disguised the occult in pop music.

Before we present the often repulsive evidence about rock's constant connection with shocking occult practices, it would help to learn why of all the arts, music is the most effective at touching the spiritual side of life and even opening doors to new spiritual experiences. The search for new spiritualism is foundational to the occult experience. Along the way we will also discover how occult beliefs and practices have infiltrated even seemingly innocuous soft rock music.

Reality check

Beethoven is reported to have said, 'Music is the mediator between intellectual and sensuous life ... the one spiritual entrance into the higher world.' John Williams, the famed movie soundtrack composer of *Star Wars, ET* and *Indiana Jones* agreed that music is 'something spiritual'.[10] Mickey Hart believes that music can 'form a union with the spirit world; it is the preferred medium for communication with the gods'.[11] When performing on stage, Pete Townshend felt 'an incredible almost spiritual experience' that was 'sacred'.[12] Robert Jourdain went even further stating that 'music possesses us — it really is as if some "other" has entered not just our bodies but our intentions, taking us over.'[13] Reflecting back on her part in the original Woodstock music festival in 1969, Grace Slick, lead singer of the rock band Jefferson Airplane (later Starship) asked, 'Were we the bands there to invoke the spirits? Were we all shamans (occult priests), channelling an unknown energy?'[14]

If music is indeed spiritual and has such power to possess us, it is worth exploring what 'spirits' are behind much of rock music. The very word 'music' comes from the Greek word for muses, the spirit guides of ancient Greece credited with inspiring men to create art, poetry and music. Many rock artists who have great influence over other musicians believe they are channelling spirits when they create their music; *but which spirits* — holy or unholy? Here are their answers, in their own words:

Tori Amos: 'It's arrogant to think you can create music on your own; there's a co-creation going on. It's really nice when they visit my body. It's an energy force.'[15]

John Lennon: 'When the real music comes to me, it has nothing to do with me 'cause I'm just a channel. It's given to me and I transcribe it.'[16]

Alanis Morissette: 'A lot of the songs were written in 15-30 minutes, very stream-of-consciousness, as though it was being channelled through us.'[17]

Robert Plant of Led Zeppelin: 'I was holding a paper and pencil, then all of a sudden my hand was writing out words. "There's a lady who's sure all that glitters is gold and she's buying a stairway to heaven." I just sat there, looked at the words and then I almost leapt out of my seat.'[18]

Members of Black Sabbath: 'Although it's just a rock and roll band, there's a phenomenon that the stuff just comes from somewhere and we just happened to be the ones it came to.'[19]

Ozzy Osbourne of Black Sabbath: 'I don't know if I'm a medium for some outside force. Whatever it is, frankly I hope it's not what I think it is — Satan.'[20]

Carlos Santana: His muse is a spirit guide named Metatron and *Rolling Stone* magazine once reported, 'Santana keeps a yellow legal pad handy to record the music when it comes to him "just like a fax machine".'[21]

It is not difficult to see that statements like these have religious overtones. Jon Anderson, the lead singer of the progressive rock band Yes, understood that music has 'always been religious … a passion and a vehicle for understanding why we are here, a re-membering of the past and ritual.'[22] To Jimi Hendrix, 'Rock music is more than music, it's like church.'[23] The background of his music was '…a spiritual blues thing. We're making our music into elec-tric church music, a new kind of Bible you carry in your hearts.'[24] Santana describes his music as 'a high you can't get at church.'[25] During concerts Paul Stanley, guitarist for KISS, thought of him-self 'as a holy roller preacher, I'm testifying and getting every-body riled up for the power of almighty rock 'n' roll!'[26] Robbie Kreiger, guitarist for The Doors, saw the band as 'revivalists and wanted our audience to undergo a religious experience.'[27] Re-call here what U2 has also said; paraphrasing a U2 song, 'church services and rock concerts are one, but not the same.'

A Grateful Dead concert was not just a rock event, it was a 'place to worship.' One fan wrote that the band was the high priest, the audience the congregation, the songs the liturgy, and the dancing the prayer. Together they 'collectively stormed the gates of heaven and entered a sacred chamber of the universe.'[28]

Thirty years later, rock is still going strong as a religion for its devotees. Dr Russell Newcombe says of all-night dance raves, 'Dancing at raves may be construed as the method by which ravers worship the god of altered consciousness.'[29] One Led Zeppelin fan said 'he grew up worshipping Zeppelin like they were church.'[30]

But who exactly is being worshipped? We begin our answer by exploring the spiritual impact on rock music made by one particular man.

The wickedest man in the world?

In the nineteen-twenties the British press bestowed this label on Aleister Crowley (1875-1947) after learning of his orgies and goat sacrifices at a former abbey in Sicily. Crowley has been variously described as a drug and sex fiend, an occult priest, a black magician, a Satanist and the most successful evangelist of pagan religion in the twentieth century and is reputed to have said about himself, 'I may be a Black Magician, but I am a ... [expletive deleted] good one.' He also referred to himself as the Great Beast 666, perhaps to bait Christians, whom he openly despised. Oddly, in 2002 he was also named in the BBC list of 100 Greatest Britons along with Johnny Rotten of the Sex Pistols.[31] Crowley's *Magick in Theory and Practice* is still a very popular book among occultists. 'Do what thou wilt shall be the whole of the Law' was his over-arching rule for living and from that rule sprang today's popular 'Do your own thing' philosophy. Another popular Crowley saying claims that 'Every man and every woman is a star'. Crowley devotee and rock musician Steven Marque says that Crowley 'belonged to an age-old tradition which saw the Eternal as the ultimate unity in which all the opposites were reconciled, including good and evil. He had lived in the East and was familiar with the scriptures of both the Hindus and Buddhists for whom these ideas were commonplace. He developed elaborate rites of sexual magick.'[32]

Given his reputation and teachings about self-deity, it is inevitable that Crowley would appeal to certain rock musicians of the late twentieth century. Jimmy Page (the Led Zeppelin guitarist behind the music used today in television commercials for Cadillac) owned Crowley's mansion in Scotland for many years and is said to possess a large collection of Crowley memorabilia. Page says, 'I've employed Crowley's system in my own day-to-day life.'[33] David Bowie once admitted that 'my own over-riding interest was in kabbala and Crowleyism, that whole dark and rather fearsome never-world.'[34]

Citing Page, Led Zeppelin and Bowie may sound very 'dated' and therefore irrelevant to a rising generation of teenagers today. Many Christians might argue that Crowley's impact ended in the nineteen-seventies and that today's rock music is free of any connection, but the fact is that his laws of 'Do your own thing' and 'Every man/woman is a star' remain central themes in rock music. These themes can be found floating through many contemporary songs. *Ordo Templi Orientis*, the religious organization associated with Crowley, maintains a web site list of what they call Magick Musick, 'recordings of interest to the occultist'. Bands on their list include Led Zeppelin, about whom the site says, 'First pressing of their third album had "Do what thou wilt..." engraved on the lead-off track. Jimmy Page provided an early soundtrack to Kenneth Anger's movie *Lucifer Rising*.'[35] Other bands or rock artists listed on the site include Ozzy Osbourne (for his performance of 'Mr. Crowley You Said It All'), Iron Maiden, Gillan (started by former Deep Purple vocalist Ian Gillan), Tod Rundgren, Ultramarine and Celtic Frost. Ministry is also listed; the title of their 1992 album *Psalm 69 — How to Succeed and How to Suck Eggs* was taken from Crowley's *The Book of Lies*.

Crowley's way is still explicitly found in contemporary lyrics. Goth-metal band Moonspell sings, 'Crowleyean erotic laws will rule at last.'[36] Alphaville sings, 'Do what you will shall be our destiny.'[37] German industrial alt-metal band KMFDM sings, 'Do what you want as you see fit.'[38] In their song 'Do What Thou Wilt', punk rock band Lords of the New Church sing, 'There is no grace; there is no guilt; there is the law: do what thou wilt.' According to *Rolling Stone* magazine, P-Nut, bass player for the funk metal/alternative band 311 who were ostensibly formed to 'make music with a positive message behind it,'[39] is obsessed with four things: music, pot, *The Simpsons* and occult figure Aleister Crowley. P-Nut's right shin has a tattoo spelling out Crowley's motto, 'Do what thou wilt shall be the whole of the law.'[40]

Crowley's religion can be boiled down to the worship of one's self as god. This is nothing new; it is the most ancient of pagan religions. At the dawn of human history, Eve was tempted by the serpent with the promise that 'in the day you eat of it [the forbidden fruit of the tree of life] your eyes will be opened, and you will be like God, knowing good and evil' (Genesis 3:5). The serpent was Satan in disguise — and the same old devil who was thrown out of heaven and down to the earth by God because he said in his heart, 'I will ascend into heaven, I will exalt my throne above the stars of God' (Isaiah 14:13).

Now exiled from heaven, Satan still seduces men and women who reject the true God to believe that they can become like gods, if only they will follow his directions. This is the ultimate 'occult' religion. This anti-gospel/pro-self message has been aggressively promoted through the New Age movement (the Age of Aquarius) and Eastern religions such as Hinduism and Buddhism, but is there proof that rock music itself is being used as a primary force to spread this new gospel?

The lads from Liverpool — revisited

The Beatles are rightfully considered to be a seminal band in the history of rock 'n' roll. When they first hit American shores, they were celebrated as the cute mop-tops from England who sang catchy pop tunes with innocuous lyrics like 'I Want to Hold Your Hand'. Paul McCartney is recognized as one of the finest pop songwriters of all time for his knack of combining simple lyrics with instantly 'singable' tunes. John Lennon's 'Imagine' may well be the most recognizable pop song across the globe today and there can be no argument about The Beatles' over-sized influence on every rock musician who followed.

Even many Christian musicians and leaders cite The Beatles as a top influence on their music. On their *Much Afraid* CD, Jars of Clay added layers of Beatles-style arrangements to the mix. Band leader Dan Haseltine says, 'Steve, our guitarist, is a Beatles fanatic and I'm sure that's had an influence on our writing.'[41] Switchfoot's Tim Foreman claims, 'I've been very influenced by the bass playing of Paul McCartney.'[42] During their 1999 Supernatural Experience tour, dc Talk performed The Beatles' 'Hello Goodbye' and John Lennon's 'Give Peace a Chance'.[43] Caedmon's Call performs a cover of The Beatles' 'We Can Work It Out' in concert.[44] Phil Keaggy was so enamoured with the music of The Beatles while growing up that one music reviewer commented, 'If there's one criticism that's dogged Phil Keaggy throughout his solo career, it's been his seeming fixation on Paul McCartney and The Beatles.'[45] Any musical group exerting such strong influence over leading Christian musicians deserves close scrutiny.

In 1966 John Lennon made this curious statement: 'I always wondered what it was about politics and government that was wrong. Now, since reading some books by Aldous Huxley, I've suddenly found out what it's all about.'[46] The Beatles saluted Huxley by including his photograph on the cover of their *Sergeant Pepper* album. Huxley (1894-1963) was described by *The Guardian* as a novelist, eugenicist, acid-head and true seer.[47] His grandfather was Thomas Huxley, popularly known as 'Darwin's Bulldog' because of his ferocious promotion of Charles Darwin's evolution theory. Aldous Huxley's book *Brave*

New World (1932) was a disturbing vision of a scientifically-engineered utopia. His psychedelic experiments, first reported in his book *The Doors Of Perception* (1954), set in motion an international drug culture involving millions. There is evidence to suggest that Huxley and Crowley met at least once, and Huxley would surely have been familiar with Crowley's *Book of the Law*, not least through his close friend John Sullivan who was also a Crowley disciple.

Timothy Leary, who popularized LSD in the nineteen-sixties and was a close friend of Aldous Huxley, also considered himself to be the reincarnation of Aleister Crowley. In his autobiography *Flashbacks* (1983) Leary recounts the following advice that Huxley gave him: 'Become a cheerleader for evolution. We must spread the word. The obstacle to this, Timothy, is the Bible.'[48] How would this gospel be spread? According to Leary, 'First you start with rock 'n' roll to spark a new religious revival. [Rock] is an instrument for evangelic education that few over 30 can grasp.'[49] And who would be the musicians to do it? 'God has come back as the 4-sided mandala[50] — the Beatles; the means by which to spread the new gospel is music. I rejoice to see our culture taken over by joyful young messiahs who dispel our fears and charm us back into the pagan dance of harmony.'[51] Is Leary's claim about the Beatles as the new messiahs of Crowley's gospel just the imagination of an acid head who used too much LSD for most of his life, or is there further proof beyond Leary that the Beatles spread this new gospel through their music?

In the summer of 1969, the Beatles' George Harrison produced the hit single, 'The Hare Krishna Mantra', performed by George and the devotees of the London Radha-Krishna Temple. The Hare Krishna chant became a household word, especially in the UK where the BBC had featured the Hare Krishna Chanters four times on the popular television programme *Top of the Pops*. At about the same time several Hare Krishna devotees joined with John Lennon and Yoko Ono in recording the hit song

'Give Peace a Chance' in Montreal. The Hare Krishna followers had been visiting with the Lennons for several days, discussing world peace and self-realization.[52]

In a 1982 interview, George Harrison said that by the time Hare Krishna came to England in 1969, 'John and I had already gotten a hold of the album *Krishna Consciousness*. We had played it a lot and liked it.' The interviewer told Harrison: 'I don't think it's possible to calculate just how many people were turned on to Krishna consciousness by your song "My Sweet Lord."' Harrison replied, 'My idea in "My Sweet Lord," because it sounded like a "pop song," was to sneak up on them a bit ... by the time it gets to "Hare Krishna," they're already hooked, and their foot's tapping, and they're already singing along "Hallelujah," to kind of lull them into a sense of false security. And then suddenly it turns into "Hare Krishna," and they will all be singing that before they know what's happened.'[53]

Nor did this proselytizing of an occult religion occur only after the Beatles had to all intents and purposes broken up. They were heavily involved in Eastern mysticism several years earlier, when the group came increasingly under the influence of the Maharishi Mahesh Yogi, an Indian Hindu guru. The band also began using psychedelic drugs, foreshadowing the 'flower children' of the following few years and in the early part of 1966 made the *Revolver* album, incorporating their new interests in drugs and Eastern religion.[54]

This brings us to the legendary *Sergeant Pepper's Lonely Hearts Club Band* album, whose cover was 'festooned with the band's wildly eclectic gallery of heroes' and included 'the paradoxical wisdom of Eastern religious philosophy in "Within You Without You" and the joys of mind-expanding drugs in "Lucy in the Sky with Diamonds"'.[55] Aleister Crowley was one of the 'heroes' featured on the cover.

The Beatles were not the only 'joyful young messiahs' envisioned by Leary. Ray Manzarek, keyboardist for The Doors, summed up the entire occult mission of rock when he said, 'We saw the music as a vehicle to become proselytizers of a new religion, *a religion of self, of each man as God*. That was the original idea behind The Doors'[56] (emphasis added).

There seems no denying that rock music has been used by dark forces to sell the Eastern religious principle that god is in everyone and everything, that we are all part of god and each man is god. But the sales pitch could never have succeeded through the blatant occultism and drug-addled behaviour of Crowley, Leary and the shock-rockers listed in this chapter. That approach frightened the masses and Leary knew it. Instead, through the 'false security' (as Harrison put it) of middle of the road rock music, millions of people have been evangelized by the 'Do what thou wilt' mantra over the last forty years.

Perhaps the best example of this subtle, middle of the road approach is John Lennon's 'Imagine', written in 1971, whose lyrics have been memorized by countless millions all over the world:

> Imagine there's no heaven
> It's easy if you try
> No hell below us
> Above us only sky
> Imagine all the people
> Living for today.[57]

The song later includes the line 'And no religion too'. This is more than just another example of rock's distant past connection with the occult. To begin the 2006 Winter Olympic Games in Torino, Italy, Italian gymnast Juri Chechi, playing a shaman, struck a golden anvil to launch the opening ceremony that included a reading by Lennon's widow Yoko Ono and featured rock musician Peter Gabriel performing 'Imagine'.[58] With a catchy pop tune and memorable lyrics, Lennon has the whole world singing that the God of the Bible does not exist and the best we can do is just live for today!

Further evidence that Lennon carried forward the 'New Age gospel' is found in his other music. Lennon's 1970 album, *Plastic Ono Band*, included the song 'God' in which Lennon boldly sings, 'I don't believe in Bible, I don't believe in Jesus, I just believe in me, Yoko and me, And that's reality.' In 1979, he wrote a song titled 'Serve Yourself', in which he instructed his listeners: 'You got to serve yourself, nobody gonna do it for you.' Lennon was mocking Bob Dylan's conversion to Christianity with a nasty parody of Dylan's song, 'Gotta Serve Somebody'.[59]

Voodoo connection

Voodoo is a pagan religion that can be traced directly to the eighteenth-century West African Yoruba people and its African roots may go back over 6,000 years. Voodoo believers worship hundreds of spirits representing nature. The purpose of the voodoo worship ritual is to make contact with a spirit and gain its favour by offering animal sacrifices and gifts. The ritual includes shaking a rattle, beating drums, dancing and chanting. The dancing and drumming build in intensity until one dancer is possessed and falls to the ground, his or her body now controlled by the spirit.

Is there a credible voodoo connection to rock music? Best known for fronting the new wave group Talking Heads, David Byrne's solo work took him deep into the realm of world music. His experiences led him to tell *Rolling Stone* magazine that voodoo-related sounds 'are a big part of where our popular music comes from... Rock 'n' roll comes from those traditions, and I believe that power and influence it has had come because it carries a small part of that energy with it.'[60] A percussionist for the Jimi Hendrix Experience remarked that he played the same guitar rhythms 'that my father played in voodoo ceremonies.'[61]

After his visit to Africa, Mickey Hart recounted his personal epiphany about rock's rhythmic heritage: 'It was my first exposure to the mother rhythms from West Africa that later mutated into my tradition becoming rock 'n' roll. The rhythm of the drum was calling up something from these sleek cosmopolitan bodies that had been asleep. There was a power I couldn't ignore.'[62] To Robert Palmer (former rock music critic for the *New York Times*), the connection between rock and voodoo is clear: 'The central paradigm of rock 'n' roll is a kind of voodoo ... that's far removed from the sober values of western culture.'[63]

Warning label

Can there be any doubt about which god and which spirits have been channelled by these rock musicians? Can there be any question that whatever or whoever inspired the writing and performance of their rock music, it was not the Holy Spirit of the Bible? However cautious we may have to be in some other areas of the rock music debate, this is one in which we must be clear, definite and decisive. If a reader remains in any doubt about the connection between rock music and the occult, here in alphabetical order is a list of rock musicians whose music, lyrics or lifestyles demonstrate occult influences of one kind or another. Let no Christian reading this book say they were not warned. Readers may be shocked by the length of this list, but we make no apology for sharing the important material it contains.

AC/DC: A hallmark of their albums is the satanic 'S'. Their album *Back in Black* has a song entitled 'Hell's Bells', including the words 'Satan's gonna get you'. The cover of the album *Highway to Hell* shows a member with horns and another wearing a pentagram (a satanic symbol). The title song includes the words, 'I'm on my way to the promised land, I'm on the highway to hell.'

Aerosmith: Their album *Get your Wings* has on the cover the Winged Globe, an occultic symbol made up of a solar disc, the wings of a sparrow hawk, rams' horns and serpents and signifying the omnipresence of the sun god.

Alice Cooper: In a story syndicated in the American national press, he told how (as Vincent Furnier) he attended a seance at which a spirit was conjured and promised him and his band worldwide success if he would change his name to that of the spirit (Alice Cooper) and allow the spirit to possess his body. During an appearance on *The Muppet Show*, fun was made of his demon possession.

Tori Amos: This female rocker once said, 'I wanted to marry Lucifer. I don't consider him an evil source — we can all tap into that energy.'[64] She also attributes her songwriting to 'a co-creation going on. It's really nice when they visit my body. It's an energy force.'[65]

The Beatles: As documented above, they experimented with LSD and promoted the false religion of Hinduism. Harrison admitted to *Rolling Stone* magazine that the drug LSD opened his mind to this pagan religion. 'The first time I took it, it just blew everything away. I had such an overwhelming feeling of well-being, that there was a God, and I could see him in every blade of grass.'[66] Lennon believed that if he meditated long and hard enough, he would 'merge with God and acquire psychic powers, like clairvoyance and the ability to fly through the air. And he wanted those powers as badly as he wanted anything.'[67] Lennon and Yoko Ono were fascinated by the occult; he purchased entire sections of occult literature in bookstores.[68]

Occultist John Green was hired by Yoko Ono in 1974 to be her tarot card reader.[69]

Black Sabbath: The name of the group refers to an occult ritual and they have been known to introduce their concerts by holding black masses on stage, complete with a nude on an altar sprinkled with chicken blood. Their first album, *Black Sabbath*, pictured a witch on the front. Group member Bill Ward declares, 'Satan could be God,'[70] while Geezer, the bass player, claims he is the seventh son of a seventh son, is Lucifer, and can see the devil: 'It's a satanic world.'[71] Lead singer Ozzy Osbourne claims he was compelled to see the film *The Exorcist* twenty-six times and on another occasion said, 'The devil is within us all the time. It's here. All this is the devil.'[72] Several members of the group admit to astral projection. Their albums include *We sold our soul for rock and roll*, with the cover featuring the satanic 'S', and *Sabbath, Bloody Sabbath* with the cover showing a nude satanic ritual emblazoned with the number 666. Included in their promotional literature is a bumper sticker with the words: 'I am possessed by Black Sabbath.'

David Bowie: In an interview with *Rolling Stone* magazine he said, 'Rock has always been the devil's music. You can't convince me that it isn't. I honestly believe everything that I've said. I believe that rock 'n' roll is dangerous.'[73] In the same interview he also said, 'Rock 'n' roll will destroy you. It lets in lower elements and shadows. Rock has always been the devil's music.'[74] At one point in his career it was reported that he drew pentagrams (satanic symbols) on his walls and made hexes (other satanic devices) while burning candles.[75] He admitted that 'my own over-riding interest was in kabbala and Crowleyism, that whole dark and rather fearsome never-world.'[76]

Terence Trent D'arby: Known more for his sexually-charged songs, D'arby also connects with New Age occult belief in the song 'Vibrator' with the lyrics 'Beautiful child of God and man, there's a messiah inside of you.'

Disturbed: The heavy metal band was a hit act at the 2001 Ozz Fest (Ozzy Osbourne's modern rock festival). Their dark lyrics include 'Bloodlust tonight, now I can't control my unbalanced soul, get back from me demon, or be exorcised!' and 'You want a Deity like me, you want a God'.

The Doors: An entire chapter could be written about the occult connections of this influential rock band. Best known for the smash hit 'Light My Fire', they took their name and inspiration from Huxley's *Doors of Perception*, the book about his psychedelic drug experiments. Lead singer and sex symbol Jim Morrison was overcome and possessed by spirit guides during concerts and 'was the shaman (occult priest) who took people on a mystical journey to a darker psychic realm.'[77] The Doors performed a song called 'Shaman's Blues'. In his poem titled 'American Prayer', Morrison writes, 'The music and voices are all around us, choose they croon the Ancient Ones', then implores us to 'reinvent the gods, celebrate symbols from deep elder forests', and asks the 'great creator of being' for a new creed and a mandala.[78] In 'Soft Parade', he mocks gospel preachers and denies the power of the God of the Bible when he proclaims, 'You CANNOT petition the Lord with prayer! We need something new to get us through.'[79] And could that 'new' thing be 'a snake who is old and whose skin is cold'?[80]

The Eagles: The name comes from the chief spirit in the Indian cosmos.[81] The group was formed under the occult influence of Carlos Castaneda (1925-1998), a sorcerer who wrote several books about traditional Native American shamanism, ancient

Toltec sorcery and experiences with the hallucinogenic drug peyote. The band members admit to writing many songs while under the influence of peyote. Several of their songs, such as 'Witchy Woman', 'One of These Nights' and 'Good Day in Hell', include satanic or occult lyrics. One of their songs, 'Undercover Angel', speaks about having sexual intercourse with evil spirits and one album bears the occult goat's head insignia.

Earth, Wind and Fire: The group's name comes from the three major elements in the cosmos. Their song 'Serpentine Fire' speaks of the sinal life entity system found in the Shah Krishna Yogi Meditation Cult. On the American television show *20/20* on 15 January 1981 they were filmed in a band member's home which was full of Eastern gods and occult symbols. On the programme, they claimed to 'have an interest in Eastern religion, astrology, numerology and the occult'. Lead singer Maurice White believes that he possesses powers from previous incarnations and has the group join hands in a circle before beginning a show, so as to tune in to the force of the 'higher powers'.[82]

Fleetwood Mac: The group had a hit called 'Rhiannon' which was dedicated to a Welsh witch.[83] Lead singer Stevie Nick is reported as having dedicated songs in concert to 'all the witches of the world'.

Jimi Hendrix: Before his death Jimi Hendrix was heavily involved in the demonic supernatural and openly admitted that he had visions in which he communed with spirits. He wore a medicine shirt from a Hopi reservation and claimed that he had come from an asteroid belt off the coast of Mars. He also claimed to have seen UFOs filling the skies above the Woodstock rock festival.[84] Hindu gods were featured on the cover of his album *Axis: Bold as Love*.

Iron Maiden: This heavy metal band has come under fire for making more satanic music than almost any other band. The title track of their album *The Number of the Beast* is a song called '666'. The opening track 'Moonchild' is supposedly sung by the devil. Many songs refer to the Antichrist and lyrics are obsessed with hellish imagery; seven out of eight songs on one album alone pertain to themes of death and assorted evils.[85]

Michael Jackson: *Newsweek* questioned dark songs like 'Billie Jean', 'Beat It' and 'Thriller', all huge hits for the megastar known as the King of Pop: 'Each one is quirky, strange, deeply personal, with offbeat lyrics that hint at Michael's own secret world of dreams and demons.'[86]

KISS: During their concerts they breathe fire, levitate their instruments and regurgitate blood. Their album covers bear the satanic 'S'. Their song 'God of Thunder' includes the words, 'I gather darkness to please me and I command you to kneel before the god of thunder and rock 'n' roll.'

Led Zeppelin: The band is currently featured on television commercials for Cadillac and is cited by Christian rock musicians as a key influence in their own ministries. The cover of *Presence* shows a strange object which guitarist Jimmy Page claimed to symbolize the force that enables the group to have such power over audiences, a power known only as a 'presence'. Page was so involved in the occult and Crowleyism that he would warrant a chapter to himself. The inside cover of the *House of the Holy* album has a picture of a naked man holding up a child in sacrifice to a mysterious light on the top of a ruined building.

Marilyn Manson: A member of the Church of Satan who rips up the Bible onstage, he proudly boasts, 'Hopefully, I'll be remembered as the person who brought an end to Christianity ... maybe through music we can finally do it.'[87] Manson claims his 1996 album *Antichrist Superstar* came via supernatural inspiration: 'I heard this album as finished, I heard it in dreams... It was like the revelations of John the Baptist or something.'[88] He wishes that every time people listen to the album 'maybe God will be destroyed in their heads...'[89]

Sarah McLachlan: Lilith Fair was a nineteen-nineties concert tour and travelling music festival that featured female musicians. McLachlan took the name from the medieval legend that Lilith was Adam's first wife and said she chose it because it represented the ultimate in feminism and celebrated the 'goddess' (a pagan religious term). But Lilith is also the name of a female Mesopotamian night demon and vampire believed to harm male children, who appears in both the Bible and the Talmud as a kind of night-demon. This led shock-rocker Marilyn Manson to comment that 'Lilith Fair is far more subversive and Satanic than anything I could have done. Here you have people playing this very innocuous folk music while providing Americans with very dangerous ideas about sexuality.'[90]

Meat Loaf: The band's album cover for *Bat out of Hell* features a demon and speaks of a mutant motorcyclist riding out of the pit of hell. The group's leader is reported as saying, 'When I go on stage, I get possessed.'[91] Their composer Jim Steinman said, 'I've always been fascinated by the supernatural and always felt rock was the perfect idiom for it.'[92]

Moody Blues: Still a favourite of the Baby Boomer generation, their album *In Search of the Lost Chord* speaks about a musical chord with supernatural properties. The inside of the album cover has a 'yantra' (the visual equivalent of a mantra in Transcendental Meditation). There are also instructions for the listener to stare at the geometric designs while the music is being played, in order to enter an altered state of consciousness. The title of one track on the record is 'OM', a Hindu Sanskrit word used for God, in which he is thought to be embodied in the very word itself.

Mötley Crüe: Their first hit album was *Shout at the Devil* featuring a black cover and a pentagram. The opening song denies the power of God and urges young people to 'Come now, children of the beast, be strong.' One of the band members admits that 'I've always flirted with the devil.'[93]

Nine Inch Nails: Band leader Trent Reznor responded to the critics by saying, 'Rock music was never meant to be safe. Your parents should hate it. If you think I worship Satan because of something you see in the *Closer* video with its images of a crucified monkey — great!'[94] He spends most of his time composing in rented Hollywood homes, including the one in Bel Air where followers of the infamous Charles Manson (who claimed to be both Christ and Satan) murdered actress Sharon Tate and four others in 1969.

The Rolling Stones: Still very popular today, their song 'Sympathy for the Devil' is a tribute to Satan's role in history and it has become an unofficial anthem for Satanists. *Newsweek* once called Mick Jagger 'the Lucifer of rock, the unholy roller' and spoke of 'his demonic power to affect people.'[95] Part of their album *Goat's Head Soup* was recorded at a voodoo ritual and the track includes the screams of those being possessed by evil spirits. The album cover design includes a colour picture of a goat's head (a satanic symbol) floating in a boiling cauldron. One of the songs is 'Dancing with Mr. D' and is about a midnight dance with the devil in a graveyard. Group member Keith Richard once said, 'There are black magicians who think we are acting as unknown agents of Lucifer and others who think we are Lucifer.'[96] On the cover of one of their earlier albums *Their Satanic Majesties Request*, the Stones dressed up as male witches.

Rush: Their album *Caress of Steel* has a cover design featuring a robed man levitating a pyramid. Most of their albums have a pentagram on the cover. They perform in front of a pentagram on stage.

Santana: Carlos Santana, the guitarist and leader of the early nineteen-seventies band of the same name, is immensely popular again today. He once was asked by *Guitar Player* magazine how he related his spiritual life to his guitar. Santana, a devotee of Indian guru Sri Chinmoy, replied, 'I am the string, and the Supreme is the musician. It's like sometimes I'm not aware I can do some of these things on my guitar, because in reality I'm not doing them, they are being done through me, which is one of the highest places anyone can reach. But when I'm really in tune with the Supreme, my guru, and my instrument, forget it, man, because it's totally beyond anything — and that's where I want to be. I just want to be in service to the Supreme. *It is the Supreme, your highest self*' [97] (emphasis added). One album was entitled *Abraxas*, the name of a leading demon spirit. Santana also recorded a hit song 'Black Magic Woman'.

Sepultura: A Death Metal band from Brazil, their *Morbid Visions* album has a song titled 'Crucifixion' with the lyrics 'We deny God and his rule, we defy his supreme force, crucified by the dark power, his death was a glory'. In the song 'Necromancer', the band sings about lost legions from hell and the wrath of demons.

Sigur Rof: The Icelandic post-rock/experimental band has a song titled 'Mother Earth' that mocks the Lord's Prayer with the lyric 'Our Mother, who art in Earth, Hallowed be Thy name'. Another song has the words, 'Naked animals beat me, and a Saviour knocks ... I want to cut and slice myself to death.'

Van Halen: The band's debut album featured the song 'Running with the Devil', which most people took as being a harmless analogy to describe the hard life of a loner on the road. But the lyrics 'I live my life like there's no tomorrow, and all I've got I had to steal' had a much darker message.

The Who: The leader is Pete Townshend, who followed the teachings of Meher Baba, an Eastern metaphysical guru. Townshend put out a solo album which included a Hindu prayer and declared that 'Baba is Christ'. Tony Palmer says that when they play 'there is a distinct feeling of the presence of evil'.[98]

That list is frightening and there is no saying how many other bands, singers and musicians may be secretly involved in the occult and whose music may be impregnated with the poison. Yet in 1983 the Christian music magazine *Buzz* assured its readers that the issue was limited to 'an occasional rock singer ... dabbling with the occult'.[99] The statement was not true then and would make nonsense if claimed today. Yet in spite of all the evidence of rock's connection to dark powers, some still approach this concern just as lightly today as *Buzz* did when telling its readers that 'to teach that to be in the same room as a Led Zeppelin record will leave oneself open to demon possession is unscriptural nonsense!'[100]

Under the influence?

A common interview question posed to Christian rock bands is, 'What are your musical influences?' John Cooper of the Christian rock band Skillet gave this reply: 'I think what happens is that you hear music, and even if you don't necessarily love it and don't know that you are influenced by it, you are. You take away a little of something from lots of different bands. And without knowing it, I kind of integrate it into an idea or something like that.'[101] Cooper touched on the common thread among songwriters which is that each one has been influenced in some way, great or small, by every other musician they allowed into their minds and souls. The co-author of this book Dan Lucarini speaks of this from personal experience as he himself has written close to 100 original music compositions. 'Sometimes the influence is obvious as we mimic another's style and someone else points out to us, "You sound just like...!" At other times it is more subtle, showing up in the riffs, the harmonies or the chord progressions we choose without even realizing that we were imitating another musician. This silent transfer of influence is a spiritual thing, and instinctively understood by songwriters, but often we cannot see the wood for the trees and someone else has to point it out for us.'

Since songwriting is a spiritual task and songwriters are in essence the embodiment of other musical influences that have been allowed into their minds and souls, it is perfectly fair to question one's musical influences, even more so if one feels called to lead music in the church. The editor of worshipmusic. com seems to agree when he poses this important question: 'Is it OK to be influenced by musicians from arenas *other* than Contemporary Christian worship circles? That's a great discussion that needs to take place in the Church today.'[102] We could not agree with him more, and would sharpen the question to ask this: 'Is it right for a Christian musician to be influenced by one who has any connection to the devil, the occult, or pagan religions?' No Christian should hesitate to answer that question in the negative.

Sadly, as demonstrated earlier with regard to The Beatles, some of the secular musicians listed in this chapter are claimed as key musical influences by Christian musicians and worship leaders (this will be discussed in more detail in another chapter). Additionally, the Christian music industry does not help matters when it compares Christian rock bands to some of these same secular bands — and almost always in a most favourable way. One Christian retail chain even offers a handy *Music Recommendation Guide* comparing Christian artists to some of the same bands mentioned above.[103]

Put out that fire!

We entitled this chapter 'Strange fire'. The phrase comes from the King James (or Authorised) Version of the Bible, where we read that Aaron's sons Nadab and Abihu 'offered *strange fire* before the LORD, which he commanded them not' (Leviticus 10:1). In the New King James Version, 'strange' is rendered 'profane' and this helps us to get a clearer picture. God had given very specific instructions about the preparation and offering of sacrifices. Certain things were taboo; precise rules had to govern what they did.

But Nadab and Abihu ignored God's commands and 'did their own thing'. As a well-known Bible commentary quotes, 'Instead of taking the fire from the brazen altar, they seem to have been content with common fire and thus perpetrated an act which, considering the descent of the miraculous fire they had so recently witnessed (in chapter 9) ... betrayed a carelessness, an irreverence, a want of faith.'[104] The result was disastrous; we read that moments later that 'fire went out from the LORD and devoured them, and they died...' (Leviticus 10:2). In his book *Gospel Worship*, the seventeenth-century divine Jeremiah Burroughs issued a stern warning to those who dare to bring profane offerings: 'If we are not careful to sanctify his Holy Name, God himself will sanctify it and sometimes by fire.'[105]

The writer of the book of Hebrews makes it clear to us that the God who did this to Aaron's sons is still the same today and is 'a consuming fire' (Hebrews 12:29).

The severity of the punishment meted out to Nadab and Abihu shows the seriousness of their sin and is a clear warning to us today, not least in the area of rock music used in God's service. But along with this warning the Bible gives us an equally clear command: 'For you were once darkness, but now you are light in the Lord. Walk as children of light (for the fruit of the Spirit is in all goodness, righteousness, and truth), finding out what is acceptable to the Lord. And have no fellowship with the unfruitful works of darkness, but rather expose them' (Ephesians 5:8-11).

Pulling the negative warning and the positive command together, our message to the Christian rock music fan is clear and simple: *put out the fire*! Demonstrate once and for all your allegiance to Christ and your opposition to Satan by clearing these musicians' material out of your life and out of your home — MP3s, CDs, memory sticks, videos, records, tapes, books, magazines, posters, clothing, badges, *everything!* God certainly intends you to have music in your life but 'What accord has Christ with Belial [Satan]?' (2 Corinthians 6:15). Advice given by Dave Roberts to *Buzz* readers over twenty years ago remains just as sound today: 'If you are serious about being a disciple of Christ you should not lay yourself open to possible demonic influence through these records. You should destroy them and discontinue buying material of that nature. Do not trot out pathetic excuses about not listening to the words either. If you don't think about what you are listening to then you will find your subconscious mind is slowly poisoned by these celebrations of lust and the occult.'[106] Learn instead to 'be imitators of God...' (Ephesians 5:1).

What about material from other groups not mentioned? You could certainly begin by checking the words, the sounds and the art on their CD covers or web sites. Closer examination might tell you a lot more than you realized! And if in doubt, *never give the benefit of that doubt to the devil.*

Of course, throwing out occult or doubtful material will not be an automatic passport to holiness. The Bible has a story about an evil spirit leaving a man, but returning later to repossess him with seven spirits worse than itself, because although the man's house was swept clean it was unoccupied (Matthew 12:44). Make sure that evil is replaced by good. That could mean better music — music that is glorifying to God in *every* way, completely free of any doubtful influence. It might also mean using your time more productively than passively soaking up anti-Christian philosophies and values carried along by the message of the music.

5.

BODY LANGUAGE

The West is the only civilization to have created an art form
whose sole purpose is to attack morality.
(Martha Bayles, speaking about rock music)[1]

A nother major reason why many Christians are concerned about rock music's suitability for use in God's service is its alleged association with sexual immorality. Of all the torrents of e-mails and letters the authors have received about their books on rock music, sex is the subject matter that has apparently created the most 'heat'. Yet even the mere mention of the charge to Christian rockers and their fans is enough to provoke intense and sometimes furious denials. All we ask at this point is that readers put aside their prejudices and preconceived notions and examine the facts we present.

We feel it right to warn our readers that some of the material quoted in this chapter will not be suitable for children or even some older Christians. Exposing extreme sexual immorality carries its own dangers, and we are mindful of the apostle Paul's admonition that 'it is shameful even to speak of those things which are done by them in secret' (Ephesians 5:12) and King David's statement, 'I will set nothing wicked before my eyes' (Psalm 101:3). In an attempt to balance the requirement for biblical modesty with the need to expose blatant sexual immorality we have deliberately left out many other quotations that are far more graphic than those we have included. We should also add that instead of immersing ourselves in the filth involved we have relied heavily on 'second-hand' research from secular sources such as mainstream magazines and newspapers, and in some cases felt it necessary to modify quotations in the interest of Christian decency.

It is hardly rocket science to know why rock music and sex are linked. At the dawn of rock 'n' roll in the nineteen-fifties, 'While a car radio in the front seat rocked, kids in the back seat were [having sex] to the hard rock beat. The back seat produced a sexual revolution and the car radio was the medium for subversion.'[2] This was at a time when the lyrics were cleverly arranged to sound so innocent that parents would hardly be alarmed — but if the *lyrics* passed the 'parent test' was it the *music* that did the trick? We are reminded of Elvis Presley's notorious appearance on the *Ed Sullivan Show* where although he sang songs with clean sounding lyrics the cameras were ordered to show him from the waist up.

By 1977 *US News and World Report* had warned, 'Hot-selling songs with sexually explicit lyrics are moving up the charts, causing widespread concern about the effects on youth across the United States.'[3] Ten years later the American philosopher Allan Bloom made this assessment in his important book *The Closing of the American Mind*: 'Rock music has one appeal only, a barbaric appeal to sexual desire — not love, not *eros*, but sexual desire undeveloped and untutored. Rock gives children, on a silver platter, with all the public authority of the entertainment industry, everything their parents always used to tell them they had to wait for until they grew up and would understand later.'

There seemed good reason for these observations. A typical Rolling Stones show was described as 'an orgy of sexual celebration, with Jagger as the head cheerleader.'[4] When they appeared on the *Ed Sullivan Show*, they were forced by the host to change the lyrics of their hit song about sexual immorality 'Let's Spend the Night Together' to 'Let's spend *some time* together'. Lead singer Mick Jagger was said to have rolled his eyes in protest when he came to the censored lyric. In 1971, Jagger told *Newsweek*, 'What I do is very much the same as a girl's strip-tease dance'[5] and in 1975 he said to *Rolling Stone* magazine, 'Sometimes, being on stage is better than [sex].'[6]

Has anything changed? Fast-forward to 2006 and American football's Super Bowl XL in Detroit. As millions of families watched the Rolling Stones' half-time show the National Football League (NFL) used special technology to make sure the sexually offensive lyrics were not heard. During the song 'Start Me Up', the microphone was turned down when Mick Jagger sang a lyric referring to a male sexual experience.

Sound was also cut off when he used a slang word for a man's sex organ.[7] The NFL may have 'bleeped out' the sexual lyrics, but an estimated one billion viewers worldwide (obviously including countless Christians) still watched Jagger's sexually-charged stage moves surrounded by scantily-clad women dancers. The more things change, the more they remain the same!

Today, our culture has become so numb to the sexual themes in rock and pop that KISS, one of the leading sex-rock bands of all time, is now considered so tame they were also invited to perform in a Super Bowl half-time show and even to do Pepsi commercials. Meanwhile sex in modern rock music has become much more pornographic, violent, sadistic and masochistic, and bands like Red Hot Chili Peppers and The Jesus Lizard even perform onstage in the nude. How did we become so numb to sexual immorality and what part, if any, did rock have in conditioning Christians to accept things that once were shunned?

From megastar Jimi Hendrix (who claimed to have slept with 1,000 women) onwards, many of rock's leading performers have made adultery, fornication, lesbianism, homosexuality or some other form of sexual deviation a way of life. Press reports of their sex lives have now become so common that they scarcely raise the readers' eyebrows. Yet we must be careful not to let this prejudice our views about their music. Sin of every kind is practised by people of every kind. There are alcoholic accountants, dishonest drivers and slimy shopkeepers — to say nothing of perverted priests — but this does not mean that their offences are inevitably tied in to their occupations. Rock performers are not the only musicians to have murky morals — even some of the best-known classical composers were decidedly off-key in their private lives. Tchaikovsky was no paragon of virtue, Chopin had a reputation as a womanizer, Mahler was hardly blameless and Mozart's leisure haunts were not exactly havens of sanctity. As for Wagner, he has been described as 'grossly immoral, selfish, adulterous, arrogant, wildly hedonistic, violently racist and ... a thief to boot!'[8]

These few examples are sufficient to show that we need to be very careful before condemning any one form of artistic expression because of the lifestyle of those who write or perform it. If we took that line to its logical conclusion we would be living in a cultural desert. The simple fact is that *all* music, even the finest, has been written by fallible men and women, but this does not mean that we must abandon everything that has been written, nor try to drive a wedge between 'sacred music' and 'secular music', nor cement everything a composer has written to his or her moral or spiritual lifestyle.

We can go one step further and say that many classical compositions have murder, violence, hatred, greed, immorality or other evils as their themes and should be judged by the same standards as any other musical production. But the point at issue is whether we can single out rock music as having specifically sexual connotations — and the best place to begin is with the musicians and their performances.

Sex on stage

The seeds of sexual excess were sown in the early years by the pioneers of rock 'n' roll music, who came from juke (African-American slang for 'bad') joints and honky-tonks, places that respectable people would never frequent because of the sexual promiscuity they knew they would find there. From Presley's twitching pelvis to the present day, there seems little doubt that sex has played a prominent part in the rock music scene, with the sexual temperature continually rising. In documenting examples of sexual immorality in rock music it is difficult to know how much to expose and when to stop and we remind the reader of the warning given a little earlier. With these issues in mind, here are some examples, with the performers listed in alphabetical order.

AC/DC (the name is deliberately bisexual) have a song which includes the words: 'Let me put my love into you, babe. Let me cut your cake with my knife.' In another song called 'You shook me all night long', the singer refers to a lover who 'took more than her share, had me fighting for air, working double time on my seduction line'.

Bang! Bang! is a 'sex rock' band described as a trio that could 'melt a tundra with its spunky, unyielding brand of sexually charged glam-punk'.[9]

David Bowie's bisexuality is such that at one stage he was voted Britain's number three male singer and number one female singer. Much of his material is depraved and vulgar.

Melissa Etheridge, a lesbian, sings about a sexual threesome in 'Your Little Secret' and threatens to disclose her lover's secret that 'one sugar ain't enough for you'.

Frankie Goes to Hollywood was an openly gay rock group who played up their stylish, camp homosexual imagery, especially in the first video for the song 'Relax'. The video was banned from British television channels.[10]

Grand Funk Railroad's music (the band sold up to ten million records a year) has been described as 'filled with sexual suggestion and power'.[11] Their manager is reported as saying, 'Listen man, what takes place on the stage of a rock concert doesn't happen spontaneously. It is carefully planned to elicit a sexual response from the audience'. He is said to have told the lead guitarist, 'Get out on stage and rape your guitar. That's what the girls want to see'. Today some Christians sing the lyrics 'He's (Jesus is) some kind of wonderful' to Grand Funk Railroad's old hit song 'She's some kind of wonderful'.

Jimi Hendrix, the first black rock sex symbol in American music, drew this comment from one observer: 'He does things to his guitar so passionate, so concentrated and intent that anyone with halfway decent manners has to look away'.[12]

KISS, who deliberately targeted the twelve to fifteen age group and had a comic book aimed at nine to eleven-year-olds, concentrated heavily on sexual abuse and perversion. In the song 'Sweet Pain' they sang, 'My whip is ever beside me. Let me teach you love in a new and different way'. The group has been described by producer Bob Ezrin as 'symbols of unfettered evil and sensuality'.[13]

Led Zeppelin was the '...horniest, most hedonistic group in rock history'.[14] Richard Cole, tour manager for Led Zeppelin throughout the band's twelve-year existence, wrote about 'shameless groupies and perverse pranks, and boasts of the band's phenomenal appetite for sex while denouncing those who say Led Zeppelin harmed the teenage girls who routinely sought rock-star notches in their bedposts.[15] Led Zeppelin songs such as 'Whole Lotta Love' and 'Trampled Under Foot' contain crude and obvious references to sex acts.

Marilyn Manson's songs contain the worst sexual perversions, with sodomy, rape and incest as recurring themes. His stage personas include an androgynous figure making crude sexual gestures.

Meat Loaf drew this comment from a teenager in a letter to *New Musical Express*: 'I have just walked out of a Meat Loaf concert. I was absolutely disgusted by the way Meat Loaf and the female vocalists were acting. Why didn't they just strip off, get down on the floor and have sex? That's what the audience would have loved.'

George Michael, heavily criticized for his highly explicit video of 'I Want Your Sex', dutifully explained that the song was about 'monogamous sex' (rock's idea of chastity).[16]

Ministry, the band that popularized industrial dance music, sings in their 2003 song 'Broken' about 'Triple XXX and filthy sex, discipline and bondage, leather mask and nuns, a topless girl' and other lyrics too vile to repeat here.

Mötley Crüe's only reason for existence according to a *Rolling Stone* magazine reviewer 'is to provide cheap thrills to jaded teens. The song "Ten Seconds to Love" boasts enough sexual innuendo to amuse the average thirteen-year-old boy until the next issue of... [a sexually explicit magazine].'[17]

Queen (another name with sexual hints) featured lead singer Freddie Mercury cranking up the group's bisexual image by wearing mascara, nail varnish and hot pants and admitting, 'We want to shock and be outrageous.'[18]

Red Hot Chili Peppers developed a stage gimmick that would soon become their trademark — performing on stage naked except for strategically placed tube socks.[19] Their best-selling albums are titled *Blood Sugar Sex Magik* and *Californication.*

The Rolling Stones' typical presentation has been called 'an orgy of sexual celebration, with Jagger as the head cheerleader'.[20] A reviewer of the album *Goat's Head Soup* commented on 'the sex and sleaze quotient' and 'explicit sex' contained in the songs.[21] The cover of their album *Sticky Fingers* came with a real zipper; underneath was a picture of thinly veiled male genitals. Their song 'Sweet Virginia' includes the line, 'I gave you diamonds, you gave me disease' (a reference to venereal disease).

Rod Stewart sings 'Tonight's the Night' and invites his angelic virgin lover to spread her wings so that he can 'come inside'. He first hit stardom with 'Maggie May', which includes the lyrics, 'Oh, mother, what a lover! You wore me out, wrecked my bed, and in the morning kicked me in the head'. He once told a magazine interviewer, 'We had an amazing experience the other night. At one point I had about fifteen bras around my waist. I've never seen so many bras thrown up on stage. That was a really good concert!'[22]

The Who drew this comment: 'They have a direct sexual impact. They ask a question — "Do you want to, or don't you?" And they don't really give the audience a chance of saying "No". It's a sort of rape.'[23]

These examples are no more than that and we have deliberately omitted many more that are too disgusting and revolting to include. To a greater or lesser degree, dozens of other top rock groups and hundreds of minor ones show the same blatantly sexual orientation, but does that prove that rock is nothing more than musical sex?

Fact or fantasy?

One of the dangers arising from the publicity given to rock stars is that we end up believing what we see and hear. But that is about as clever as believing everything claimed by television commercials. The point is well made by Steve Lawhead: 'Since rock musicians are image manipulators, most often what they say and do is calculated for a purpose. Usually that purpose is attention.'[24] He gives Alice Cooper as an example: 'Alice Cooper was fairly well known for his shocking stage performances — such as beheadings, cavorting with live snakes, hangings, surrealistic nightmare sequences. But Vincent Furier (Alice's real name) does not sit around at home wearing torn leotards and grotesque facial makeup. According to numerous interviews, he plays golf, softball, watches television and goes about his life much the same as anyone else. His life off stage is dull compared to what he projects in the spotlight.'[25] Malcolm Doney agrees. He calls Alice Cooper's activities 'the product of a crass commercialism'[26] and says, 'The decadent image of David Bowie and Lou Reed was part of the same game-playing mentality.'[27]

No doubt the illusion is widespread. Elton John once said, 'There is nothing wrong in going to bed with somebody of your own sex. I think people should be very free with sex — they should draw the line at goats.'[28] Of course it produced widespread publicity — but was it serious? Separating fact from fantasy in this area is not easy. Yet this does not make objectionable lyrics, obscene gestures and deviant sexual claims any more acceptable, nor does it lessen their impact on the morals of the listeners.

In compiling this chapter we and our publishers had many discussions about which quotations to include and which to leave out. As we explained earlier in the chapter we have left out many we could have included and have deliberately curtailed others, in the interest of biblical modesty. In doing so, we have inevitably lost some of the 'shock value' — and this makes the point that the modern rock music business has made vast quantities of money by selling sex in increasingly graphic forms and appealing to every perverted sense of rebellion that exists today. We make no apology for editing the available material.

The filth connection

The mucky picture we have painted would explain why a leading rock magazine could refer to 'prophylactic rock'.[29] But is that how the performers and their agents see it? It is one thing to act out sexual fantasies to music on stage and play the game, but what is their personal philosophy of rock? Do they see any connection between rock and sex? Here, without comment, are the views of over a dozen of those in the upper echelons of the rock music scene.

Adam Ant: 'Pop music revolves around sexuality. I believe that if there is anarchy, let's make it sexual anarchy rather than political.'[30]

Aerosmith's manager: 'When you're in a certain frame of mind, particularly sexually-oriented, there's nothing better than rock and roll.'[31]

The band's front man, *Steven Tyler,* adds, 'Rock 'n' roll is synonymous with sex and you can't take that away from it. It just doesn't work.'[32]

Roy Brown, composer of 'Good Rockin' Tonight': 'I had my mind on this girl in the bedroom. I'm not going to lie to you. Listen, man, I wrote them kind of songs. I was a dirty cat.'[33]

Duran Duran: 'You've got to be pretty sexless to hold a guitar, dance with it on stage and not put over some kind of sexuality.'[34]

Glenn Frey of The Eagles: 'I'm in rock music for the sex and narcotics.'[35]

Mick Jagger: 'You can feel the adrenalin flowing through your body. It's sort of sexual. I entice my audience. What I do is very much the same as a girl's strip-tease dance.'[36]

Freddie Mercury of Queen: 'I do deliver sex appeal. It's part of modern rock. I sell sex appeal with my body movements on stage.'[37]

Jim Morrison: 'I feel spiritual up there. Think of us as erotic politicians.'[38]

John Oates of Hall and Oates: 'Rock 'n' roll is 99% sex.'[39]

Andrew Oldham, manager of The Rolling Stones: 'Rock music is sex and you have to hit them [teenagers] in the face with it.'[40]

Jimmy Page of Led Zeppelin: 'Rock 'n' roll is sexually ... you music.'[41]

Gene Simmons of KISS: 'That's what rock is all about — sex with a 100 megaton bomb, the beat!'[42]

Frank Zappa, superstar of Mothers of Invention fame: 'Rock music is sex. The big beat matches the body's rhythms.'[43]

These comments are more serious than those we quoted earlier, as they have less obvious publicity value. They may therefore take us a little closer to the truth — and what the rock stars here are saying is that there is a very definite connection between sex and the music in which they are involved. Have they all got it wrong?

What's in a name?

To anyone dropping into today's rock music scene from, say, a hundred years back, even the terminology we use would be totally incomprehensible. What would 'rock' mean to them in musical terms? How could we explain to them that 'punk' and 'funk' are variations of 'rock'? What would they make of 'grunge' or 'glam'? Even more to the point, what does 'rock music' mean to us? As we have seen, 'rock' is a post-Beatle refinement of 'rock 'n' roll' — but what does 'rock 'n' roll' mean? What has it got to do with a particular musical style? Where did the name come from? How did it come to be used to describe the music?

The phrase itself seems to have been born in the American black ghetto communities at the end of the Second World War, where it was a slang phrase for fornication. As such, it soon found its way into the very earthy rhythm-and-blues songs of the time. In 1951 Alan Freed, a disc jockey in Cleveland, Ohio, was looking for a phrase to describe the growing spill-over of rhythm-and-blues music, which he was beginning to play on his white radio station, a phrase that would capture the spirit of the music and mirror the growing excitement it was generating among young people. The phrase he chose was 'rock 'n' roll'. It has been said that Freed chose the phrase to make the music more acceptable to white listeners. That may well be the case, but that was not why it was originally coined and his choice may have been more significant than he realized. One thing is certain; the sexual connotation remained and the fear of many is that it fits the music too well to be merely coincidental.

Not the last word

The secular press can never be accused of undue bias in favour of biblical standards, or of being overly concerned about morality in general. It is interesting, therefore, to read the following comments on the subject of sex and rock.

Time magazine once observed that 'In a sense all rock is revolutionary. By its very beat and sound it has always implicitly rejected restraints and has celebrated freedom and sexuality.'[44] The *Daily Mail's* television critic Herbert Kretzmer wrote, 'Songs, in short, have become the new pornography. Only the deaf, uncaring or wholly distracted will fail to notice this.'[45] Peggy Chrimes, the *Daily Mirror's* television critic, writing about the tendency to screen and censor rock programmes earlier in the evening, complained, 'It is a ready-made excuse to take the sex out of rock 'n' roll, which is a pity, because that's what it's all about.'[46] The *Daily Mail's* Lynda Lee-Potter wrote an article about the dangerous sexual pressures being brought to bear on young girls, in which she commented, 'The entire pop world is geared to titillating the young, in arousing children to frenzied ecstasy as erotically dressed pop stars scream invitations to sexual behaviour far beyond their audience's years.'[47]

Jazz musician and entertainer George Melly has no doubts about the sexual impact of certain kinds of music. In his book *Revolt into Style*, he writes, 'The effect of a top pop group on an audience of pubescent girls is clearly... [sexual deviation deleted].' Later he adds this: 'The pop idol is transformed into a ... fantasy object for adolescent girls. Not all girls are prepared to leave it at fantasy level. Some are so stimulated that they are prepared to make do with anyone even tentatively connected with the group, as many a middle-aged manager or young band boy will substantiate.'

This particular feature of rock is a nauseating fulfilment of something prophesied as long ago as 1965 by Jan Berry of Jan and Dean, who was reported to have said, 'The throbbing beat of rock-and-roll provides a vital sexual release for its adolescent audience,' and suggested that 'The next big trend in rock-and-roll will be to relieve the sexual tensions of the pre-adolescent set.' Musicians have always attracted attention from young girls. Groupies (young girls who follow rock bands and often perform sexual favours for band members) emerged in the nineteen-sixties, a sad but logical outcome of the sexual tension created by Elvis Presley and other rockers in the previous decade. It was only a matter of time before the young girls who in a fit of passion threw their underwear on stage at Elvis would graduate to groupie status. Many wild tales of sexual escapades by groupies have now become part of rock music lore.

All of these statements coincide exactly with those of the rock musicians we quoted earlier, and many observers of the social scene have come to the same conclusion. At a 1981 conference in Oxford, England, representing over 200 public schools, The Rev. Professor Moelwyn Merchant told his audience, 'I think explicit sex is much less dangerous than the plugging of pop records that lower the whole tone of human relationships… It is the disc jockeys and their plugging of debased sensory material and the debasement of images who are the real pornographers.'[48] At about the same time in the USA the Music Television Network (MTV) became very popular in part by broadcasting pornographic and lewd videos made by rock bands. Viewing things from quite a different angle, an acute observer of the British social scene once described BBC Television's *Top of the Pops* as 'sex to music, when young people go through the motions of going to bed without actually doing so'. Author David A. Noebel was just as succinct: 'Rock 'n' roll is musical pornography.'[49]

The argument about the relationship between sex and rock goes on. Even Steve Lawhead (who is by no means 'anti-rock') admitted in the nineteen-eighties, 'There is more blatant immorality being peddled in popular music now than ever before.'[50] But is rock a cause of today's immoral ethic or just a carrier? Exactly how much blame should it bear? Do we indict it or excuse it? Christians must make up their own minds on the evidence they have, relating that evidence at all times to the clear teaching of Scripture.

However, there is another important question we should ask: can we use rock music without any danger of becoming tainted by its immoral associations? Some Christian leaders confirm what we are saying here about the link between sex and rock music. At an event held recently in San Francisco, 'More than 25,000 teens converged on San Francisco's AT&T Park on a windswept Saturday for a daylong rock concert — with none of the sex and drugs that go hand in hand with rock 'n' roll. Kids screamed and swooned while smoke poured from the stage and electric guitars screeched. But the lyrics could have been ripped from a hymnal, and one rocker actually took a break to read from the Bible.'[51] The event featured top Christian rock acts Jeremy Camp and TobyMac and was sponsored by a Christian youth ministry whose goal is 'to encourage evangelical Christian youth to fight back against a pervasive popular culture they say promotes sex, violence, drugs and alcohol.'[52] While their motives are certainly noble, is their choice of music styles equally noble? Can they without a doubt assure us that there is no linkage between the rock music itself and the sexual permissiveness it has always fostered? Can their message of sexual purity succeed when it is mixed with the powerful message of rock music?

Richard Taylor, author of *A Return to Christian Culture*, is in no doubt about the answer: 'We cannot foster an erotic type of music and expect to succeed in avoiding the erosion of standards and ideals. Rock music has a message and it is the message of sexual permissiveness. As music affects your body you instinctively want to put motions to it. So what kind of motions fit rock music? Basically sensual motions. If the message of rock music produces that sort of response, then it is not good music for a Christian.'

Rock music styles may have changed over the years and the lyrics in many mainstream songs are no longer outright sexual but have reverted back to our earlier double-meaning lyrical style, yet the basic themes in rock have not changed. Illicit sex and lewdness are still distinctively a part of rock music culture today, as Steve Bonta illustrates in *New American:* 'From Elvis' gyrating hips and the phallic symbolism in rock stars' stage gestures and props, we've regressed to popular bands like Red Hot Chili Peppers and The Jesus Lizard, who sometimes play in the nude and perform unmentionable bodily functions onstage. Other groups, including megastars like Madonna and Marilyn Manson, as well as lesser-known bands representing the new "porn rock" subculture, feature strippers and act out sexual perversions for their feverish audiences. And rock's lewdness isn't confined to the performers. Popular tastes have moved to the Dionysian chaos of "rave" parties, where participants sometimes disrobe and perform sexual acts on the dance floor.'[53]

MTV pumps rock 'n' roll sleaze into millions of homes twenty-four hours a day. Bonta went on to point out that 'From the smutty dialogues of the enormously popular animated series *Beavis and Butthead*, to the annual coverage of US college Spring Break bacchanalia on the beaches of the Caribbean, to the endless stream of pornographic rock videos, MTV uses the power of visual images catering to man's baser instincts in order to strengthen rock music's appeal.'[54] Yet this is also part of the daily diet of many Christians, who are not only enthusiastic about Christian rock but addicted to secular rock music in general. We can only assume that many have no idea of the conflicts that are being set up.

Our final pointer to the truth about sex and rock comes not from the performers, but from the fans. Eric Holmberg, producer of the *Hells Bells* video series, travels around the United States speaking at schools and youth meetings and gathering research from those who go to secular rock concerts. In all of his sessions he asks the same question: can you name three rock songs that you feel will encourage people to remain sexually pure before marriage? Nobody can do so, and the typical reaction is one of incredulity that someone would be silly enough to ask the question. These fans' failure to answer Holmberg's question surely speaks volumes about rock and sex — and to those who would say, 'But this is just a lyrical problem' we should add that these same fans also told Holmberg they just like to listen to the *music*!

Nearly 2,000 years ago, the apostle Paul gave the seven-days-a-week solution: 'Let us purify ourselves from everything that contaminates body and spirit, perfecting holiness out of reverence for God' (2 Corinthians 7:1, NIV). He also commanded us that 'among you there must not be even a *hint* of sexual immorality, or of any kind of impurity ... because these are improper for God's holy people' (Ephesians 5:3, NIV, emphasis added). Fifteen centuries later, Martin Luther connected Paul's words to the music scene of his day when he wrote, 'I wish that the young men would have something to rid them of their love ditties and wanton songs and might instead ... learn wholesome things and thus yield willingly to good.'[55]

Every Christian has a responsibility to apply those principles to every part of life. For many Christians, following Luther's application would mean a transformation of their musical tastes. It might also call for a bonfire!

6.

BAD COMPANY

Do not be deceived:
Bad company corrupts good morals.

(The apostle Paul)[1]

In the last two chapters we looked at occultism and sexual immorality, two of the more sinister elements associated with rock music, though it could be argued that these flow into the music rather than out of it. Having said that, few would seriously deny that the connection is clear and close. There can be no doubt that rock music, regardless of the lyrics, is a powerful medium for communicating and fostering such damaging philosophies. As Eric Holmberg, a respected commentator on culture, puts it, 'One would have to be either ignorant or a liar to deny any linkage'.[2]

But that is by no means the end of the story. Rock music must by now have been blamed for almost every evil under the sun, from atheism to the crime rate. It is likely that someone, somewhere, is on the verge of blaming it for global warming or crop failure! Perhaps it is not too surprising that rock gets a lot of 'flak', as it has kept some pretty unsavoury company over the years. Mick Jagger could have been speaking on behalf of the entire genre when he mused upon the Rolling Stones' induction into the Rock and Roll Hall of Fame, 'After a lifetime of bad behaviour, it's slightly ironic that tonight you see us on our best behaviour.'[3] During its journey on the long and winding road from the first fusion of rhythm and blues with country honky-tonk all the way up to the latest emo rock and new metal music, rock music has picked up some other nasty hitchhikers.

Pills and needles

Drug abuse is an obvious example. Much of this can be traced to the rise of the hippie movement in the nineteen-sixties. Many of the pop songs which became all the rage at that time encouraged young people to get turned on to drugs, while others included drug-related lyrics without comment — and the lead came from the top. The Beatles' record-breaking album *Sergeant Pepper's Lonely Hearts Club Band* was described by *Time* magazine as 'drenched in drugs'.[4]

One of the songs on the Beatles album *Magical Mystery Tour* invited the listeners, 'Roll up your sleeve, roll up your sleeve, the magical mystery tour is coming to take you away.' In 'Rainy Day Woman', Bob Dylan advocated 'everybody must get stoned', while his song 'Mr Tambourine Man' has been called 'the best of the drug songs'.[5] By the end of the nineteen-sixties the Le Dain Commission, appointed by the Canadian Government to study the drug problem, reported, 'The pop music industry has played a major role in encouraging drug use in general and marijuana in particular.'[6] In testimony before a U.S. Congress subcommittee investigating the recording industry's marketing practices, paediatrician Michael Rich stated in 2002 that 'During the past four decades, rock music lyrics have become increasingly explicit — particularly with reference to drugs... Heavy metal and rap lyrics have elicited the greatest concern, as they compound the environment in which some adolescents increasingly are confronted with substance use...'[7]

During the Vietnam War, the United States Government wanted to send a top rock group to entertain the troops, and had possible groups screened first to ensure that they were clear of drugs. The plan had to be abandoned because a 'clean' group could not be found. The psychedelic rockers of the nineteen-sixties openly encouraged their listeners to be under the influence of LSD or other hallucinogenic drugs. Grateful Dead counted among their inner circle Ken Kesey, author of *One Flew Over the Cuckoo's Nest* and who conducted 'Acid Tests' — LSD parties where the band played. Also prominent were Neal Cassady, the inspiration for Jack Kerouac's Dean Moriarty character in *On the Road*, and Owsley 'Bear' Stanley, the most famous maker of LSD who also built the first of the band's famous sound systems.[8]

By 1979 not much had changed. A leading rock group manager told *Circus*, 'No matter what anyone tells you, drugs will always be a part of the rock scene,'[9] while in the same magazine rock critic Robert Forbes added, 'Drugs are a necessary ingredient for many rock musicians.'[10] Among those who have admitted to taking drugs are Mick Jagger, The Bee Gees, Jerry Garcia, the Doobie Brothers, Glenn Frey of the Eagles, Linda Rondstadt and Gregg Allman; how many others there are is anybody's guess. The Rolling Stones are among a number of groups still pushing drug songs in the twenty-first century, with 'Brown Sugar' (slang for S. E. Asian cocaine), 'Sweet Sister Morphine' and 'Cousin Cocaine' as examples. Eric Clapton's song 'Cocaine' is still a concert favourite today.

Drug problems continue to plague rock bands. The late Kurt Cobain of the band Nirvana struggled with a heroin addiction. Some bands boast that although they shy clear of so-called 'hard drugs' like heroin, cocaine and crack they are addicted to marijuana. A *Rolling Stone* magazine reporter spent time on tour with the band 311 and wrote that, 'Not two minutes after the journey begins, bassist P-Nut pulls out a rainbow-coloured bong and a large zip-lock bag that is swelling with more than an ounce of strong marijuana buds, and proceeds to pack himself a bowl.'[11]

The perception of the rock star as an alienated, self-destructive and mentally unstable tragic hero is one of the most pervasive myths in rock music, yet there is much evidence to support the notion. It was sparked in the late nineteen-sixties, when a string of musicians emerged whose overindulgence in LSD led to varying degrees of mental collapse. These included Pink Floyd's Barrett, Fleetwood Mac's Peter Green, Brian Wilson and the late Skip Spence of Moby Grape. This tragedy was codified by David Bowie's 1972 concept album, *The Rise and Fall of Ziggy Stardust and the Spiders From Mars*, which was partly based on the earliest LSD casualty, minor English rock 'n' roller Vince Taylor.[12] There is a tragic list of those who have died as the result of drugs. It includes Jimi Hendrix, Janis Joplin, Jim Morrison, Al Wilson (Canned Heat), Gram Parsons and Gary Thain (Uriah Heep), Vinnie Taylor (Sha Na Na), Keith Moon (The Who), Tommy Bolin (Deep Purple), Robbie McIntosh (Average White Band), Sid Vicious (Sex Pistols) and Lowell George (Little Feat).

Not surprisingly, one university student told us that drugs are 'as easy to get as coffee'. How drugs and music merge is unclear, but there are alarming stories of the result. Jean Alison told *Reader's Digest* the story of her son's LSD trips being set off again by 'one of the tunes he had been singing'.[13] Even more alarmingly, the British youth magazine *Young Life* reported that a young man, converted to Christ ten years previously and miraculously healed of hard drug addiction, went to the Greenbelt Christian music festival in 1981 and as soon as he got there started hallucinating for the first time since he became a Christian![14] Can we just dismiss that out of hand? What we can be sure about is that anything that might help to create that kind of syndrome should be avoided like the plague. As to the connection between drugs and rock, Steven Tyler of the group

Aerosmith might have summed it up best when he said, '[Rock music] is the strongest drug in the world.'[15]

Rebels without a cause

Other elements have also helped to give rock a bad name. One of these is violence and not just when Alice Cooper split open live chickens and threw their intestines over the audience back in the nineteen-seventies. Groups like Eric Clapton's Cream produced 'a sort of subliminal violence with which their audience could involve themselves.'[16] Ted Nugent, who called his music 'combat rock' (and wears earplugs while performing it), speaks of raping his audience.[17] A group called Napalm Death, claiming to be the fastest thrash rock band in the world, released an album called *From Enslavement to Obliteration*. Reviewing a record by a band called Festering Pus, one writer said, 'It is bilious, bullying and bloomin' brutal.'[18] Allen Lanier of Blue Oyster Cult admitted that 'Rock and roll brings out violent emotions. There's a lot of violence, a lot of aggression in the music.'[19]

Violence in rock has progressed to the point where we now have an abomination called death metal. Mick Thompson of the nu-metal shock rock band Slipknot may have the best explanation for how things could have sunk so low: 'I used to watch gory horror movies and at first I was disturbed, but then I became numb to it. With hard rock, it's the same way. People who listened to Korn now want something even harder.'[20] There is a mindless and numbing brutality about heavy metal, punk and the like, and no Christian should have anything to do with it.

Rebellion has been another of rock's companions. 'The essence of rock music is rebellion,' said Lemmy Kilmister of the heavy metal band Motorhead.[21] Kilmister is not alone: a great deal of rock music speaks of rebellion of one kind or another, not merely against specific aspects of our society, but against authority in general. Warning that most adults are only concerned about the *noise* of heavy metal music, *Newsweek* said, 'It's not just about the ear-splitting sound and the relentless beat. Kids at a heavy metal concert don't sit in their seats; they stand on them and move — it's the spirit of rebellion.'[22] David Lee Roth of the band Van Halen told *USA Today*, 'We like the fact that the masses see us as rock 'n' roll rebels.'[23] George Melly even suggests that 'A pop movement is attractive precisely because it proposed a revolt.'[24]

Speaking on the BBC Radio 4 programme *Crooning Buffoons*, Ray Gosling went even further: 'Rock 'n' roll is a beast. Well-intentioned people thought you could pick it up and cuddle it. They forgot it had claws ... Next time you pass a record shop window ... look at the names of the bands — The Slits, The Damned, Bad Manners, The Vibrators, The Stranglers and Meat Loaf. The march of the Mods in 1964 was no twentieth-century version of the Durham Miners' Gala. It was sawdust Caesars putting the boot in ... nasty as a boil, every one of them. I know, because I was one of them. Behind every sweet doowop and bebop is an unfettered sexuality and sympathy for the devil: violently anarchic — in the face of all harmony, peace and progress. People could see that when it first happened and it hasn't changed. Anybody with a penn'orth of grey matter could see it was trouble.'[25]

Rock music has been associated with rebellion from the very beginning. In its early years, the combination of rock and roll's sexually-suggestive lyrics and wild, animal-like physical responses by teenagers shocked parents, who immediately called for their children to stay away from it. But most teens chose to ignore their parents' wishes. The movie industry, never one to miss a commercial opportunity, churned out rock 'n' roll rebel films designed to horrify parents and thrill teens: *Rock Baby Rock It* (1957) — billed as 'a sizzling story of hot rock as you've never seen it before!'; *Carnival Rock* (1957); *Don't Knock the Rock* (1957); and *Hot Rod Gang* (1958 — released in the UK as *Fury Unleashed*). This last movie included 'great rock and roll by Gene Vincent and the Blue Caps; hot rods, cops, juke joints, fist fights and cute chicks; and Kay Wheeler doing her sexy Rock 'n' Bop dancin'.[26]

The rebellious theme gradually hardened, and Eric Burdon and the Animals scored a big hit with the lyrics 'It's my life and I'll do what I want, it's my mind and I'll think what I want'. Perfectly expressing the rebellion against parental authority embodied in the rock 'n' roll ethos, the song was quickly adopted by teenagers in America and elsewhere as their anthem whenever they disagreed with their parents' or teachers' orders.

As time went by and the original teen rockers matured, rock music became an accepted thread in our popular culture. Television commercials and film and television soundtracks began to feature rock songs and bands. As mainstream rock music lost its ability to shock or offend middle America, new forms of music like shock rock, punk rock and heavy metal emerged to fill this role. Rock groups like KISS, Alice Cooper, David Bowie, Queen and Blue Oyster Cult openly promoted Satanism, transgender sexuality and sado-masochism. Punk rock groups advocated anarchy and lawlessness.

Today's rock has not lost its ability to shock a civilized society with its love for anarchy and rebellion. From recent BBC documentaries on new wave bands we learn that, 'There's a new spirit of punk rock rebellion sweeping the nation. Go in search of the bands who have a whiff of rock and roll rebellion about them … a new bunch of bands riding a wave of beer, violence and stupidity — all claiming to be the voice of the working class. Swear words on their tee shirts, spit, fight and smash things up.'[27]

Rock music and tattoos have also seemed to go hand in hand, at least in Western society in the last twenty years. Heavy metal and punk rock bands gradually popularized this trend among musicians and today it is rare to find any rock musician without a tattoo. Rockers like Tommy Lee of Mötley Crüe exalt in their tattoo-covered bodies; members of the rock band P.O.D. promote the glorification of tattoos among Christians. We have even heard of youth group leaders who are proud of their rock-related tattoos. Christians who question the practice on biblical grounds usually point to the specific command, 'You shall not make any cuttings in your flesh for the dead, nor tattoo any marks on you: I am the LORD' (Leviticus 19:28) but the rebellious element is often overlooked. Encouraged by their favourite musicians, some Christian teenagers are rushing to get a tattoo, usually overriding the objections and concerns of their parents — and in direct violation of the fifth commandment, 'Honour your father and your mother' (Exodus 20:12), which the apostle Paul reinforced (Ephesians 6:1; and Colossians 3:20).

The advice Christians and others are receiving from the promoters of tattooing is totally predictable — that it is good to be a rebel! One web 'zine dedicated to 'body modification' (the politically correct term for tattooing and ritual cutting of the human body) publishes advice to Christians and others who are struggling with the decision whether or not to get a tattoo, or who already have done it but are criticized for it by 'religious people'.[28] In an article titled 'What the Modified can learn from Satan', the writer teaches that 'Body modification is the safest key to unlocking the doors to personal freedom, individual affirmation, and spiritual enlightenment that I've ever seen.' The article is about the supremacy of the individual and how the Church of Satan can teach us something about not conforming to the Christian herd. Another article is titled 'Does God hate your tattoo?' in which the same writer cleverly tries to break down Christian resistance to tattoos and offers to connect the sceptical Christian to other Christians who have tattoos. The saddest part is that his 'Do what you want' teaching has been adopted by Christians who want to justify their tattoos and repeated by them on blogs and chat rooms on the Internet. If Crowley, Huxley and Leary were alive today, they would be delighted at how easy it is to insinuate their satanic principles into young, rebellious Christians.

The Bible's teaching is the exact opposite of 'do your own thing' individualism. It clearly declares, 'Let every soul be subject to the governing authorities. For there is no authority except from God, and the authorities that exist are appointed by God. Therefore whoever resists the authority resists the ordinance of God, and those who resist will bring judgment on themselves' (Romans 13:1-2). Incidentally, this points indirectly to the dangers of the popular fad of speaking about Jesus as a 'rebel'. On a *60 Minutes* television broadcast in December 2004, Cameron Strang, the publisher of *Relevant* magazine said, 'The Christian rock thing is almost rebelling against the rock establishment. Rock 'n' roll is rebellion.'[29] Rather than thinking in terms of any kind of revolt, Christians should concentrate on their responsibility to be 'blameless and harmless, children of God without fault in the midst of a crooked and perverse generation, among whom you shine as lights in the world' (Philippians 2:15).

In God's name

Another sinister element in rock music is widespread blasphemy. As long ago as 1964 the Beatles' press officer Derek Taylor said, 'It's as if they'd founded a new religion. They're completely anti-Christ. I mean I'm anti-Christ as well, but they're so anti-Christ they shock me, which is not an easy thing.'[30] In John Lennon's book *A Spaniard in the Works* he refers to Christ as a 'garlic eating, stinking, little yellow greasy fascist bastard Catholic Spaniard'. David Bowie sank even lower and once stated, 'Jesus Christ was a strange boy himself.'[31] Others are equally blasphemous and anti-Christian in their beliefs, their behaviour and their music, but have found ways of expressing their philosophies more subtly as we learned in our chapter 'Strange Fire'. But can rock co-exist with God? Little Richard, one of the founders of the rock 'n' roll era, knows the answer to this one: 'Rock 'n' roll doesn't glorify God. You can't drink out of God's cup and the devil's cup at the same time. I was one of the pioneers of that music, one of the builders. I know what the blocks are made of because I built them.'[32]

Blasphemy became the state of the art with the two hugely popular rock musicals, *Godspell* and *Jesus Christ Superstar*. The script of *Godspell* is partly paraphrased from the words of Matthew's Gospel and was hailed by many Christians as an exciting breakthrough in communicating the gospel to the masses —a marvellous way to get the name of Jesus out to millions of people who would seldom if ever darken the doors of a church. Even the now defunct Christian magazine *Crusade* wrote approvingly of it. But the musical's author Stephen Schwartz took a very different line: 'I hadn't been brought up Christian. And so I was not someone coming in with reverence.'[33] He proved that by having the cast wear clown costumes to follow the example of Jesus, an idea taken from the 'Christ as clown' theory propounded by Harvey Cox of the Harvard Divinity School.[34] In one scene he has John the Baptist baptize Jesus with a sponge, making sure to clean behind the ears. Schwartz also thought it would be fun for one of the female cast members 'to do a Mae West[35] style number' because she had 'a kind of Mae Westian naughty/naive quality to her character'.[36] Commenting on his recent musical *Children of Eden*, he says he believes the book of Genesis is mythical and as a result, 'I feel more comfortable about playing slightly loose with these Bible tales.'[37]

Jesus Christ Superstar, which became the biggest money-making musical in history at the time, also received an enthusiastic reception from many Christians — yet it was financed by Robert Stigwood, a homosexual rock promoter, and written by Timothy Rice and Andrew Lloyd Webber, both of whom admitted to being atheists at the time. Interviewed on an American radio station, Rice said that the idea of the whole opera was to have Christ seen through the eyes of Judas, Christ as man and not as God, and the fact that Christ himself was just as mixed up and unaware of his identity as was Judas. On another occasion he admitted, 'It happens that we don't see Christ as God, but simply the right man at the right time in the right place.'[38] As one reviewer wrote, 'The story is as consistently cynical and agnostic a deconstruction of the life of Jesus as anyone has ever put on film. Jesus, as presented here, is just an innocent weakling caught, almost off his guard, amid the power games of mindless zealots and ruthless political leaders.'[39]

Those are very significant statements. They show that although Bible words were being used they were twisted into conveying a message far removed from biblical truth. The tragedy is that multitudes of Christians fell for it then and still do today. In 1999, the *Godspell* album was reissued by the Christian label Gotee, with endorsements in the liner notes from Michael W. Smith.[40]

The secular press was not always so gullible, with the film critic of *Newsweek* making this comment on the film version of *Superstar*: 'It is one of the two fiascos of modern cinema. It has fatal foolishness everywhere ... We danced and sang and Jesus was crucified and a good time was had by all. Lord, forgive them. They know not what they are doing.'[41] Yet the very fact that these two musicals were generally so popular among non-Christians should have warned believers of their dangers.

Those two superhits are now part of modern musical folklore, yet in some measure they paved the way for a situation now so bad that what Graham Cray said of rock music has come true: 'Most of it is used as a vehicle for anti-Christian propaganda.'[42] At the 1997 MTV Music Awards, shock rocker Marilyn Manson, standing at a podium with a sign that read 'Antichrist Superstar', exclaimed to the audience, 'We will no longer be oppressed by the fascism of Christianity.'[43] Frank Zappa thinks the best way to raise a happy child is to 'keep him or her as far away from a church as you can.'[44] Courtney Love feels she has 'a duty ... to impose my worldview on the culture'[45] using hard rock music as the vehicle.

Blasphemy in rock has got progressively worse in recent years. There are bands with names like JesusEater (a band of four tattoo artists from Baltimore playing hardcore with a punk attitude), The Jesus Lizard (a leading noise rock band who perform in the nude), Lamb of God (a death and black metal band), Fear of God (heavy metal band with an album titled *Toxic Voodoo*), Denial of God (known for emulating the Satan-worshipping death metal masters Deicide), and Blind Idiot God (speed rock and reggae dub). None of these bands pretends to honour Jesus or God's name; on the contrary, their music and credos are blatantly opposed to God, often in an aggressive fashion. Industrial dance music band Ministry mocks the second coming of Christ in their 2004 song 'Waiting', taunting 'Waiting for Christ in the USA, waiting till I die.' In 'Bad Religion', the Boston-based alternative metal group Godsmack, with its devout Wiccan leader, mocks preachers and the Word of God, quoting from Scripture and then screaming 'Oh, it's a bad religion, from a broken nation, it's a contradiction, and I can't take it any ... [expletive deleted] more.'

Marilyn Manson is positively vitriolic in his hatred towards God and Christianity. His 1996 album *Antichrist Superstar* contained songs including one heralding the Antichrist's imminent return, 'Little Horn' (alluding to the book of Revelation), and 'The Reflecting God' with the lyrics 'I went to God just to see, and I was looking at me, saw heaven and hell were lies.' He also claims that 'God will grovel before me, God will crawl at my feet.'

The Christian's response should be obvious. No matter how much he may like the sound of the music he has no warrant to surround himself with material created by artists whose philosophies and values are in blasphemous opposition to the one who alone is 'King of kings and Lord of lords' (Revelation 19:16).

Body blows

There are further danger signals for those who listen to rock music and the first of these warns us that rock music can be physically damaging. We touched on this in an earlier chapter when we looked at loud amplification as one of the essential elements in rock and we can take our cue from there.

Articles in the secular press have made the point. Writing in the UK's *Leicester Mercury* under the headline 'Will the sound of music drive us mad?' Charles Fraser said, 'Irate parents have suspected it for years and now medical authorities are coming to the same conclusion ... deafening rock music can drive you mad.'[46] A leading educationalist Dr D. M. Beaumont asked, 'Why have music that can lead to hysteria and in the long term to schizophrenia?'[47] At an international conference on noise pollution, a World Health Authority expert testified that loud rock music could cause deafness, psychiatric problems and even temporary insanity.[48]

There is certainly no questioning the physical assault mounted by some forms of rock, such as heavy metal and punk. As Dave Roberts wrote, 'Heavy rock is body music designed to bypass your brain and with an unrelenting brutality induce a frenzied state amongst the audience.'[49]

This unrelenting audio brutality is even to be found in so-called 'Christian rock' today. In a November 2005 article in *Salon* titled 'The Devil's Music', writer Daniel Radosh raised this very disturbing question: 'Does it matter that David Ludwig — the 18-year-old alleged killer of his 14-year-old girlfriend's parents — was a huge fan of hardcore Christian rock?' The article relates, 'On the night of October 6, David Ludwig and his girlfriend, Kara Beth Borden, went to the Lancaster Bible Church in Manheim, Pennsylvania, for a Christian rock concert. As the punishingly loud guitars of Audio Adrenaline and Pillar strained the limits of the church sound system, the kids screamed and pumped their fists and banged their heads. "Pillar and Audio A rock my face off!" David wrote on his blog the next day. Kara spent almost all the money in her pocket on a Pillar sweatshirt. She was wearing it the morning of Nov. 13 when, police say, David shot and killed her parents and fled with her at his side.'[50] The article went on to say, 'It should go without saying that Pillar isn't even remotely responsible for Ludwig's actions, any more than Marilyn Manson was responsible for Columbine.'[51] Pillar plays rap-core, a furiously propulsive mash-up of hard rock and rap. Audio Adrenaline plays very loud, driving rock.

For many performers the avalanche of decibels is a deliberate and important part of their total intention. It is meant to blast the emotions and the mind — not to reflect truth, honesty, integrity or beauty, nor to encourage a discerning response or produce any beneficial result. When David Porter says of rock music that 'It is primarily a physical thing,'[52] he hits the nail on the head. So does Mick Farren when he says, 'Rock music is not something you understand, it is something you feel with your body and you know.'[53] In an article in *Reader's Digest* titled 'We're poisoning ourselves with sound', James Stewart-Gordon detailed some of the serious effects of noise on the human body. One of his conclusions was that 'Noise is most damaging when it is loud, meaningless, irregular and unpredictable,'[54] an unintentional but accurate description of a great deal of today's rock music. There are hidden dangers, too. Equipment used by today's rock groups delivers sound at both infrasonic and ultrasonic levels (below and above the hearing range) and scientists are becoming increasingly disturbed by the potential threat to health that this poses.[55]

The sounds of music

There are other even less obvious dangers associated with certain sounds. Timothy Leary claimed evidence that music of a certain kind had effects similar to those produced by toxic drugs. Adrenalin secretions generated by over-stimulated glands led, he claimed, to imbalanced and harmful physical reactions. More recently, others have confirmed this. David Noebel says, 'Under rock music, the secretion of hormones is more pronounced ... which causes an abnormal imbalance in the body's system, lowers the blood sugar and calcium levels and impairs judgement.'[56] Noebel also cites medical evidence that 'The low frequency vibrations of the bass guitar, along with the driving beat of the drum, affect the cerebrospinal fluid, which in turn affects the pituitary gland, which in turn directs the secretions of hormones in the body.'[57] Even more remarkable is this statement by Cyril Scott: 'Our research has proved to us that not only the emotional content but the essence of the actual musical form tends to reproduce itself in human conduct.'[58]

We are not left guessing as to the kind of 'human conduct' to which hard rock can lead. In 1982 the *Daily Mirror* reported, 'A night out at a rock concert ended in tragedy for schoolboy Chris Tyrer. He died after joining in a "head banging" session. It is the dance in which youngsters shake their heads from side to side in time to the music. Chris was seen "head banging" as 1,000 fans watched the rock group Saxon at Wolverhampton Civic Hall. The next morning his parents found him paralysed down one side. He died in hospital eight days later.'[59] Even more horrendous is the story of Mark Silman. The teenager from Reading, England, a former Elvis Presley fanatic, killed a fifteen-year-old girl by stabbing her eighty-five times with a ten-inch butcher's knife. The *Reading Chronicle* reported that he had modelled himself on a rock singer with the group The Meteors, who sing about blood and violence and drink blood on stage.[60]

These cases may be extreme, but they are certainly not unique — and we can assume that there are countless other young people who are being physically damaged because of exposure to the kind of sound rock singer Ted Nugent had in mind when he said, 'Rock is the perfect primal method of releasing our violent instincts.'[61] Yet so many Christians seem strangely oblivious to the danger. This leads to the obvious question: has any Christian, whose body is 'the temple of the Holy Spirit' (1 Corinthians 6:19), the right, for the selfish satisfaction of his own musical tastes, to expose himself for even one moment to the kind of music that can potentially lead to such consequences?

It's all in the mind

Not only can rock music be physically damaging; another area of danger is that it opens the door to psychological manipulation. Dr William Shafer is quite blunt about it: 'Rock music is a tool for altering consciousness.'[62] So is Robert Palmer, the former chief rock critic of the *New York Times* and author of *Rock and Roll: An Unruly History*, who claimed that using music to induce altered states of consciousness had become one of the most significant musical trends of the nineteen-eighties and that rock musicians were beginning to explore the possibilities of rhythmic and modal repetition, which seeks through absolute control of limited musical means to induce certain psychological states. In their book *Super Learning*, Sheila Ostrander and Lynn Schroeder write, 'The idea that music can affect your body and your mind certainly isn't new ... For centuries, from Asia to the

Middle East to South America people have used music to carry them into unusual states of consciousness. The key has always been to find just the right kind of music for just the right kind of effect.'

The now defunct Communist regimes made intensive studies into ways of conditioning people. One Bulgarian doctor, after fifteen years' research on the use of music in conditioning, concluded, 'Certain drumbeats act as a kind of pacemaker, regulating brain-wave rhythms and breathing, which leads to biochemical changes that produce altered states of consciousness. If you listen to a different drummer, you do see a different world.'[63] In a remarkable book called *The Science of Yoga*, I. K. Taimni comes to the same conclusion: 'There is a fundamental relationship between vibration and consciousness, because each level of consciousness has a specific vibration associated with it.' In his book *Subliminal Seduction*, Wilson Bryan Key tells of advertising companies spending fortunes researching how music can be used to influence people. Some discovered that a seventy-two-beats-a-minute rhythm increases suggestibility and that a television commercial with such a beat produced the headache symptoms that the product being advertised was supposed to cure.

But the evidence for psychological manipulation does not come from outside sources alone. Rock musicians have been saying the same thing for a long time, though in simpler, cruder ways. Timothy Leary was certainly on to it. His song 'Turn on, tune in, drop out' became an anthem for millions, and Leary's comment on it was 'Don't listen to the words, it's the music that has its own message ... I've been stoned on the music many times ... the music is what will get you going.'[64] Graham Nash of the megagroup Crosby, Stills and Nash, said, 'Pop music is the mass medium for conditioning the way people think.'[65] Drummer Spencer Dryden was quite clear how this power should be used: 'Get them when they're young. Bend the minds.'[66] Jimi

Hendrix knew what to do next: 'You hypnotize people to when they go back to the natural state. And when you get people at their weakest point, you preach into their subconscious what you want to say.'[67] Mick Jagger said much the same thing: 'We're moving after the minds and so are most of the new groups.'[68] In another interview he said, 'Communication is the answer to the whole of the world's problems and music is the key to it all because music opens the door to everybody's mind.'[69]

High or deep?

Of course it is not only rock music that can be used in psychological manipulation. The same can be true of classical music. Hitler used some of Wagner's music to crank up the crowds — and even parts of Handel's *Messiah* when he wanted to create a pseudo-religious atmosphere. Even the best of music can be used from the worst of motives.

One secret of music's great power is that it can appeal directly to the subconscious. As a result, people soak up the meaning of music without being aware that they are doing so. Add to that the volume level, constant repetition and incessant beat which are so much a part of rock music, and the scene is set for the conditioning process. As Cedric Cullingford wrote in *The Guardian*, 'Far from being a palpable alternative culture with its own clear ideas, pop music is something absorbed at a subconscious level.'[70] Many young Christians have told us that they feel perfectly safe in listening to records containing perverted lyrics because just like their secular counterparts, 'We don't listen to the words, we just love the music.' But they have missed the vital point that the music itself is affecting them at an even deeper level *without their knowing it.*

Surely the dangers of all this are obvious — and not least in communicating the gospel. Evangelists have sometimes been told during a lively gospel concert, 'Don't worry, we'll bring them down before you speak.' Preachers face the same problem in church services now that the rock concert has moved inside. But why do the listeners need to be 'brought down' before hearing the Word of God? What were they 'up' on in the first place? An emotional 'high'? Then why were they taken up there? Presumably as a preliminary to the preaching! The whole thing becomes a tragic nonsense. Why is it important to get a crowd 'high'? There is certainly a right kind of preparation for the hearing of God's Word, but excessive volume, driving beat, repetitious phrases and the like are not the biblical way to go about it. Musical conditioning is not the same as the Holy Spirit challenging the mind to think, the spirit to be still, and the heart to be humbled in the presence of God.

In closing this chapter, let us ask a very important question. In loading our worship and evangelistic services with manipulative music, are we not greatly increasing the risk of producing 'conversions' that are psychological rather than spiritual? Are we not in danger of manipulating the emotions so that people have a false worship experience? The set-up could not be more perfect. Impressionable people can be so conditioned by the music that they are much more likely to accept whatever the preacher says. This is especially dangerous in evangelism. Add a good communicator and the chances are that he will produce an impressive number of 'decisions'. However, the danger is that these 'decisions' are the result of musical conditioning rather than spiritual conviction. We will take a closer look at this in the next chapter.

It might be claimed that evangelists and preachers can also be manipulators, even those who use little or no music. We agree, but would argue that when they are, the eventual results are just as disappointing. It would not be difficult to prove that the best 'manipulators' among evangelists and preachers are those who produce the most impressive immediate statistics, but the numbers that count are those that continue in the faith, moving from worldliness toward godliness, and showing evidence they are being conformed ever more closely to the image of Christ.

Everybody enjoys music of one kind or another. With its power to stir the emotions of its listeners and the fact that rock music in particular is such a tremendous attraction to young people, the idea of using it in worship and evangelism seems at first thought to be sensible and natural. But worship and evangelism are *not* about the natural; they are about the spiritual. We are serving a God who says, 'My thoughts are not your thoughts, nor are your ways my ways' (Isaiah 55:8) and in worship and evangelism, as in every other area of life, the all-important thing is not to go along with the majority, not even the Christian majority, but to find out 'what is acceptable to the Lord' (Ephesians 5:10).

7.

RED FLAGS

We can come and sing hymns in this church and only enjoy the dignity of the music as a relief from rock 'n' roll.

(American preacher A.W. Tozer)[1]

On the first Sunday in November every year a Veteran Car Run takes place from London to Brighton, on Britain's south coast. It commemorates the 1896 abolishment of the Locomotive Act, popularly known as the Red Flag Act. This law forced automobile drivers to have a man walking in front of the car, waving a red flag to warn pedestrians and horse carriages that something new and dangerous was approaching; cars were, after all, able to tear along at a terrifying four miles per hour!

Both before and since 1896 red flags have been used in many contexts to warn of danger and we want to use the same symbol to point up a number of serious issues relating to the use of rock music in worship and evangelism, all of which we believe need to be addressed. We have looked at some of these in earlier chapters, but now want to turn to a number of others. It should go without saying that in doing so we have no interest in attacking music as a whole. From our introduction onwards we acknowledge not only music's value but its place in God's economy. Our aim is to examine the suitability of using rock music to stimulate Christian worship and energize the taking of the gospel to unbelievers.

We are concerned for the glory of God, which should always be the ultimate aim of every Christian. We are concerned for the good of the whole church, whose members are our brothers and sisters in Christ, but especially for those who are stumbling over the rock music issue. We are concerned for the integrity of the gospel, anxious not to see it dragged in the mud. We are concerned for the spiritual welfare of young Christians, who are at times so cynically manipulated by the music industry. All of these concerns are undoubtedly shared by the many conscientious objectors to rock music in the church.

When the American evangelist D. L. Moody visited Scotland in 1873 for his great evangelistic campaigns his partner was song leader and musician Ira D. Sankey, whose organ-playing and singing attracted great crowds. But when the team went to hold a Sunday afternoon service in a church in Edinburgh the leaders took one look at the (portable) organ and cried, 'We're no havin' such a kist fu' o' whistles in our kirk,' and promptly dumped it out onto the street. When prejudice is in control of the music debate, reasoning is usually rationed!

In this chapter we want to marry reason and resolution by pinpointing seven specific concerns showing exactly how and why rock is so divisive in the church. We hope that as a result those who can influence things at a local church or wider level will see rock music as a 'stumbling block' (Romans 14:13) and respond accordingly.

What's the difference?

In the first place, we are concerned that the rock music idiom (a style or form of artistic expression) so easily encourages worldliness. To explain what we mean, the following reviews may help:

144

'The thing that the band has going on for them live is their fans singing along. Man, were those 13 to 16 year old girls going nuts over Matt and company!'[2]

'Shrill screams reverberated off the sky-high ceiling. The beginning riff followed by an overwhelmingly loud "Whoa-oh" sent shockwaves through the violently undulating teenage sea. Small groups of girls stood in tight circles clapping like cheerleaders, practically running in place with mouths agape in screams as if the Beatles had just stepped on American soil.'[3]

'The pulsating techno music builds to a deafening crescendo as space-age-sounding zaps punctuate the heavy bass and drum beat. Red and green laser lights etch twisting torsos against blackened walls as coloured glow sticks slice through manufactured fog. Two hundred teens, ages 14-18, have come to dance to cutting-edge house, trance and jungle music, while light patterns of "gobos" and "moonflowers" wash the room in a bright array of colour.'[4]

'The crowd was stoked and ready to rock as the music started to play and the audience could still only see the silhouettes of the band members behind a pale illuminated curtain. Stuart worked the fans into a frenzy when he left the stage.'[5]

'At the first chords, the crowd began pogo-jumping in unison to the crisp guitar, driving rhythm and sweet harmonies. A funky, retro spiral light projector swirled behind the band, accentuating the hipness already fighting the fog machine for control of the room's atmosphere. Owen dedicated the next song "to the ladies". The laid-back southern groove brought the crowd back to a head-bobbing frenzy.'[6]

'Offering the best that "crunk" rock has to offer, the five-piece masters of funk moved the crowd with their intriguing show, leaving quite an impression. The lead vocalist encouraged the crowd to make some noise as they performed a personalized cover of Nirvana's "Smells Like Teen Spirit."'[7]

What kind of events do you think are being described here? Thoroughly secular ones, with no holds barred? Wrong! Each quotation describes a Christian rock concert. Without making any judgement on the sincerity or integrity of anyone involved, the question we want to ask is this: what kind of spirit does all of this suggest? Does it not seem to be one which is merely aping the world, using its language, its values and its images? The emphasis is on the performance, the showmanship and the crowd's adoration; is this spiritual and helpful, or worldly and unhelpful? The basic question we are asking here is whether this religious cloning of the rock music idiom makes it spiritual or leaves it in its worldly state. There is a crucial difference between being worked up by animal spirits and being anointed by the Holy Spirit.

Worldliness has also crept into the local church ministry by the same means, as the following letters to the authors illustrate:

'I went in to the Youth Building where some of the guys were playing a familiar "Christian Rock" song on their guitars and drums. Across the room a girl turned her head to see who may be watching her as she danced seductively to the music. Immediately I asked myself the question, "Now what was it about that song that caused her to do that?" The words of the song spoke of Christ's sacrifice on the cross. No, it was not the words that caused her to feel like dancing seductively. I had to conclude that the music accomplished exactly what it was designed to do. Since that visual image, I have never wavered in my position against Christian rock.'

(From a concerned mother of teenagers)

'We used to look forward to church, now it has become literally a test of endurance to put up with it. I often feel as though I have blundered into a disco joint by mistake; the only things missing are the smoke and drinks — the light show and driving over-amplified music are the same.'

(From a Christian college professor)

'This weekend our church hosted a circus sponsored by the local Christian youth organization. There were half a dozen bands like Skillet, Relient K and Five Iron Frenzy. Thousands of kids came and tore up the lawns and caused other damage. They decorated the bathrooms with black paper and silver hangings, black and silver rugs, all kinds of stuff to make them look, frankly, like a nightclub — and I've seen nightclubs! The local TV station ran a story last night, featuring irate neighbours complaining about the music noise. Our youth department tried to bribe the neighbours by offering them tickets for dinners and movies. This is Christianity? No, this is the world, the flesh and the devil. This is youthful arrogance.'

(From a church staff member)

Let us take this a little further. The Bible makes it clear that we are not to dress or behave in ways that might create moral problems for other people. When secular rock stars do so, we are right to condemn their actions. Then can we excuse the Christian rock star when he struts his stuff on stage and has thirteen-to-sixteen-year-old girls 'going nuts'? What is the difference? Do 'Jesus' words' or the musicians' claims that they are performing for God's glory somehow sanctify their actions?

This highlights one of the greatest problems in Christian rock: it blurs the distinction between Christian and non-Christian value systems by trying to incorporate them both. The distinction is even more blurred when church leaders such as the man named America's Pastor by *Time* magazine[8] 'surprised an audience by declaring, "I've always wanted to do this in this stadium." He then sang an impersonation of Jimi Hendrix's hit song "Purple Haze". As the audience erupted into laughter, the church band joined in playing back-up to it.'[9]

This audience's response leads us to ask another question: do the people involved understand what is meant by 'worldliness'? Once a universally understood term in the church, there seems to be widespread ignorance of this biblical concept (or even a wilful disregard for its significance) among today's rock lovers and performers. But this is a dangerous position to take, as the Bible warns: 'Do you not know that friendship with the world is enmity with God? Whoever therefore wants to be a friend of the world makes himself an enemy of God' (James 4:4). No Christian in his right mind would want to play around with this warning! What is more, the Bible tells believers that friendship with the world causes 'wars and fights ... among you' (James 4:1). If it can be shown that rock music is a worldly love, it is not difficult to decide what has brought about the tragic worship wars that have caused so much heartache among God's people.

Romans 12:1-2 offers us a stark contrast between 'worldliness' and 'godliness'. In this passage the apostle Paul implores his readers to 'present your bodies a living sacrifice, holy, acceptable to God'. In this context, 'holy' means physically pure and consecrated, set apart to God from the world. No shadow of worldliness can exist around the pure light of holiness. Neither are we permitted any liberty to 'do our own thing' and choose a brand of 'holiness' that fits our lifestyle. It must all be 'acceptable to God', whose command to all believers is crystal clear: 'Be holy, for I am holy' (1 Peter 1:15-16).

Paul then goes one step further and explains the steps that need to be taken in the lifelong quest for holiness: 'And *do not be conformed to this world*, but be transformed by the renewing of your mind, that you may prove what is that good and acceptable and perfect will of God' (emphasis added). The Greek word translated 'conformed' is the root of our English word *schematic*. Paul's first readers would immediately have understood his meaning as an allusion to dressmakers using a pattern; it speaks of a sense of fashion and style and of conforming to what we might now call a template. The common-sense application for Christians is obvious. We are not to fashion ourselves according to the same pattern as the world. But what is meant by 'the world'? The nineteenth-century scholar Adam Clarke helps here: 'By "world" may be understood the customs and fashions of the people at that time. The world that now is — THIS present state of things, is as much opposed to the spirit of genuine Christianity as the world then was.'[10] Albert Barnes sums it up well in reminding us that Christians should not conform to the prevailing habits, style and manners of people who are without God: 'They (Christians) are to be governed by the laws of the Bible; to fashion their lives after the example of Christ; and to form themselves by principles different from those which prevail in the world.'[11] This is not to say that only godly people are capable of writing and performing music that is glorifying to God (and we deal with this issue elsewhere in these pages) but it does warn us against slavishly adopting musical styles that are deliberately and thoroughly godless. In the light of all that we have already seen, it should not be difficult for Christians to decide whether the rock music idiom is worldly or otherwise. Having done so, they should then respond honestly and wholeheartedly to the Bible's clear direction: 'Denying ungodliness and worldly lusts, we should live soberly, righteously, and godly in the present age' (Titus 2:12).

Then how did worldliness slip into worship? We agree with A. W. Tozer's assessment that much of the blame can be placed on a growing acceptance of a worldly secularism that seems much more appealing in our church circles than hungering or thirsting for the spiritual life that pleases God: 'We secularize God, we secularize the gospel of Christ, and we secularize worship. No great and spiritually powerful man of God is going to come out of such a church.'[12]

Steve Camp, a Christian rock star who eventually became so sickened by the compromise, sin and worldliness he saw in the Christian music industry that he pulled out of it, had a clear grasp of the situation: 'When Christian artists today take the old song of the world, dress it up, modify it and say it now represents the person of Jesus Christ, a Christian message or describes the character of God, they (unexpectedly) assault the gospel and diminish the gift that has been entrusted to them. This is inappropriate at best and sacrilegious at worst. We cannot pour new wine into old wineskins.'[13]

True Christianity will be attracted to godliness yet offended by worldliness — never the reverse. When someone offers a wineskin, it will recognize the old wine at first taste and will spit it out of its mouth. If the old wine is offered week after week and the new wine is put aside, does it surprise us that we have division in the church over the issue of music?

American (and other) idols

Our *second* concern is that the rock music idiom encourages exhibitionism and self-promotion, even in Christian circles. In an article called 'Rape of the Ear' in the British Youth for Christ magazine *Vista*, Ben Ecclestone wrote: 'All musical performance carries with it a built-in temptation to put on an act,' and there is no doubt that he is right. Provided one is not petrified with fear, there is something powerfully attractive about going on stage in front of a crowd. We know this to be true in our own ministries and believe the danger to be even greater for rock musicians whose appeal is so much more directly to the emotions.

Self-promotion is one area of worldliness where rock musician Keith Green was in no doubt that many Christian artists had failed to get it right. In *Can God use Rock Music?* he wrote, 'Frankly, I have been just as much offended by most of what I've heard and seen as any sweet ole Christian grandma who accidentally stumbles into a blaring-loud gospel concert ... It isn't the beat that offends me, nor the volume — it's the spirit. It's the "Look at me!" attitude I have seen in concert after concert, and the "Can't you see we are as good as the world?" syndrome I have heard on record after record.'[14]

Michael Tait of the immensely popular rock/rap group dc Talk spoke about their struggles with rock's star attraction in *CCM* magazine: 'I've always wanted to be the front guy of a band of guitar-toting, drum-slinging rock 'n' rollers because my personality is one of such flamboyancy and energy. Rock 'n' roll embodies and exudes all of that.'[15] Kevin Max (another member of dc Talk and described by *CCM* magazine as 'a man in black whose shocking blonde hair and rock-star sideburns sizzle with cool') admitted, 'As a performer, you're constantly neurotic about what you look like, how you're performing on stage, what you come off like to the public. And I think that has a lot to do with a lot of the mistakes I've made.'[16]

This tendency for the idiom to produce stars instead of servants is clearly reflected in the fawning adulation found in the advertising and review material published in the Christian music press. Here is just one example from a concert review: 'Audio Adrenaline was worth the price of admission by themselves. Singing some of their greatest hits, illuminating the stage with an awesome light show and all the pyrotechnics you could want, this band lived up to the words of their own song "Worldwide" when they sang:

Four corn-fed boys from the heartland
Brought together for some rock 'n' roll
From Kentucky, Minnesota, Missouri and Ohio
Tonight we're gonna put on a show!'[17]

How does all this tie in with the apostle John's statement that '...the cravings of sinful man, the lust of his eyes and the boasting of what he has and does — comes not from the Father but from the world' (1 John 2:16, NIV)? Is it not also faintly ridiculous? To make the point, we have taken reviews from *Christianity Today's* Favourite Worship CDs of 2003 and 2004 and substituted our own names and ministries for those of the worship artists. This is the result: 'John Blanchard deserves high praise for combining multiple interests into a single, cohesive preaching style. Dan Lucarini's talents are undeniable and promising. Blanchard is wildly ambitious, intriguingly varied, and remarkably thought-provoking. Lucarini is known for his great opening lines, stunning delivery, amazing production, and enthusiastic storytelling. It seems only fitting that we pay tribute to John Blanchard, this pivotal Christian writer. Together Lucarini and Blanchard are a ridiculously talented team!'

Would that kind of nonsense be acceptable in advertising our ministries? *If not, why not? And if not, why should it be acceptable in any part of God's service?* The apostle Paul's approach was exactly the opposite: 'For we do not preach ourselves, but Christ Jesus the Lord, and ourselves your bondservants for Jesus' sake' (2 Corinthians 4:5). He refused to accept adulation from anyone: 'Nor did we seek glory from men' (1 Thessalonians 2:6). Christian rock stars may protest that they are not singing their own praises, but are simply victims of overzealous fans, but they fail to see that such fans can only be responding to an image that is being presented to them. The way to avoid people becoming star-struck is for the star to do everything possible to remove the cause.

The Christian rock star syndrome is further accentuated by the annual Dove Awards, which typically honours the Male Vocalist of the Year, Female Vocalist of the Year, Band of the Year, Rock Song of the Year, Worship Song of the Year etc. The *About Christian Music* web site promotes a Male and Female Artist of the Week. *Worship Leader* magazine lets their readers vote for award-winners in categories like Best Praise and Worship Song; Best Worship Project; Best Scripture Song; and Breakthrough Artist.

This kind of thing may seem perfectly harmless; but is it? Is it helpful to the fans to concentrate their thoughts in this way on the performance of the artists? Is it helpful to the artists themselves to be the centres of this kind of attention? Acknowledging the very problem we have raised, *Worship Leader* magazine tries to take the moral high ground by claiming that awards are not 'a popularity contest that glorifies celebrity',[18] but this seems to us to be ingenious rather than ingenuous. We are tempted to ask, 'How many shouts of "Praise the Lord" does it take to balance out one Breakthrough Artist award?' What percentage of praise and honour is God willing to share with an award-winning worship leader? When the awards are handed out, does the obligatory 'It's not about me, it's about God' truly give to him the unshared glory he rightfully deserves?

As a final and fitting example of the rock-star cancer in the church today, Christian musicians have been lining up to audition for the TV show *American Idol*. In this hugely popular programme on Rupert Murdoch's Fox Channel, young people sing in front of a panel of musical talent judges and compete for the top prize of becoming 'America's Idol'. One Christian wrote to the authors with her reaction when she watched it: 'I must admit that it wasn't until this year that I stopped watching the show. It sucks you in like a vacuum, but why? Why does it do that to us Christians? Shouldn't we know better? The songs, the immodest dress, the sexy dancing — it is everything we shouldn't be.'

Jeff Johnson, a full-time worship leader in an evangelical church, competed on *American Idol* in 2005 and claimed that it was all part of God's perfect plan for his life: 'When the show aired, it promoted my ministry to 30 million people. It's ... part of God's plan for what He has called me to do.'[19] One of the celebrity judges on the panel that day was Gene Simmons, from the infamous rock group KISS. In a moment of supreme irony Simmons (of all people) 'gently tried to nudge him towards country music, warning him that rock and roll's focus on sexuality would contradict his religious focus.'[20] Johnson thought it was interesting that Simmons 'was trying to give me spiritual advice about not singing pop music.'[21] Tragically, Johnson seemed to lack Simmons' discernment.

When one pastor's teenage daughter announced that she was trying out for *American Idol*, a concerned lady in the congregation wrote to him as follows: 'I was very disturbed when I heard that she was going to audition for *American Idol*. The first commandment is "Thou shalt have no other gods before me". Well that is what these American Idols become to other teens — their god, no matter how strong a Christian that individual is.' The pastor's defence was: 'We have been commanded to be in the world but not of the world. The world has been invading the church too long without the church invading the world. If she tries in her flesh she will fail. If she goes in the Spirit she will succeed.' This seems extraordinary, coming from a church leader whose Bible warns us against 'the lust of the flesh, the lust of the eyes, and the pride of life' (1 John 2:16). How could he fail to see that *American Idol* is a blatant demonstration of all three?

The worship pastor at another church announced that while enjoying the 2005 season finale of *American Idol* he came up with three lessons for worship leaders, the first of which was 'authenticity counts.'[22] One hardly knows whether to laugh or cry. How can there be anything approaching authenticity in such a show? All the modern tricks of camera angles, audio techniques, make-up artists, wardrobe consultants, image consultants and faked music were given their full rein, yet this Christian teacher still found it 'authentic' enough to become an example to God's worship leaders!

Any honest Christian knows that genuine humility is hard to come by, and that fighting pride is a constant and costly struggle. To a greater or lesser extent we all have an appetite for appreciation, a liking to be lauded. Voting for worship leaders or any Christian musician on the basis of how professionally they perform in playing and singing about the one who deliberately 'made himself of no reputation, taking the form of a bondservant' (Philippians 2:7) is not only unhelpful to all concerned but a total contradiction of a central truth of the Christian faith. So is *American Idol*. Steve Camp put it well: 'We fail to glorify Him when we praise the servant through awards and accolades rather than exalt the Master.'[23]

The well-known British preacher Alan Redpath put his finger on the spot in his book *Blessings out of Buffetings*: 'The principle of the world is "self-glorification" and the principle of the Christian is "self-crucifixion". The principle of the world is "exalt yourself" and the principle of the Christian is "crucify yourself". The principle of men is greatness, bigness, pomp and show; the principle of the cross is death ... There is never a breaking through of communication of [Christ's] life in your heart and through you to others in heavenly conviction and authority which will challenge or bless them unless at that point there has been a personal Calvary.'

It is surely not difficult to apply these principles in the case of the Christian rock music performer? One of the inherent problems about the rock music idiom is that the attention is focused first on the singer and then on the song — whereas the objective of evangelism is to focus on the gospel and the objective of praise and worship is to focus on God. We can come at this from another angle. When trying to convey a verbal message to someone, it is unnatural to back up the words by swaying, squirming, dancing, slinking or gyrating various parts of one's anatomy. When these things are done on stage they are an act, part of a show — and showmanship of any sort on the part of a preacher or gospel musician is an abomination. Our sole duty is to point people to Christ; to draw attention to ourselves not only fails to help in getting biblical principles across, it positively hinders any attempt to do so. It also places the performer in a dangerous position in the light of God's very clear statement, 'I am the LORD; that is my name! *I will not give my glory to another* or my praise to idols' (Isaiah 42:8, NIV). There is no questioning the fact that the rock music idiom encourages self-promotion and that in Michael Green's words, 'What we need is not just a message of crucifixion, but the crucifixion of the messenger.'[24]

Some might point to examples of 'humble' Christian rock musicians and say, 'It's not the music, but the person's heart that matters', but we would remind them that the strategy of appealing to the man rather than to principle has not served the church well in the past. Tragically, there are too many historical examples of Christian leaders who appeared in public to be righteous but whose private lives completely contradicted their image.

Others will rush to the defence of rock music with the reply that any music style can be used to exalt the performer and therefore it is simply not fair to pick on rock alone. That is partially true. The church has wrongly placed other musicians on a pedestal and even those who lead hymn-singing in a more formal and traditional fashion can so easily become centres of attention and 'put on a show'. We side with A. W. Tozer when he says, 'I have done everything I can to keep performers out of my pulpit. God has never indicated that proclamation of the gospel is to be dependent on human performances.'[25]

Rock performers face a particular problem in this area in that whereas many other music problems could be solved by correcting the performer, the rock idiom defies individual correction because it is by design an individualistic and narcissistic form. Nothing can change that and nothing short of its complete removal can solve the self-promotion problem.

True Christianity is directly opposed to exhibitionism, self-promotion and showboating. When an idiom such as rock music emphasizes these in church we must in all conscience demand that it be removed.

On with the show?

The *third* concern we have is that the rock idiom mixes worship and evangelism with a stimulating form of entertainment. This is one of the 'crunch' issues on the whole subject and we will therefore need to look at it thoughtfully, carefully and honestly. Let us begin by making our definitions clear.

Firstly, what do we mean by 'entertainment'? The verb 'to entertain' has at least twelve different meanings,[26] but we can soon whittle the list down. Five are now obsolete and can immediately be dropped. Also, 'to entertain' can mean to provide food or shelter, to treat hospitably, to take something into consideration, to hold something in the mind, or to meet or experience something; and none of those meanings applies here. That leaves us with three: 'to hold the attention or thoughts of', 'to hold the attention of pleasurably', and 'to amuse'. We accept that in general neither the first nor the third of these fits the Christian rock bill. Music's primary appeal to the emotions makes the first definition somewhat exaggerated; 'to amuse' is commonly associated with making fun, and although some Christian musicians do take unbiblical liberties in that area, it would be unfair to tar them all with the same brush. That leaves us with 'to hold the attention of pleasurably'. To use the dictionary's noun, 'entertainment' in this sense is 'a performance or show intended to give pleasure'[27] — and it seems to us that given all the evidence we have presented that is a perfectly fair description of Christian rock music. The debate can therefore move on to ask *whose* pleasure is the primary result — God's or the worshipper's?

Secondly, what is worship? We will present the biblical definition of worship in a later chapter; at this point it will be sufficient to say that worship is characterized by reverence, modesty and humility, and has nothing that even remotely aims at our pleasure and entertainment. Anything that deviates from that detracts from the glory due to God and Jesus Christ. As we will discover later from Scripture, our songs of praise are to be spiritual, not carnal, and should be marked by a deference to serve our fellow believers.

On a preaching tour in South Africa, John Blanchard was asked to speak at a large evangelical church on the subject of death and the afterlife. With such a serious message he anticipated that the service would be suitably sobering, but the entire time before he preached was taken up by a worship group that enthusiastically ripped into its repertoire. Reflecting on the service afterwards, four obvious flaws came to mind. There had been an unhelpful element of exhibitionism; there had been no doctrinal structure or development in the songs; there had been a futile attempt to drum up an atmosphere of worship; and about 75% of the congregation had apparently been disenfranchised, as they did not join in the singing when asked to do so. We have seen similar flaws in countless churches in which we have ministered in recent years, even when the music has not been exceptionally loud. There is an increasing tendency for pastors to hand over responsibility for the conduct of services to worship teams whose grasp of the significance and sanctity of corporate worship often seems to fall a long way short of their driving enthusiasm.

We need to be alert to the same dangers when proclaiming the gospel. There is no gospel apart from Christ, no gospel without Christ and no gospel outside of Christ. Simply put, the gospel is solidly centred on who he is and on what he did — and there is not a single element of entertainment in either. There is nothing entertaining about the eternal deity of Christ, bathed in the glory he had with his heavenly Father 'before the world was' (John 17:5). There was nothing entertaining about his coming into the world, 'taking the form of a bondservant, and coming in the likeness of men' (Philippians 2:7). There was nothing entertaining about his miracles; they were performed 'for the glory of God, that the Son of God may be glorified through it' (John 11:4). There was nothing entertaining about his lifelong struggle against temptation; he 'himself has suffered, being tempted' (Hebrews 2:18). There was nothing entertaining about his prayer life; we are told that he 'offered up prayers and supplications, with vehement cries and tears' (Hebrews 5:7). There was nothing entertaining about his experience in the Garden of Gethsemane, when 'his sweat became like great drops of blood falling down to the ground' (Luke 22:44). There was nothing entertaining about his agonizing death on the cross when the burden of our sin forced him to cry out, 'My God, my God, why have you forsaken me?' (Matthew 27:46). There was nothing entertaining about his resurrection, by which he was 'declared to be the Son of God with power' (Romans 1:4). There was nothing entertaining about his ascension into heaven, when he was 'received up in glory' (1 Timothy 3:16). There will be nothing entertaining when he returns to earth, when 'every eye will see him, even they who pierced him' (Revelation 1:7). There will be nothing entertaining when all of humanity stands before him on the day of judgement and when as 'judge of the living and the dead' (Acts 10:42) he will pronounce men's eternal destinies.

We dare not miss the significance of this last paragraph. If not one single element in the gospel message is entertaining, *how can the gospel possibly be presented as entertainment?* The life of Jesus was not a religious road show. He did not come to give a performance, but to give his life! At the end of the day, this is the fatal flaw in entertainment evangelism or worship — they are both contradictions in terms. The objective of entertainment is to give pleasure (and there is nothing essentially wrong with pleasure), but the aim of truly biblical evangelism is to warn people of their appalling spiritual condition and to point them to the one who 'came into the world to save sinners' (1 Timothy 1:15). As Paul Bassett rightly says, 'The danger is just as great today as it was in Paul's day of producing a crossless Christianity whose flattering appeal creates fans, but not followers.'[28]

The whole emphasis on entertainment becomes even more absurd when we realize that although the gospel is good news, it does not appear so to the sinner. The Bible speaks of 'the offence of the cross' (Galatians 5:11); it describes Christ as 'a stone that causes men to stumble and a rock that makes them fall' (1 Peter 2:8, NIV); it says that 'The message of the cross is foolishness to those who are perishing' (1 Corinthians 1:18) and that the message of a crucified Saviour is 'to the Jews a stumbling block and to the Greeks foolishness' (1 Corinthians 1:23). To the unconverted, the glorious message of the gospel is sheer nonsense. To tell him that he is by nature a guilty, depraved rebel against his Maker and that his only hope of the forgiveness of sins and eternal life lies in the hands of a young Jew who was murdered and rose from the dead 2,000 years ago insults his intelligence, offends his sense of decency and hurts his pride. Then how can we get such a message across and entertain him at the same time?

All of this underlines the seriousness of the work of evangelism. The apostle Paul could tell the Ephesians that he served the Lord 'with all humility, with many tears and trials' (Acts 20:19) and 'for three years I did not cease to warn everyone night and day with tears' (Acts 20:31). Can the evangelistic entertainer honestly claim to have that kind of burden and to have performed with that kind of spirit? In genuine evangelism, the church is a lifeboat, not a showboat!

Perhaps we should add a paragraph here to expand on what we mean by that. In pointing out the fundamental folly of entertainment evangelism or worship we are not suggesting that the Christian message is one of gloom and doom, best presented by people with personalities and styles to match. After all, the Bible says that 'the kingdom of God is not eating and drinking, but righteousness and peace and joy in the Holy Spirit' (Romans 14:17). The order of those key words — 'righteousness', 'peace' and 'joy'— is not accidental. The Christian life is certainly meant to be one of joy, but a Christian's real joy depends on the extent of his peace (of heart, mind and conscience), while his peace depends on his righteousness (his right relationship with God). To offer joy before peace, and peace before righteousness, is to put both carts before the horse. There is never true joy without peace and no real peace without righteousness. So the first aim in evangelism is not to bring joy (let alone superficial happy feelings) but to bring home to people their need to get right with God. As Dr Martyn Lloyd-Jones succinctly said, 'The business of preaching is not to entertain but to lead people to salvation, to teach them how to find God.'[29]

Larry Norman, called by some the father of Christian rock and the CCM business, has admitted the impossibility of combining entertainment and evangelism. Asked, 'What is the main aim of your ministry?' he replied, 'I don't think music is a ministry. Music is just a bunch of notes.'[30] Later in the same interview, when asked what he was trying to achieve through his music, he said, 'I never achieve evangelism through my music. If I'm going to say anything evangelistic, I say it with words and not music. Music is art, not propaganda.'[31] Norman's honesty is helpful. Rock music aims at pleasing people — biblical evangelism aims at saving them; and true worship aims to please God. Pleasing people is a perfectly legitimate aim, of course — in the right context. Holiday Inn, the international chain of motels, used to call themselves 'The People Pleasin' People' and countless satisfied customers will say that they have succeeded. But pleasing people must never be a factor in evangelism or worship.

One of the principles that governed New Testament evangelism and worship was, 'We ought to obey God rather than men' (Acts 5:29). Paul could say, 'We speak, not as pleasing men, but God who tests our hearts' (1 Thessalonians 2:4) and testify a moment later, 'Nor did we seek glory from men' (1 Thessalonians 2:6).

This poses a constant and fundamental problem for the Christian rock artist. He is trying to please men and God at the same time but, as we have already shown, the idiom he is using imposes what we might call 'popularity pressure'. The publicity, the spotlights, the presentation, the applause — all the attention is on him rather than on his message. When John the Baptist was preaching, his stage was the desert, he wore his ordinary clothing, his message was clear and uncompromising, he made no attempt to please men and his attitude was one of utter humility. We might almost say that it was the most natural thing in the world for him to point to Jesus and say, 'Behold! The Lamb of God who takes away the sin of the world!' (John 1:29). It is almost impossible for the Christian rock singer to have that same spirit, because of the pressures the idiom imposes on him. However sincere his motives, however genuine his personal devotion to the Lord, whatever his songs are saying, what so often comes across is not 'Behold! The Lamb of God...' but 'Look at me saying, "Behold, the Lamb of God..."' His real dilemma is put in a nutshell by David Porter when he says, 'The problem is that art was never meant for preaching with at all.'[32]

A truly biblical response to the Word of God is to worship him in spirit and in truth, and to resist anything that mixes entertainment values into worship or evangelism.

Tailor-made Messiah

Our *fourth* concern is that the rock music idiom tends to water down the holiness of God and the cross of Christ. In his book *The*

Divine Conquest, A. W. Tozer writes, 'If I see aright, the cross of popular evangelicalism is not the cross of the New Testament. It is, rather, a new bright ornament upon the bosom of a self-assured and carnal Christianity. The old cross slew men; the new cross entertains them. The old cross condemned; the new cross amuses. The old cross destroyed confidence in the flesh; the new cross encourages it.' In *Of God and Men* he adds this: 'Much that passes for New Testament Christianity is little more than objective truth sweetened with song and made palatable by religious entertainment.'

Those are serious charges, but we believe them to be true. Of course, Tozer is referring to church life in general, but his comments particularly apply to the Christian rock music scene. There are essential elements of biblical truth that cannot be fitted into the narrow and shallow confines of the rock idiom. Can a rock 'n' roll song explain what is meant by God, sin, judgement, the death of Christ, repentance, faith or justification? *If not, how can it convey the gospel?*

We have already touched on another problem for entertainment evangelism in that doctrines such as the holiness and sovereignty of God, the depravity of man, the substitutionary death of Christ, the need for genuine repentance and the call to holiness of life, all cut and hurt and offend the natural man. He hates these things. How then can they possibly be conveyed to him in a worldly and tainted entertainment idiom, which is designed to be pleasurable to his senses? This same question must be asked of worship. Can we truly touch people's hearts by tickling their ears? The Australian-born preacher J. Sidlow Baxter made this comment in his book *Rethinking our Priorities*: 'Pop style, lilty, swingy airs or strummings simply do not fit the rich, deep, urgent, serious truths of the Bible and the gospel.' In other words, the music does not fit the message. The music may be popular, but as the English composer and musicologist Erik Routley says, 'If any music is composed or performed with an eye simply to attracting the unconverted, it is likely to fall into the same error we find in the parson who, in order to make users of bad language feel at home, uses bad language himself.'[33]

One of the results of trying to convey the whole biblical picture by rock music is that one ends up conveying only part of it — which means that the listeners receive a fragmented (and therefore false) message instead of a full one. All too often the end result is that people enjoy hearing the 'gospel' and love the pop preacher's 'life messages' because the message has been tailored to suit their wants rather than to meet their needs. They are quite happy to 'make a decision for Christ' or profess some other kind of commitment, but largely because the Christ they have heard about is not the Christ of Scripture. Instead, he is often closer to the one spoken about by Stewart Henderson (adopting a persona) in his poem 'Splintered Messiah':

I don't want a splintered Messiah
In a sweat-stained, greasy grey robe;
I want a new one.
I couldn't take this one to parties;
People would say, 'Who's your friend?'
I'd give an embarrassed giggle and change the subject.
If I took him home, I'd have to bandage his hands.
The neighbours would think, 'He's a football hooligan.'

I don't want his cross in the hall;
It doesn't go with the wallpaper.
I don't want him standing there
Like a sad ballet dancer with holes in his tights.
I want a different Messiah, streamlined and inoffensive,
I want one from a catalog,
Who's as quiet as a monastery.
I want a package-tour Messiah, not one who takes me to
    Golgotha.

I want a King of kings with blow waves in his hair.
I don't want the true Christ;
I want a false one.[34]

All too often, this is the one the listener gets. The real Christ is still 'despised and rejected by men' (Isaiah 53:3). That is what makes him such poor box office and leads some well-meaning Christians to try and make him 'cool' and acceptable to today's culture. True Christianity must reject this presentation of Christ, even if it causes divisions in the church.

Generations

Our *fifth* concern is that the rock music idiom widens the generation gap and splits the church into musical camps by age group. Rock 'n' roll was the first music in the history of the world specifically aimed at the teenage market. Its beat appealed to their awakening senses. It spoke of rebellion, revolution, freedom and independence, and the more adults objected to it, the more the young took it to their hearts. It eventually became an international anthem for young people and a major factor in establishing the 'youth culture' we have today.

An advertisement placed by *Rolling Stone* magazine in the *New York Times* said, 'Rock and roll is more than just music. It is the energy center of a new culture and youth revolution.'[35] In Mick Jagger's words, 'There is no such thing as a secure, family-oriented rock 'n' roll song.'[36] Bob Dawbarn wrote, 'Rock 'n' roll, if not actually inventing the teenager, split the pop followers into the under-twenties and the rest.'[37] The Beatles' George Harrison made it clear that alienating adults was no accident: 'Music is the main interest of the young people. It doesn't really matter about the older people now because they're finished anyway.'[38] Prominent music critic George Lees was even more specific: 'Rock music has widened the inevitable and normal gap between generations, turned it from something healthy — and absolutely necessary to forward movement — into something negative, destructive, nihilistic.'[39] Jazz artist Ira Gitler agreed: 'Above all other considerations, rock is definitely the music of today's youth and its importance is more social than musical … It sets them apart from the values and attitudes of the adult, establishment world in a more emphatically schismatic manner than ever before.'[40]

It is not difficult to see that philosophy reflected in the life of the church, with young people either becoming increasingly segregated from the rest of the congregation or the rest of the congregation being forced to accept their rock music in the same service. We believe that this tendency to create a 'youth church' or 'youth-oriented worship services' is unnatural and unhealthy. The Christian church is a family and the members of a family ought to demonstrate their common solidarity, rather than their differences. We are not suggesting that there should be a law demanding that every Christian should have the same musical tastes, as that would be absurd. What we are saying is that rock music has always placed an unnatural emphasis on 'youth culture' as a separate entity in society and that such an emphasis is damaging to the life of the church.

This is not empty theorizing; we have seen its effect in countless churches during the past thirty years. We corresponded with the widely-respected former president of an international Christian broadcasting company, who wrote that the message being sent loud and clear is this: 'Young people matter — you don't. It is a way of confirming that the wisdom of the older people must give way to the desires of the younger.' In another letter, a married couple expressed well the frustration felt by many older members of churches: 'Our small town church has slowly been simmering us in the lukewarm pots. The drum trap set arrived on the platform about two months ago. The respect, reverence and humility have vanished from our sanctuary. Pastor has told those of us who are concerned that if we don't like it, we can leave. If anyone questions the new format, their reply is "We'll do whatever it takes to get to the young people." They realize they're losing their older group, but are firm on concentrating on the younger ones. The new movement is rude. Where is the love? Where is the Holy Spirit?'

Yet there is no such thing as a 'youth church', nor is there a 'youth gospel' or 'youth worship style'. There is 'one body and one Spirit ... one Lord, one faith...' (Ephesians 4:4-5). If we are segregated by age and drive out the 'non-youth' with music styles that offend, how can the church carry out Paul's instructions that the older women train the younger women to love their husbands and children, and that the young men learn to be self-controlled from the example of the older men (Titus 2:1-6)?

True Christianity rejoices in the glorious truth that believers are 'all one in Christ Jesus' (Galatians 3:28) and nothing should be encouraged which tends to blur that beautiful picture. Our senior saints should not be marginalized by a musically-defined youth movement, yet sadly this is happening everywhere, persuading many fine Christians that they have no option but to leave the church they love.

Sound barrier

The old chestnut tells of the preacher writing in the margin of his sermon notes, 'Shout here, argument very weak' and both authors must hold their hands up and admit that we are among the many who have been guilty at times of unwisely cranking up the volume when addressing a crowd, especially when feeling the need to do something to get our listeners' attention. Rock music constantly faces the same issue (if not for the same reason) as it tends to be louder than other forms of music, especially when amplifiers are used to raise the decibel level. We have looked at the volume problem earlier in this book and drawn attention to the physical damage that loud rock music causes, not least to the musicians themselves, with Pete Townshend admitting his part in inventing and refining a type of music that is in danger of causing deafness.

We have also seen the way in which the volume can so often smother the value of the words and would like to back this up by another illustration. During a nationwide UK tour in 1987 singer Sheila Walsh's Worthing concert was reviewed by *Christian Herald* music editor David Hotton. He wrote quite favourably about some aspects of the evening, but then came the punch line: 'For some of us, however, *communication ended when she sang* because, more often than not, the band was too loud for us to catch the words.'[41] We could not have made our point any better than that — and Sheila Walsh's style would be thought decidedly tame today!

However, at this point we want to extend the volume test by considering its effect on those who are not fans of rock music but who have no option but to listen to it — unless they walk out of a given service, concert or meeting, or leave the church altogether. The former president of an international Christian broadcasting company highlighted the problem: 'The loudness of the music is unjustified. The noise alienates older people. Their ears cannot tolerate the sound. I know many godly people, including my own parents, who have stopped going to church for the simple reason that the loudness of the music is intolerable to their ears.'

He is not alone in drawing attention to this cause for concern. The following responses received from readers of *Why I Left the Contemporary Christian Music Movement* are typical of many others:

'I've tried to stay and show that I will do anything to bring unity to our church. But the band is so loud, and I don't want my children to be subjected to such noise. When the band was told that three families left because of their music, they said that they didn't care. I knew then that they were out to glorify themselves and not God.'

'The music was at discotheque volume. Within two minutes of playing I had to leave the sanctuary due to this ill feeling that swept over me. My heartbeat raced, my hands shook with uncontrolled nervousness, I felt nauseated, my thoughts were scattered, and I felt winded. I sat outside the sanctuary and wept bitterly because I knew this would mean we would have to leave.'

'It's too bad when you have to take ear plugs to church because the music is so loud it's offensive. My mother has suffered from a stroke and gets upset if there is a lot of loud noise and commotion. I took her to a church in Colorado, where the music was so loud and wild that it upset her to the point that we had to leave with her in tears. Some worship THAT was!'

'They crank the amplifiers up SO LOUD that it is painful. A visiting music leader said that anyone who doesn't like loud music is out of the will of God. Once upon a time I used to love to sit in the front of the church. Now I sit in the back away from the speakers. The doctors, audiologists and hearing aid manufacturers are going to end up with a lot of patients.'

'I have a Jewish friend whom I was evangelizing so I took her to a church that is pro-Israel. They had a guest rock band that morning with music so loud and irreverent that she said it was blasphemous and told me she would wait outside.'

'The audience was mostly older folks, in their sixties or above ... the music was deafeningly loud due to the massive sound system.

After 15 minutes or so, I left because my ears were hurting from the high decibel level of the music.'

What is the reaction of the worship leaders and pastors who are in charge of these audio assaults? Several correspondents complained that we were exaggerating the noise issue in *Pop Goes the Gospel* and *Why I Left the Contemporary Christian Music Movement*. They protested that only a few people had a problem with it and that if they did they should tell the church leaders to address the matter. This seems a reasonable response, but messages from our readers show that this is often futile:

'Last Sunday the music was a lot louder than usual; several people complained who normally never complain. I went to the worship leader who was running the sound board and told him several thought the sound was too loud. He replied it wasn't and he was not going to change it for a few people.'

'For the past nine months I have been talking with the "worship" music committee and expressing my concern with the volume (to the point of causing some people physical pain) as well as the way the "praise band" is performing. The response I receive is varied depending on the week: "We are looking into the situation" or "Maybe it's where you are sitting in the sanctuary." Obviously, the impression I'm receiving is that they are only telling me what they think I want to hear and really don't plan on doing anything about it.'

Some may argue that the Bible more than hints at endorsing very loud music by its exhortations to make a 'joyful noise' to the Lord, but this can fairly easily be countered. Phrases such as 'joyful noise' are to be found only in older versions of the Bible, whereas modern versions tend to replace 'noise' with 'shout', as in 'Shout to God with the voice of triumph!' (Psalm 47:1). The shout of triumph seems often to have been an important part of a sacrificial worship ritual, perhaps a blast of trumpets in unison, and it seems very likely that shouting and singing were always two separate expressions of joy and praise. In fact, through the history of music from then onwards, there seems no acceptable pedigree of music being expressed by loud shouting. Nor, surely, can there be warrant for Christian music being turned up to such a volume that it virtually obliterates the words it is meant to be conveying to its hearers, or for being so selfishly indulged in that it drives away godly Christians who long to be part of their local church and to support its ministry in every way they can.

Worship Inc.

A. W. Tozer watched in disbelief in the nineteen-fifties as evangelical churches adopted three methods which he saw as being diametrically opposed to New Testament principles. He identified them as big business methods, show business methods and Madison Avenue advertising methods. He then made this prediction: 'You can be sure of this: to attempt to carry on a sacred, holy work, after these methods is to grieve the Holy Ghost and remain in Babylonian captivity.'[42] Today, we see the fulfilment of his prophecy.

This is not a book about 'big business' in church life, with all of its associated problems. For readers wishing to pursue that subject we recommend books like *This Little Church Went to Market* by Gary Gilley, a fellow Evangelical Press author. Our focus is on rock music and how that impacts the worship of God and the clear communication of the gospel. We have already seen that the rock idiom encourages a show-business mentality and uses worldly advertising methods. Our concern here goes deeper and asks whether the Christian rock music industry uses the same business methods to market the very heart of worship itself.

On 24 October 2002, Dan Lucarini received an e-mail from his daughter with a subject line that immediately caught his attention.

FW: Re: Chevy+Lucado+Third Day+Michael W. Smith= Christian automarket?

She had forwarded an article from the previous day's *Detroit Free Press* headed, 'Chevy has faith in tour, but Christianity-themed concerts spark controversy'. The article began, 'Chevrolet Presents: Come Together and Worship stage shows, debuting November 1 in Atlanta, already are sparking outrage and praise.'[43] The tour was described as 'a multimedia worship service with an evangelical flair — complete with preaching by the Rev. Max Lucado and a distribution of free evangelical literature. The headline musicians, Michael W. Smith and the rock band Third Day, are among the hottest acts in the contemporary Christian music genre.'[44] It went on to say that the promoters expected the tour would play at venues with seat capacities averaging 14,000.

The Christians involved in the tour were excited to have Chevrolet as a sponsor, and the public relations machinery moved into gear. 'We consider this to be a breakthrough for our industry,' said Frank Breeden, head of the Christian Music Trade Association in Nashville, Tennessee.[45] A talent agent for the tour was quick to note that 'This is not necessarily an entertainment experience. It's really a vertical experience between believers and God ... much like a church service.'[46] If successful, Breeden said, this could become 'a new wave in entertainment marketing.'[47]

As a successful sales and marketing executive in the software industry and an expert on product marketing tactics, Dan Lucarini was naturally curious to find out what was in it for

Chevrolet and how they would market to the Christians. He discovered that the company was eager to reach 'a demographic niche that was largely untapped by secular manufacturers'.[48] A Chevrolet marketing team doing earlier field research at an amusement park noticed a large crowd drawn to a Christian rock concert being held there. To the trained eye of the marketing professionals, 'These were young families with disposable income, a fact that made them ideal Chevy customers. Clearly, *the way to catch their eye was through their faith*'[49] (emphasis added). After research, the Chevrolet marketing manager said, 'We've found that in 26 of our 44 markets in the Southeast, Bible and devotional reading is the No. 1 leisure activity. So it's huge. This is the Bible Belt.'[50]

The manager then said what we might expect from any marketer salivating at the prospects: '"We think we've got a great venue here, but honestly, this is a business thing that we're trying to accomplish here. *This is about selling cars.*" In three Southern markets, Chevrolet also offered churchgoing customers who test-drove a car ... a free worship-tour CD.'[51]

Readers seeing this for the first time should be shocked, as were we, at this crass commercialism conducted in the name of Jesus. Some Christians voiced their protest, and in what he called an 'open letter to the church', the Christian musician Steve Camp spoke out in strong opposition to this mixing of Christian and secular practices. As of February 2006, the entire letter was still available on his web site *www.a1m.org* — a source we commend to our readers. Brilliantly noting that 'this gave a whole new meaning to the phrase "corporate worship"', Camp summed up his (and our) concerns by pinpointing the following four unbiblical practices:

1. Charging people money to come and worship the Lord and hear his gospel.
2. Partnering with unbelievers in the work of the ministry.

3. Inviting and condoning secular corporations to do their business and trade in the midst of the worship of God.
4. Purposely soliciting from non-believers to finance the work of the ministry.[52]

Camp went on to confront three enormously popular Christian icons, and we can all learn something useful from his approach: 'At the outset, I want to affirm my love and prayers for Michael W. Smith, Third Day, and Max Lucado. The arduous thing is, though this issue is not about them specifically, they do share culpability for their willingness to associate themselves and financially profit from a Worship Tour.'[53]

This happened four years ago — but did the Christian music industry learn anything from it? To our knowledge, none of the people involved in the Chevy Worship Together tour has publicly repented or disavowed their support, nor have they expressed the slightest concern about their share in it. As Camp has commented on his web site: 'The issues sadly remain the same. The world is finding favour and much "legal tender" these days; profiting from ministry ... worship being no exception. The only two things left in the church that do not command a fee today are communion and baptism.' Can we be absolutely sure that this will always be the case?

This is a sensational story yet we must be careful not to be fooled into thinking this was an isolated incident. Time-Life, a leading television infomercial company known best for pitching rock and soul hit music collections, promoted 'praise and worship lifestyle' CDs from Integrity Music. The commercials were aimed directly at middle-aged women. According to a CCM radio manager we interviewed (and confirmed by an article in the *Los Angeles Times*) this also happens to be a target audience for the Christian music industry because these women have plenty of disposable income to buy the products. The infomercial included women testifying that the worship music

— not God — was responsible for comforting and encouraging them in times of trouble.

The president of Integrity has said, 'The whole mission of our company is to help people worldwide experience the manifest presence of God,'[54] but any thoughtful Christian will surely have serious concerns about the motives behind this blatant marketing of worship.

Christians should also be concerned that EMI CMG Publishing has recently extended its publishing agreement with Kingsway's ThankYou Music to sign, develop and promote worship music songwriters. EMI CMG is an operating unit of EMI Music, the home of The Rolling Stones as well as a new cartoon band called Gorillaz who have a CD titled *Demon Days* and a demonic receptionist with an upside-down cross on her forehead; and many other objectionable rock acts. The Christian managers involved call this 'a partnership that has been none other than God-inspired', and a privilege to 'join together in such an awesome endeavour.'[55] Are they absolutely certain that this partnership was inspired by the same God who commands his people to 'have no fellowship with the unfruitful works of darkness, but rather expose them' (Ephesians 5:11) and not to be 'unequally yoked together with unbelievers' (2 Corinthians 6:14)?

What exactly does this partnership mean to the churches? At the present time several of the top worship songs used in churches are distributed by the companies involved in this agreement. They include 'Here I Am To Worship', the current No. 1 worship song in the world (as of August 2005 according to CCLI), 'Blessed Be Your Name', 'Heart of Worship', 'Better is One Day', 'Lord Reign Me In', 'Hallelujah', 'In Christ Alone', and 'How Deep the Father's Love For Us'.

CCLI is Christian Copyright Licensing International, the company that collects money from churches who use these worship songs and many others, and then distributes the money to the copyright owner. How much do songwriters earn for their songs? We are told, 'That depends very much on the usage of the song by churches. A song reproduced by one church only may earn a matter of cents, while a song used in many other churches will earn more.'[56] While that may seem like a mere pittance, we need to keep in mind that there are over *225,000* churches and ministries paying for this and that those pennies can add up fast. This is a multi-million dollar business and a proportion of royalties goes to the music publishing companies. This means that a portion of the money Christians spend buying worship songs from ThankYou Music and part of the church funds that go to CCLI are contributing to the profits of EMI Music.

Sadly, much more could be said about worldly business methods and partnerships with unbelievers, all in the name of producing a better worship experience. Of all the concerns and grievances we have covered in this book, none concerns us more than that the sheep are being fleeced by men and women masquerading as good shepherds, preying on their victims' God-given desire to worship God.

To those who would protest that this odious business can hardly be pinned on rock music and that the blame is with *people* we would say five things:

1. The rock music idiom encourages precisely this kind of practice.
2. The people involved in it are *not* polka bands or Irish fiddlers, but rock musicians.
3. The vast majority of music styles pushed here are part of the rock family tree.
4. The people concerned say they are *not* at fault, as we have heard no apologies or confessions.
5. If Johann Sebastian Bach in his time had peddled his music as a 'total worship lifestyle hub designed to bring you into God's presence everyday', and we had been alive to witness this, our objections would have been equally strenuous.

True Christianity does not profit commercially from the gospel, nor from the true worship of God. It stands in full agreement with Jesus himself who, in cleansing the temple in Jerusalem of those who were commercializing the worship of God, overturned the tables of the moneychangers and told those who sold doves, 'Get these out of here! *How dare you turn my Father's house into a market!'* (John 2:16, NIV, emphasis added).

Of course the marketing of Christian books such as ours, and even those with no reference to music, must come under the same scrutiny. The printed page does not have the same visceral impact as a rock music presentation — it is difficult to imagine hordes of Christians leaping about in London's Evangelical Library! — but Christian publishers and authors need to be scrupulously honest in exercising their ministries and do all they can to ensure that they have 'a conscience without offence toward God and men' (Acts 24:16).

8.

SQUARE ONE

Music is the language spoken by angels.
(American poet Henry Wadsworth Longfellow)[1]

After a long chapter flagging up some of our major concerns about rock music's relationship to worship and evangelism, this would be a good point at which to take a breather and to focus our attention on a truly fundamental factor that should govern all of our thinking and ultimately determine all of our decisions.

Discussion on a controversial subject (and rock music is one!) can begin with things such as a news item, a high-profile person's opinion, or an obvious change in social or cultural trends, but for the Christian there is one bedrock principle that needs to be absolutely predominant at every point.

Anything from God?

About 589 B.C. Zedekiah was the puppet King of Judah, then held in captivity in Babylon. He was a thoroughly unpleasant character, and we are specifically told that neither he nor any of those he influenced 'gave heed to the words of the LORD which he spoke by the prophet Jeremiah' (Jeremiah 37:2). He even allowed Jeremiah to be imprisoned on a trumped-up charge of trying to desert to the Babylonians. But when the going got really tough he sent for the prophet and asked one crucial question: 'Is there any word from the Lord?' No doubt the place was buzzing with all kinds of rumours and speculation. There must have been dozens of ideas as to the cause of Judah's problems, and just as many as to what the solution might be. But when the chips were down Zedekiah knew in his heart that there was only one thing that mattered: *What does God say?*

In the book

For any Christian facing an issue on which there is a strong difference of opinion among believers, Zedekiah's question can be put like this: 'What does the Scripture say?' (Romans 4:3). We are not left at the mercy of our feelings on matters of either belief or behaviour, because God has not only spoken but also given his written word for us to read, study, understand and obey. As the Bible itself claims, 'All Scripture is given by inspiration of God, and is profitable for doctrine, for reproof, for correction, for instruction in righteousness' (2 Timothy 3:16). This means that the Christian should come to the Bible not as a last resort (desperately ransacking it to find statements which he hopes will back up his own opinions) but as a first resort, so that his views will be grounded, governed and guided by a word that 'is settled in heaven' (Psalm 119:89). The Christian who desires to 'do all to the glory of God' (1 Corinthians 10:31) understands that his life must continually be purified, that he must be separated from ungodly beliefs and habits, and that the Word of God must govern his motives and methods. He also rests in the assurance that Scripture alone is perfectly able to judge 'the thoughts and intents of the heart' (Hebrews 4:12).

Great Christian leaders over the centuries have expressed this submission to Scripture in memorable ways. Augustine, who died in A.D. 430 yet remains one of the most influential Christians in history, once said, 'We must surrender ourselves to the authority of the Holy Scripture, for it can neither mislead nor be misled.' Martin Luther wrote, 'Before the Word everyone must give way.' John Calvin said, 'The Bible is the sceptre by which the heavenly King rules his church.' John Wesley claimed, 'I am a Bible bigot. I follow it in all things, both great and small.' Yet we must not think that it is only spiritual giants who consider these views relevant. *This is normal Christianity.* Opinions are interesting, trends are significant, arguments are fascinating; but the Christian must be governed by God — and that means being governed by Scripture. As the seventeenth-century preacher William Gurnall put it, 'The Christian is bred by the Word and he must be fed by it.' The Christian who is determined to begin at square one must do so by setting aside his magazines, chat rooms, web sites, newspapers and history books, and sitting down with his Bible.

Five hundred plus

Trying to find a specific reference to particular subjects in the Bible is sometimes like trying to find the proverbial needle in a haystack. (Not that that makes those references unimportant; God does not have to repeat himself for his words to have authority.) What is more, some important subjects are mentioned surprisingly seldom. For instance, there are no more than four references to the Lord's Supper in the whole of the Bible, yet no straight-thinking Christian would say that the sacrament is only a 'fringe thing'. When we come to the subject of music, the situation is quite different. The Bible contains no fewer than 550 references to music, musicians and musical instruments, and our problem is not where to find them but how to assemble and understand them.

In the beginning — singing stars

Although the Bible is scientifically accurate, it is not a scientific textbook, and its accounts of the creation bear this out. They are very brief and sometimes almost lyrical. For instance, speaking of the creation of the world, God asks Job, 'To what were its foundations fastened? Or who laid its cornerstone, when the morning stars sang together, and all the sons of God shouted for joy?' (Job 38:6-7). No doubt the phrase relating to stars singing is metaphorical, but it is also meaningful. If God can speak of the pure response of his created works to the majestic glory of his creation in terms of song, surely singing must be something which God welcomes and in which he delights?

That's an order!

We can confirm God's approval of music by noticing the many times when the inspired writers of Scripture command his creation to praise him in song. Here are some examples: 'Let the heavens rejoice, let the earth be glad; let the sea resound, and all that is in it; let the fields be jubilant, and everything in them. Then all the trees of the forest will sing for joy; they will sing before the LORD'; 'Let the rivers clap their hands, let the mountains sing together for joy; let them sing before the LORD'; 'Praise the LORD, all his works everywhere in his dominion' (Psalms 96:11-12; 98:8; 103:22, NIV). Again, whatever the metaphorical elements here, these statements clearly speak of something God ordains and desires. If these were the only biblical references to music and singing they would be sufficient for us to know that music has a God-given place in his universe.

All people that on earth do dwell

If stars and trees, mountains and rivers are told to praise God, we should surely expect to find the same response demanded from man, the crown of God's creation — and we do, on page after page. Here are just some of the dozens of instances we could quote: 'Sing praise to the LORD, you saints of his, and give thanks at the remembrance of his holy name' (Psalm 30:4). 'Rejoice in the LORD, O you righteous! For praise from the upright is beautiful. Praise the LORD with the harp; make melody to him with an instrument of ten strings. Sing to him a new song; play skilfully with a shout of joy' (Psalm 33:1-2). 'Make a joyful shout to God, all the earth! Sing out the honour of his name; make his praise glorious' (Psalm 66:1-2). 'Sing to the LORD! Praise the LORD!' (Jeremiah 20:13).

These references are nearly all in what we might call a 'general' context, but many others are more specific, with people being told to sing praise to God for his goodness to them in particular circumstances, such as for special blessings received or for deliverance from their enemies. Even more important than the context is the focal point of all this worship, praise and thanksgiving — and this is God himself. In fact, God and the praising music of his people are so wrapped up together that Moses and the Israelites could sing, 'The Lord is my strength and song' (Exodus 15:2). As they celebrated their miraculous deliverance from the hands of the Egyptians, their song of praise had God not only as its object and inspiration, but also as its theme. In the fullest possible sense, their song was sung to the glory of God.

God's gift

Another factor we must note in this general look at the place of music in Scripture is that music is not only *for* God but *from*

God. In praising God for delivering him from a difficult situation, David says, 'He has put a new song in my mouth — praise to our God' (Psalm 40:3). Even that one reference is important. It tells us that it is not enough to think of music merely in terms of human culture but of divine creation. Music is certainly an art, but it is primarily a gift. As John Calvin put it, 'All arts proceed from God and ought to be held as divine inventions.'[2] Elsewhere, he went on to say, 'Among other things adapted for men's recreation and for giving them pleasure, music is either the foremost, or one of the principal; and we must esteem it a gift from God designed for that purpose.'[3] Some years earlier Martin Luther said much the same thing more colourfully: 'Music is to be praised as second only to the Word of God because by her are all the emotions swayed ... When natural music is sharpened and polished by art, then one begins to see with amazement the great and perfect wisdom of God in this wonderful work of music ... He who does not find this an inexpressible miracle of the Lord is truly a clod and is not worthy to be considered a man!'[4] We agree with both men. No Christian can legitimately be opposed to music in and of itself. He may prefer one style or type to another, but to reject music out of hand is to run contrary to God's intention and to be less than the whole person God wants him to be.

The farmer, the musician and the toolmaker

Some Bible students believe that the first reference to any subject in the Bible is of particular importance. This may be open to debate, but it would certainly seem to be so in the case of music. The first reference comes just a few generations removed from Adam and Eve, when the Bible tells us about the three sons born to Lamech and his two wives, Adah and Zillah. This is how they are introduced: 'Adah bore Jabal. He was the father of those who dwell in tents and have livestock. His brother's name was Jubal. He was the father of all those who play the harp and flute ... Zillah ... also bore Tubal-Cain, an instructor of every craftsman in bronze and iron' (Genesis 4:20-22).

That sounds like nothing more than part of somebody's family tree, but there is much more to it than that. These three brothers were the 'founding fathers' of three important groups of people. The first was a farmer and the third a toolmaker — and agriculture and industry are obviously vitally important for man's well-being. But the middle brother was a musician, with the obvious inference that man is more than just a food-eating worker. He has other dimensions beside the physical and material — and the needs of one of those other dimensions are properly met by music. In the words of the American classical pianist Sam Rotman, 'Here, within the compass of but a few verses, God reveals that the provision of man's material needs is not enough; in addition, man must have an outlet for his aesthetic sensitivities. Even from the beginning music was more than a mere pastime which could be viewed as something pleasant but essentially unnecessary. Simply stated, God has created in man a certain aesthetic need which can be best satisfied in music, and in his love and wisdom he has provided for this need.'[5]

Music is not merely something that is potentially pleasant; it is meant to contribute something essential to man's total needs and God has lovingly provided us with the ability to create it. The picture is simple and beautiful. The very existence of music should cause us to praise the God who gave it to us.

Yet there is at least one other important lesson we can learn from Jubal, which is that musicians, like all other human beings, are fallen men and women always prone to being seduced by the wickedness of their culture. There were two lines that proceeded from Adam, the line of Cain to which Jubal belongs and the line of Seth of whom it was said they 'began to call on the name of the LORD' (Genesis 4:26). From Seth came great men of God like Methusaleh, Noah and Enoch. On the other side Cain, who caused the original worship dispute and then murdered his brother in a fit of jealousy, produced a far different type of descendant. There is no record in Cain's line of the godliness seen in Seth's line. Cain and his descendants were cursed by God, condemned to wander the earth and destined to be failures at farming (Genesis 4:11-12). With meagre crops to sustain their nomadic lifestyle, it is quite possible that Jubal's brother Jabal raised the livestock not only for milk but also for slaughter. If this is the case it would have meant rebellion against God, who did not permit men to eat meat until after the Flood had subsided. Jubal's grandfather Lamech was the first bigamist (Genesis 4:19) and a murderer (Genesis 4:23). Ultimately Cain's wicked line corrupted Seth's godly line through intermarriage and the result was such incredible wickedness that God judged the earth with the Flood as recorded in Genesis 6.

This all tells us that the father of all musicians was born into a rebellious family of pagans and violent men, not into a godly line. Then how did he exercise this creative gift of making music? Was his music pleasing to God or was it no more commendable than that of the false priests of Amos' day to whom God said, 'Take away from me the noise of your songs, for I will not hear the melody of your stringed instruments' (Amos 5:23)? To be completely honest, we have no idea what Jubal's music sounded like or what God thought of it, but we do know enough about Jubal to be discerning and cautious about the music created by men.

Feelings and faith

We ought at this point to ask ourselves one very basic question about music: what is it for? Put very simply, the answer is that music is one of the ways by which we can give audible expression to our common emotions such as joy, sorrow, love, sympathy, heroism and compassion, and as we turn the pages of the Bible, we find it used in all of these areas. As Erik Routley puts it with particular reference to the Old Testament, 'Music was in very wide use in the culture of Israel at all its stages ... we can distinguish epics and dirges in secular contexts (insofar as any context for Israel was secular), and songs of praise, thanksgiving, instruction, personal experience, and liturgical significance in the religious context.'[6]

Yet most Bible references to music occur in direct connection with the worship and service of God, with man's religious faith rather than with his general feelings. The first of these references is in Exodus 15, where we have the great 'freedom song' of Moses and the Israelites. By the time we reach 1 Chronicles religious music has become highly sophisticated and organized, with King David appointing no fewer than 4,000 singers to praise the Lord with 'musical instruments "which I made ... for giving praise"' (1 Chronicles 23:5) and 288 master musicians 'instructed in the songs of the LORD, all who were skilful' (1 Chronicles 25:7).

The entire book of Psalms formed a 'hymn-book' for Old Testament believers, with some of the instructions (which are part of the text of Scripture) being quite specific in giving details of the musical instruments to be used. For example, Psalm 4 has the note 'with stringed instruments', and Psalm 5 'with flutes', presumably to ensure that the music matched the words. These 'forewords' are not merely interesting, but instructive. God's praises were not to be sung in a shoddy or haphazard way. Instead, great care was taken to meet certain criteria.

The point is important, because many of those involved in worship and evangelistic music today would point back to Chronicles and the Psalms and claim that it gives them all the licence they need for 'doing their own thing' musically — but closer examination tells a different story. It has been pointed out that of the eight musical instruments used by the Israelites, only four (harp, lyre, cymbal and horn) were specifically authorized for use in the temple. Timbrels were taboo, as were flutes, pipes and dulcimers, even though these are mentioned in the Psalms and could properly be used elsewhere. What is more, the musicians had to come from certain families, they played only on certain limited and special occasions, and only at specific times during the service. There was no question of a free-for-all, with anyone who could play an instrument being invited to join the band and turn the service into an informal music festival. Instead, music was rigidly controlled in the temple worship service, presumably to ensure it was never the predominant factor but certainly due to the fact that the Israelites paid close attention to what God required. The broader lesson is that neither in music, nor in any other area of life, has God given us licence to 'do what is right in our own eyes'.

What happened to the hyssop?

The contemporary Christian musician who tries to lean on chapter and verse in the Old Testament to justify all of his musical output has further problems, because if he continues reading his Bible he will soon discover that all the musical organization we have just noted was a purely temporary arrangement. It was part of the Old Testament ritualistic and sacrificial system that was abolished by the death of Christ. All the paraphernalia of temple worship, though ordained by God, was part of a system of types, figures and shadows that was done away with when Christ instituted the new covenant. Those who justify rock music in God's service purely on the grounds that 'similar' musical instruments were used in Old Testament worship could find the same justification for putting tassels on their clothing, asking God to purge them with hyssop, walking about Zion and waving bits of dead sheep! Would it not be more biblical to agree that all of these types, systems, rituals and sacrifices (ordained by God to accommodate the particular spiritual darkness of Old Testament times) have now been abolished, and replaced by the simple beauty of Christ's statement that true worshippers are those who worship 'in spirit and truth' (John 4:24)?

The New Testament

What is extraordinary about the 500 musical references in the Bible is that they are virtually all in the Old Testament. The other remarkable division is that of all the New Testament references, only ten or so refer to Christians here on earth, all of the others being related to the heavenly hosts mentioned in Revelation. Of the 'earthly' references, two are quotations from the Old Testament. Of the remainder, two merely tell us that Jesus and his disciples sang a hymn before they left the Upper Room to go to Gethsemane (Matthew 26:30; Mark 14:26); another records that while in prison at Philippi, Paul and Silas were 'praying and singing hymns to God' at midnight (Acts 16:25); and another that Paul was determined to sing God's praises in a language that could be understood by the hearers (1 Corinthians 14:15). There was 'music and dancing' in the parable of the prodigal son (Luke 15:25), while James gives the simple instruction: 'Is anyone cheerful? Let him sing psalms' (James 5:13).

That leaves just two places in the whole of the New Testament where there is direct instruction given on the subject — and they are parallel passages, saying virtually the same thing. Writing to the Ephesians, Paul says, 'Be filled with the Spirit, speaking to one another in psalms and hymns and spiritual songs, singing and making melody in your heart to the Lord' (Ephesians 5:18-21). Writing to the Colossians he says, 'Let the word of Christ dwell in you richly in all wisdom, teaching and admonishing one another in psalms and hymns and spiritual songs, singing with grace in your hearts to the Lord' (Colossians 3:16).

It is interesting to notice the identical lists Paul mentions: psalms, hymns and spiritual songs. What were these? 'Psalms' would be mainly, but perhaps not exclusively, the Old Testament Psalms as we know them; 'hymns' would be current compositions in praise of God the Father and the Lord Jesus Christ (we may have snatches of some of these here and there in the New Testament, such as Mary's words at Luke 1:46-55); while 'spiritual songs' seemed to have covered a rather wider range of lyrical compositions, but could have included the other two groups.

The New Testament has nothing else to say on the subject! Those who would appeal to 'the sacrifice of praise to God, that is, the fruit of our lips' (Hebrews 13:15) as connecting with the Old Testament musical service and the towdah praise offering miss the important fact that the writer borrowed the words from Hosea 14:2, where in context they referred more to a broken and repentant prayer of confession than to a 'happy-clappy' praise tune.

Yet even these brief phrases in Ephesians and Colossians have lessons for us. An obvious one is that variety is encouraged in Christian music. As the Bible scholar Derek Kidner puts it, 'Our garden of praise, if we may put it so, is not to be all vegetables, or even all one kind of flower.'[7] Yet variety does not mean licence to do anything we please. 'Psalms' and 'hymns' had direct reference to God, but the songs, too, had to be 'spiritual' — an important qualification. Music about God should reflect his glory, beauty, holiness and order, and should direct men to him and to his ways. We should also note their emphasis on vocal worship. As Albert Barnes wrote, 'The prevailing character of music in the worship of God should be vocal. If instruments are engaged, *they should be so subordinate that the service may be characterized as singing*'[8] (emphasis added). Lastly, and particularly relevant to our discussion about music as a divisive force, it is clear that in context Paul is teaching us that music is not to be used to satisfy our personal desires and preferences. Instead it should be an important element in fostering unity and edification in the church. There were to be no worship wars! If we could take serious note of this alone, how many church splits and needless scandals might be avoided!

Each of these principles is important. If our music is truly to be 'to the glory of God' (1 Corinthians 10:31) it must draw attention to him, mirror his majesty, and meet all the biblical criteria we have before us. Quite apart from anything else, this also means that we should take any composition of words or music to Philippians 4:8 and ask these questions: 'Is it true? Is it noble? Is it just? Is it pure? Is it lovely? Is it "of good report"? Is it praiseworthy?' If it fails to meet these standards we have no right to use it in God's service. Using these criteria, how can we possibly claim that all music styles are suitable for God's worship and service and that personal preference is the only guideline we need?

We can take this a step further. Scripture describes the worship of God as a serious and reverent act of humility. The Hebrew word used in over 95% of Old Testament references to worship is *shachah*, whose literal meaning is 'to be prostrate in homage to God; to bow down and humbly beseech; to do reverence'. *Shachah* appears in over 160 verses, and where it is not translated as 'worship' it is usually translated as 'bowed down their face on the ground'.

In the New Testament, fifty-four out of some seventy verses containing the word 'worship', 'worshipper' or 'worshipping' are translated out of the Greek *proskuneo*. In Middle Eastern societies, especially Persia, which had exerted much influence over the region, the ancient mode of greeting one another was determined by rank. The Greek scholar Spiros Zodhiates vividly describes the cultural meaning of *proskuneo*: 'Persons of equal

191

rank kissed each other on the lips. When the difference of rank was slight, they kissed each other on the cheek. When one was much inferior, he fell upon his knees and touched his forehead to the ground or prostrated himself, throwing kisses at the same time towards the superior.'[9]

The writer of Hebrews gives Christians two non-negotiable rules for worship, capped off by a solemn reason why we must pay heed: 'Let us have grace, by which we may serve God acceptably with reverence and godly fear. For our God is a consuming fire' (Hebrews 12:28-29). The Greek word translated 'serve' literally means 'to render our religious service' and is translated 'worship' in some modern versions. The word translated 'reverence' means with modesty or shamefacedness. Adam Clarke summed it up well when he wrote, 'When Abel sacrifices, God is well pleased; where Cain offers, there is no approbation [approval]. We have boldness to enter into the holiest by the blood of Jesus, but let that boldness be ever tempered with modesty and religious fear; for we should never forget that we have sinned, and that God is a consuming fire.'[10] This is the heartbeat of worship that the early church would have known and practised; can we say that ours is the same?

In the November-December 2005 issue of *Reformation Today*, Mark Troughton, a pastor with experience in England and Switzerland, wrote a perceptive piece under the intriguing title 'Christian Misanthropy'. With the kind consent of *Reformation Today's* editor we want to quote the following passage:

> I, for one am worried by some 'liberal evangelical'(?) worship meetings where Truth and Word are scarcely to be heard because most of the time is given over to what is, in essence, entertainment and cheap emotionalism. Am I mistaken or is the 'music/worship group' in danger of becoming a New Priesthood which mediates the presence of Jesus/God to the congregation through music/emotion

at the expense of the Word/Truth? (I'm not arguing for the 'Priesthood of One Believer' by contrast.) Am I on the wrong track when I get the distinct impression that we are being corporately encouraged to 'reach out and touch Jesus' (somehow) when the rhythm and emotion are at its highest point? Why does this remind me of the Baal priests in 1 Kings? Am I being uncharitable when I conclude that these are the hallmarks of pagan hysteria and mysticism — of mystical 'encounters with God', of 'happenings'? Or even the Roman Catholic Mass? I hope I'm wrong. I'm not a devotee of techno-trance parties, but I sometimes wonder what the differences are. And if evangelism happens primarily by attracting people to this great experience of 'worship' then the mind boggles at what they are becoming converts to.

Eloquent silence?

Before ending our look at music in Scripture, there is one important point to be made about the use of Christian music for evangelistic purposes. In the entire Old Testament, *there is not one instance of music being used to help communicate Judaism to the heathen.* There is no record, for instance, of God's people organizing a Jewish religious folk festival to try to convert the Hittites, Hivites, Jebusites or Amalekites. Even David's 'new song' (Psalm 40:3) was a testimony to his fellow Israelites, urging them to continue trusting in God, whatever their circumstances.

Even more significantly, there is no reference in the New Testament to the early church using music to reach non-Christians with the gospel, even though it obviously had the means at its disposal. All the music references are to the church at worship; there are none to the use of music in evangelism.

Some people have rejected this and claimed that when Paul and Silas were 'praying and singing hymns to God' while in prison in Philippi, they were reaching out to the unconverted jailer, but this idea does tend to lose a little impetus when we note that the jailer actually slept throughout the singing session and only woke up when God sent an earthquake! (Acts 16:26-27). The fact is that his subsequent conversion had nothing to do with evangelistic singing but everything to do with the fear of God.

Is our general point not very striking? Here is the early church, bursting with new life, longing to tell the world about the risen Christ. Here are its Spirit-filled leaders, willing to give everything, even their own lives, to reach men and women with the gospel. Here is the apostle Paul saying, 'I have become all things to all men, that I might by all means save some' (1 Corinthians 9:22). Yet we never once read that they used the powerful (and available) medium of music to get their message across. Nor did they adopt pagan rituals or entertainment tricks of any sort to present the gospel. Did they miss the boat — or did they know something we have either forgotten or ignored?

Of course, there are those who will say, 'But that is an argument from silence.' Yet if we are absolutely honest we have to ask ourselves this question: is the silence saying something — something crucially important?

9.

MOTIVES UNDER THE MICROSCOPE

I should be sorry … if I have only succeeded in entertaining them;
I intended to make them better.

(George Friedrich Handel)[1]

In earlier chapters we have reviewed evidence that, at the very least, rock music in all forms is controversial, closely associated with ungodly behaviour, and at times downright dangerous. Why then would Christian musicians choose it to accompany the praise and worship of God or to proclaim the gospel of his grace? Why would they risk causing false conversions and creating soft disciples who may fall away as soon as the going gets tough and they realize that music will not meet their needs? Why would they choose to offend millions of other Christians such as those we discussed in chapter 1? Why, too, would respected preachers and other Christian leaders throw their unqualified support behind Christian rock?

Question time

What prompts the preachers? What motivates the musicians? Are we to imagine that they are all devil-inspired 'moles', infiltrating the Christian church in order to destroy it from the inside? Of course not — though it goes without saying that in an industry of this size there are bound to be rogues of one kind or another. Not all of those involved in hyping the Christian rock market do so from motives that are as pure as the driven snow; some of the performers would not even claim to be Christians.

Tom Morton, then a full-time musician with British Youth for Christ, wrote quite openly about this in 1981: 'What has happened over the last fifteen years in Britain has been the formation of a Christian music "scene", featuring record companies, management agencies, tour organizers, full-time performers, concert promoters and assorted hangers-on. Instead of this subculture being rooted in Christian standards in fact as well as in name, it appears that some of the Christian music scene has become, in effect, sub-Christian. Some Christian musicians seem excessively concerned with fame, with their image; some record companies seem profit-orientated at the expense of their artists' ministries, and since their "package" is wrapped up in pseudo-evangelical language and justification, few people have realized what was happening.'[2] Elsewhere, Morton made this frank admission: 'The rock music industry is perhaps one of the most corrupt in existence, and the unthinking transfer of its techniques to the Christian sphere has resulted in some of the uneasy mixtures of gospel and garbage which have in the past gone under the name of "gospel concerts".'[3]

Those are serious statements — and they were made by someone with inside knowledge of the Christian music scene. With warnings like these, you might imagine that by 2006 the industry would have 'cleaned house' and rid itself of the influence of ungodly performers and their worldly techniques. But quite the opposite has happened and Morton's words are as relevant today as when they were first written. A great deal of Christian music today, even our worship music, is controlled and produced by secular music companies. Christian bands come under the influence of thoroughly pagan managers and image consultants who also promote the vilest and most ungodly of secular musicians, while Christian music videos are often produced by the same people who produce degraded material for MTV. Some Christian bands even boast of having recorded with talented secular musicians who are involved in work far removed from a Christian ethic.

Be that as it may, let us be as positive as we can and assume that the vast majority of those in the Christian rock scene are sincere believers seeking to serve God through their music. What motives do they have for believing that they are right in doing so? Here, in their own words, are some of their responses to that question.

'It draws the crowds.'

There is no point in denying this. The crowds that attend worship services or evangelistic events where rock bands perform easily outnumber those attending gatherings with a more formal structure. But should that surprise us? In the first place, rock music has become an indispensable part of today's youth culture and rock worship gives young Christians an apparently irresistible opportunity to express their Christianity in this way without resisting the pressure of their cultural peer group.

Secondly, we are living in a time of spiritual depression, when the church has a much greater appetite for the trivial and amusing than for the biblical and searching. If we are honest, A. W. Tozer's words have a tragic ring of truth about them: 'It is scarcely possible in most places to get anyone to attend a meeting where the only attraction is God.'[4] But that must never be an excuse for conceding to man's lack of spirituality. As Paul Bassett says, 'One of the subtlest ways of flattering man is to communicate the gospel in a way he wants rather than the way he needs.'[5]

Having said all of that, the claim about popularity is irrelevant, because our real concern should be with truth and principle, not polling statistics.

'It communicates to unchurched people in a language they can understand.'

Again, we agree. Rock music communicates in a specific language quite apart from the lyrics, and what may seem to be disjointed lunacy to 'golden oldies' is a dynamic language to the 'cool' crowd. Like all other music, rock is bound up with its culture, in this case the culture of the 'teens to thirties'. Although there are times when there is no mistaking what the music is communicating, there are many instances when its language is virtually unintelligible to many others.

This 'inside track' leads many pro-rock Christians to claim that their music has the apostle Paul's endorsement when he says, 'I have become all things to all men, that I might by all means save some' (1 Corinthians 9:22). Our response would be that to argue like this is to wrench the Bible's words out of context, because they are part of a passage in which Paul is focusing on *the primacy of preaching*, not suggesting that he is open to a limitless number of alternatives.

The big question remains: does rock music effectively communicate the Word of God? We maintain that it does not, for the crucial reason that the medium has a distorting influence on the message. David Hesselgrave makes this point very powerfully in a statement which does not specifically have rock music in mind: 'Missionaries must divest themselves forever of the naive notion that the reception of the gospel message is the same irrespective of how it is conveyed to the world — whether by book, magazine, radio, television, film, sound recording, etc. Perhaps no fiction has had wider currency than if you put a gospel message into any of these media at one end, it will come out at the other end as the same message... *The media must always affect the message*[6] (emphasis added).

So does rock music communicate the gospel effectively and without distortion? After all, it is vitally important that the message of the gospel is not only biblically given but biblically received. The Bible's primary appeal is to the mind. God declares: 'Come now, and let us reason together' (Isaiah 1:18); Christ's summary of the First Commandment includes the need to 'love the LORD your God ... with all your mind' (Mark 12:30); Paul makes it clear that the way to prevent conformity to the world is 'by the renewing of your mind' (Romans 12:2). Yet, as Graham Cray admits, 'In all rock music, lyrics are secondary. Rock is music of feeling, spoken primarily to the body and only secondarily to the intellect.'[7]

That is a very significant statement, made by an expert in the field, and it is backed up by Christian rock legend Larry Norman: 'In order to decide whether Christian music has any great weaknesses or strengths you have to decide what its purpose is. If it's for non-Christians — to convince them that Christ is an important alternative to seek in their life — then most Christian music is a failure because it doesn't convincingly communicate that particular message.'[8]

There is another and fundamental point to be made here, namely the Bible's clear statement that the unconverted man cannot understand the gospel: 'The natural man does not receive the things of the Spirit of God, for they are foolishness to him; nor can he know them, because they are spiritually discerned' (1 Corinthians 2:14). This does not give us an excuse for sitting back and doing nothing — we must do all we can to communicate the gospel clearly, lovingly and persuasively — but at the end of the day only the Holy Spirit can carry the truth into the mind, the heart, the conscience and the will. So to say that the unconverted 'understand Christian rock' is a dangerous half-truth. They may understand rock (whatever may be meant by 'understanding' it) but apart from the grace of God they cannot grasp the gospel. To suggest that music can bypass this is downright unbiblical.

'Music is essentially neutral — only the words count.'

As this is undoubtedly one of the strongest arguments put forward in favour of Christian rock we must give it careful attention. If this one argument were true, no critic of Christian rock would have anything more than personal taste to lean on. Two statements will be sufficient to summarize what is being said. In Larry Norman's words, 'The sonic structure of music is basically neutral. It's available to anyone to express any kind of message they choose'.[9] Rock musician John Fischer says, 'Basically, music is neutral. Art forms are neutral.'[10]

In his bestseller *The Purpose-Driven Life*, Rick Warren elevates the argument from the level of basic music concepts all the way up to music styles by stating that 'God loves all kinds of music, because He invented it all, there is no biblical style, and God likes variety [of music] and enjoys it all.' This raised the stakes even higher, as it infers that any critic of rock is potentially opposed to something that has God's unqualified approval.

We could not disagree more with Warren's thinking here. His words remind us of a private discussion with a Christian music superstar who suggested to us that the first music heard on earth might have been a raindrop falling on a tautly-drawn leaf. He then claimed that since that sound was 'neutral' and created by God, all music was both neutral and God-given. But to jump from a raindrop to a rock concert and to lump them together with everything in between is laughably naive.

It is obvious that a single note (dictionary definition: 'a tone of a definite pitch')[11] does not of itself have any influence, good or bad. It has neither message nor meaning. In that sense, we agree that it is 'neutral'. But the debate is not about single, isolated notes, but about music (dictionary definition: 'the art and science of combining tones in varying melody, harmony, etc. so as to form complete and expressive compositions').[12] The words 'expressive compositions' are important — they tell us that when single notes or tones are deliberately brought together in a musical work they are no longer neutral. When music is composed, it is not composed into a neutral nothing, but into a specific something, a meaningful form with distinct colour and character.

We can illustrate the same principle by comparing music to the printed word. The text of Psalm 23 in one modern version of the Bible has 442 letters of the alphabet. Before they were assembled by the printer, these letters were neutral. They were complete and perfect, but they meant nothing, they had no message. But in Psalm 23 they have been grouped together to form an expressive composition. Now they are saying something, and the order in which they have been composed precisely determines what they are saying.

If you take those same 442 characters and arrange them differently, instead of spelling out a message of assurance, comfort and faith for the Christian believer (as they do in Psalm 23), they could convey a message of hate, greed or violence. Compose them in some other way and they could form a shopping list. The individual letters would be the same, but they would have lost their neutrality in the composition. The American popular scientist Benjamin Franklin once claimed that with twenty-six lead soldiers he could conquer the world. The 'lead soldiers' were the letters of the alphabet and Franklin's point was that when assembled together in the right numbers and in the right order they had power to change men's lives. Once assembled, the soldiers would no longer be neutral — nor are musical notes and tones when assembled into an expressive composition.

The point is so important that it is worth listing a number of statements to back up our contention that music apart from lyrics is *not* neutral. The outstanding Greek philosopher Plato (428-348 B.C.) wrote, 'Musical training is a more potent instrument than any other, because rhythm and harmony find their way into the inward places of the soul.'[13] Aristotle (384-322 B.C.), Plato's most famous student, wrote, 'Music has the power to form a character.' Boethius (c. 480 - c. 524), the Greek philosopher and statesman, wrote, 'Music is a part of us, and either ennobles or degrades our behaviour.'[14] The great French reformer and theologian John Calvin (1509-1564) claimed, 'There is hardly anything in the world with more power to turn or bend, this way or that, the morals of men ... it has a secret power to move our hearts in one way or another. Wherefore we must be the more diligent in ruling it in such a manner that it may be useful to us and in no way pernicious [destructive].'[15] The authors of *A History of Western Music* said that Richard Wagner's music was able 'by its sheer and overwhelming power to suggest or arouse or create in its hearers that all-embracing state of ecstasy, at once sensuous and mystical.'[16]

Coming to the present time, one authority after another could be quoted along the same lines. David Tame observed that 'of all the arts, there is none that more powerfully moves and changes the consciousness than music.'[17] Musicologist Jean Maas wrote, 'Music is the greatest power I have ever experienced, I doubt if anything equals its power to act upon the human organism.'[18] In *Super Learning*, Sheila Ostrander and Lynn Schroeder stated: 'The idea that music can affect your body and mind certainly isn't new ... The key has always been to find just the right kind of music for just the right kind of effect.' In *Music: its secret influence through the ages* Cyril Scott wrote, 'Music affects the minds and emotions of man-kind. It affects them either consciously or sub-consciously, or both. It affects them through the medium of suggestion and reiteration. It affects them either directly, indirectly, or both.'

Dr George Stevenson, Medical Director of the National Association for Mental Health Inc. in the UK, makes the same point: 'The widespread occurrence of music among widely distributed people and various cultures is evidence that in music we have a great psychological force.'[19] Dr Howard Hanson, Director of the Eastman School of Music at the University of Rochester, agrees: 'Music can be soothing or invigorating, ennobling or vulgarizing, philosophical or orgiastic. It has powers for evil as well as for good.'[20] Even Michael Green, President of the Recording Academy, unwittingly adds to the evidence, because while denying the power of music to provoke any harm he goes on in the same sentence to praise its power to heal and help![21]

Over and above all of these statements, we have the overwhelming testimony of human history that music has moved man in a vast variety of ways. It has calmed his fears, summoned up his courage, soothed his sorrows, stimulated his memory, stirred him to violence and prepared him for death. There is a striking illustration of the power of music in the Old Testament when Saul, Israel's first king, called for David to play his harp to him during his recurring bouts of melancholia: 'And so it was, whenever the spirit from God was upon Saul, that David would take a harp and play it with his hand. Then Saul would become refreshed and well, and the distressing spirit would depart from him' (1 Samuel 16:23).

To suggest in the light of all this evidence that music in and of itself has no influence is to swim against an overwhelming tide, but what about rock music, which is our primary concern? Does it share this kind of influence? We will allow the musicians to answer for themselves. U2's Bono thinks, 'Music is love. You can dress it up as different things, but music for me is magic and love ... music is the language of the spirit. It's how God speaks to us, and that is why it is so often trampled on and why it's turned into, you know, a piece of ... [expletive deleted].'[22] Rocker Tori

Amos says, 'Music is the most powerful medium in the world.'[23] Keith Richards believes that 'Music works in mysterious ways. It goes in and you don't have a say in what it does to you.'[24] To Carlos Santana, hugely popular today, the power of music is both physical and spiritual: 'You hit one note and every hair on your body is gonna stand up and you feel like you just made love or touched God's feet or both.'[25] Gene Simmons of KISS was amazed 'by the power of it [music]. You could say "Kill" and watch this surge happen in the audience.'[26]

Phil Keaggy, the Christian guitarist, agrees: 'On the instrumental side, I've had people say about my music that, although there were no words, something about the melodies and rhythms really touched them.'[27] So does Mickey Hart of Grateful Dead: 'Transformation. That's the power of music. If the music has that, then it has power. The grooves that I spoke about earlier — those were powerful grooves. They had the power to transform, to take you there. To make you dance, to trance you, to put you into a rapturous state.'[28]

Rock music has even been cited as a factor in bringing to power the New Left radical political movement of the nineteen-sixties. Radical left leader Jerry Rubin said, 'The New Left sprang from Elvis' gyrating pelvis. Hard animal rock energy beat surged through us, the driving rhythms arousing suppressed passions.'[29] Frank Zappa said much the same thing, 'I realized the music got through to the youngsters because the big beat matched the great rhythms of the human body. I knew there was nothing anyone could do to knock it out of them, they would carry it with them for the rest of their lives.'[30]

This issue is tremendously important in considering the whole subject of Christian rock music, especially in light of these words by Dr Max Schoen, in his book *The Psychology of Music*: 'Music is the most powerful stimulus known among the perceptive senses. The medical, psychiatric and other evidences for the non-neutrality of music is so overwhelming that it frankly amazes me that anyone should seriously say otherwise.'

One further point: if music is neutral, if it can say whatever the musician intends or what the hearer wants it to say, then why are certain kinds chosen as background music played on airplanes, in supermarkets, or in places likely to be stressful? If music is neutral, why would we consider the theme music from Alfred Hitchcock's iconic film *Psycho* unsuitable to be played in doctors' and dentists' waiting rooms? The obvious reason is that the music is chosen by men to do something; and the reason it can do something is that it is not neutral. It seems incomprehensible to us that Christians should persist in arguing otherwise.

'The church has always borrowed from secular music.'

'Hymns were the top 40 of their day,' says studio musician Carl Stewart. 'Many of the hymns took their melody from popular bar-room drinking songs, and the writers did so with the hopes that the general population would be able to identify with them.'[31]

We have heard this argument time and again, often drawing in Martin Luther, the early Methodists John and Charles Wesley, and William Booth (the Salvation Army founder) to reinforce the claim. Yet this argument often gives the impression that the church has borrowed secular music indiscriminately and has led many Christians to pass on the resultant half-truths and exaggerations. The issue has been greatly oversimplified and the resulting battle lines falsely drawn between the 'sacred tune' and 'secular tune' camps.

What do the music history experts say? The early church (before A.D. 312) shunned the forms and types of music connected with great public spectacles such as festivals, competitions and dramatic performances, as well as the music of more intimate occasions. It was not that leaders of the church disliked music itself, but that they wanted to wean converts away from everything associated with their pagan past. Excluding certain kinds of music from early church worship also had practical motives. Through long habit, the first converts associated elaborate singing, large choruses, instruments and dancing with pagan spectacles.[32]

From early Church Fathers such as Jerome, Basil and Chrysostom, we hear that it was better to be 'deaf to the sound of instruments than to give oneself up to diabolical choruses and lascivious and pernicious songs'.[33] In addition to secular songs, there were also many religious songs in the Middle Ages that were not intended for use in church but only for home or private use.[34] As a matter of fact, secular music turned the tables and borrowed polyphony from the church, so that the motet, originally a sacred form, had become largely secularized by the end of the thirteenth century. From earliest times, English sacred music had a close connection with folk style.[35]

The Renaissance (c.1450-1600) marked a rebirth and rededication of human values as opposed to spiritual values. It was no longer considered evil to enjoy the pleasures of the senses. Sacred musicians turned to secular styles in an effort to make their work more understandable and delightful to people. This humanistic change in outlook made music more directly appealing and meaningful to listeners. Examples of putting secular melodies to religious use were extremely common in this period.[36]

Martin Luther lived in the golden age of unaccompanied choral music. The Netherlands school of composers had brought the art of multi-voiced choral singing to a high point. He did borrow tunes but mostly from an unexpected source, the Roman Catholic Church! In his own words, 'To set a good example, we have made some selections from the beautiful music and hymns used in the papacy ... However, we have changed the texts and have not retained those used in the papacy ... The songs and the music are precious; it would be a pity, indeed, should they perish.'[37]

Between 1524 and 1545, Luther composed and compiled nine hymnals, whose melodies were a mixture of Latin hymns, popular religious songs, and secular tunes recast in a religious context. Luther found it necessary to discard some secular chorale melodies, such as *'Aus fremden Landen komm' ich her'*, because this and other similarly adapted melodies retained their popularity in the taverns and dance places. He said he was 'compelled to let the devil have it back again.'[38] He also wrote, 'Together with several others I have collected a number of spiritual songs ... in the interest of the young people, who must receive an education in music if we are to wean them away from carnal and lascivious songs and interest them in what is good and wholesome.'[39]

John Calvin is rarely mentioned in this discussion but we can also learn something from him about the use of secular tunes. Calvin hired Louis Bourgeois, a composer to the French Court, and asked him to set the Psalms to simple and modest tunes, resulting in the famous Geneva Psalter (c. 1562). As Erik Routley has noted, 'Calvin's philosophy of church music hinged upon two basic factors: simplicity and modesty. Since music was to be used by the people, it needed to be simple, and because it was used to worship a sovereign God, it needed to be modest.'[40] (Modesty in this context would have included not only humility, but also the sense of innocence and purity.)

Calvin also wrote, 'Music of itself cannot be condemned; but forasmuch as the world almost always abuses it, we ought to be so much the more circumspect [cautious]... The Spirit of God condemns the vanities that are committed in music ... because men delight too much in them, and when they set their delight and pleasure in these base and earthly things, they think not a whit upon God.'[41] Under this strict caution, Calvin's composers created new melodies, adapted popular tunes from their culture, and borrowed from principles of the sacred plainchant.

Johann Sebastian Bach, one of the greatest composers who ever lived, is often quoted by Christian rockers as a defence that if anyone claims they play for the glory of God, then their style of music is beyond criticism. They regularly quote Bach as saying, 'The aim and final end of all music should be none other than the glory of God and the refreshment of the soul', yet they almost never include or even know of the rest of the quotation: 'If heed is not paid to this, it is not true music but a diabolical bawling and twanging.'

A popular myth about the Methodist tradition is that John and Charles Wesley used drinking and tavern songs as the melodies for their hymns. But according to The Rev. Dean McIntyre, director of music resources at the United Methodist Board of Discipleship in Nashville, Tennessee, 'The Wesleys did no such thing. Given their aesthetic and theological sense, it would [be] unthinkable for them to do so. Wesley's aesthetic to above all sing spiritually simply would not allow drinking songs to accompany hymn texts.' McIntyre goes on to say, 'In no hymn book or other publication of the Wesleys can there be found any example of or encouragement to use drinking songs to sing hymns.' As he then points out, the deeper issue is that people have used the Wesleys as an 'excuse for importing the secular music culture into worship.'[42]

Shortly after McIntyre's article was published, a Methodist pastor was compelled to reply, '*Mea culpa, mea summa culpa.* I have been an agent of misinformation. Over the years, I have repeated the story that Charles and John Wesley used the tunes of drinking songs for some of their hymns. Like most people who said this, I was encouraging people to be open to "secular" influences in church music. I now know that my sources were misinformed.'[43]

To summarize, the argument that the church has always borrowed music from the world can be answered in the following ways:

- Throughout history Christian musicians have borrowed secular tunes and wedded them to sacred lyrics. We have no problem with that in principle, as God is the ultimate author of melody and any musician, sacred or secular, is capable of creating a good tune.

- Until the eighteenth century, church musicians gave far more to secular music than they borrowed from it. The top musicians of the Renaissance and Baroque periods were church composers who also wrote reams of secular material and had a positive effect on the music of their time. Instrumental music was nurtured and refined by church musicians. They were the leaders, not the borrowers. Can the same be said of today's Christian rock musicians?

- Historically, church leaders have been cautious and careful about their music choices. The early Church Fathers were concerned about the spiritual health of their new converts from idolatry. Luther's writings included warnings about 'carnal' music, not just lyrics. Calvin allowed tunes with secular origins for worship, but only under strict guidelines. John and Charles Wesley were much concerned with personal holiness, as evidenced by the eighteenth-century standards of Methodist piety. Since we have seen little or no proof to the contrary, we must safely conclude that these men would not have 'raided the bars' for tunes to fill their hymnals.

- Folk music has always been used by Christians, but not just *any* folk music. Luther described the music he appreciated with phrases like 'voices sweetly singing' and 'music so charmingly gay', and spoke of compositions that 'are like the song of the finch'.[44] Even the upbeat music of his day was dominated by sweet melody, but in our times we are dealing with a troublesome style called rock and we seldom hear similar descriptions of its tunefulness. A rock song may well contain a pleasant melody but all too often it is eclipsed by the repetitive beat and volume of the rhythm instruments.

We conclude that there is simply no historical precedent for the wholesale and uncritical adoption of every secular music style for worship and evangelism. The church today should be just as cautious as the early church leaders, Luther, Calvin and the Wesleys when it comes to the music it chooses.

'There is a distinctive difference between Christian rock and secular rock.'

This argument is strongly advanced by some of those with interests in the Christian rock scene, but other thoughtful observers disagree and see more similarity than difference. We cited earlier a quotation in the *Los Angeles Times* that 'Hawk Nelson and Kutless [Christian bands] are simply a few more inspirational lyrics and a lot fewer expletives removed from Good Charlotte and Bowling for Soup.'[45] Rock singer Chuck Girard made this honest admission: 'If you took the lyrics away and changed them to a secular message, I don't think you would be able to tell the music apart from pop, rock-oriented music.'[46] Steve Turner went even further: 'The difference between a Slade concert and many Jesus rallies is negligible.'[47] Professor Verna Wright reported that when gospel and secular rock records were played in a controlled test held in a Belgian youth club, the hearers 'couldn't tell the difference.'[48]

This exactly confirms the contention of Dr William J. Shafer, who says, 'Rock is communication without words, regardless of what ideology is inserted into the music'[49] and that of Professor Frank Garlock, who claims, 'The words only let you know what the music already says ... The music is its own message and it can completely change the message of the words.'[50] What all of this is saying is that rock music is rock music, not just a plastic medium that can be bent in any direction. Even John Fischer, who believes that music is neutral, admits, 'Some art forms have been created to express certain philosophies and are so wedded to those philosophies that they convey that kind of outlook.'[51] Even more significantly he adds, 'We can't assume that we simply plug in a Christian message and everything will be okay.'[52]

Surely it is not difficult to relate this to today's Christian rock scene? Richard Taylor sums up the fatal flaw in the argument that Christian rock is somehow different: 'We cannot change the basic effect of certain kinds of rhythm and beat simply by attaching to them a few religious or semi-religious words. The beat will still get through to the blood of the participants and the listeners. Words are timid things. Decibels and beat are bold things, which can so easily bury the words under an avalanche of sound.'[53] Those who still cannot tell the difference may have fallen victim to what A. W. Tozer saw as a weak and twisted philosophy of godliness: 'Good hymnody has been betrayed and subverted by noisy, uncouth persons who have too long operated under the immunity afforded them by the timidity of the saints.'[54]

'It helps us to worship God better.'

This argument is more difficult to counter because it is so subjective. After some thirty years of Christian rock there are countless millions of Christians who seem almost incapable of worshipping God without it and it seems virtually indispensable as the recommended music to enhance one's worship experience. The worship music industry aggressively promotes the idea that the ultimate worship act is listening to or singing certain styles of pop/rock music and that this music experience even has the power to conjure up the presence of God.

Michael W. Smith, a mega-star rock musician who is also a worship leader at his local church, makes the point with rock music mainly in mind: 'I really believe all this new interest in worship — the people getting interested and the new music that's coming out — it's all a great new thing God's doing. Can you hear it? It's in the music. When music helps you enter into the presence of God, you know it. It's you and God.'[55] The British rock worship group Delirious? is said to have the power to 'create a *truly spiritual mood* by the way they segue [move without interruption] from one song to another. Nobody does it better.'[56]

Since 2002, Integrity Music has sold over one million copies of its iWORSHIP Total Worship Experience, described as 'a total worship lifestyle hub designed to bring you into God's presence everyday'. The blurb goes on to claim, 'Integrity's iWORSHIP CDs feature the world's most powerful worship songs from premier worship artists for an incredible worship experience. This double CD set is presented in a seamless flow for a nonstop worship experience.'[57] The President of Integrity rams the message home: 'The whole mission of our company is to help people worldwide experience the manifest presence of God.'[58] Even children are targeted: 'Integrity's iWORSHIP Kids is a new line of resources specially designed to help kids experience God in new, exciting ways! This comes as the answer to what many of today's parents and children's pastors are seeking — fun, easy-to-learn lyrics with a hip beat kids love.'[59] Since the vast number of songs contained on the iWorship CDs are rock music it should leave us in no doubt that the Christian music industry is passionate about rock-enhanced worship experiences.

But why is this an issue? Quite simply, there is not even a hint in the Bible that worship is about seeking an emotional musical experience to make us feel God's presence. Nowhere in Scripture are we told that we should manipulate anyone into a worshipping mood through musical means, nor does the Bible teach that music has any special powers to invoke the presence of God. The absence of biblical support should be enough for every thinking Christian to pause and take stock. When there is that kind of difference between what the musicians are telling us and what God says in his Word, something, somewhere, is seriously wrong. It is time to get our thinking straight on this issue. As we try to do this, we need to recognize that throughout history pagans have used music with a strong and hypnotic beat to summon *their* gods and demons: as Frank Zappa reminds us, 'The loud sounds and bright lights of today's rock are tremendous indoctrination tools.'[60]

We need to ask another question here: is it possible that the manipulative and mind–body–soul altering power of rock music is producing a *counterfeit* spiritual experience? A. W. Tozer thought so: 'It is plainly possible to have religious experiences and forms of worship that are not at all acceptable to God.'[61] Does anyone in the rock worship camp (which even quotes Tozer at times — though very selectively!) have the courage to admit this may be possible? Or have we sunk to the pitiful level that Tozer decried: 'Because worship is largely missing, do you know what we are doing? We use artificial means to try to induce some kind of worship. I think the devil in hell must be laughing, and I think God must be grieving, for there is no fear of God before our eyes.'[62]

'We don't associate rock with immorality and worldliness.'

As we saw earlier in this book, young Christians who were raised on 'Christianized' rock say they see no issue because their generation has its own redeemed version of the music that is not the same as the old, bad rock music. Feedback from readers of *Why I Left the Contemporary Christian Music Movement* under the age of twenty-five includes statements like these: 'I am of a generation that has always had "cool Christian music" so rock honestly does not carry a negative stigma with it for me' and 'I fail to see the link between the rock beat and the sexuality and other sins you mentioned that go along with it.'

This argument seems to rest on two assumptions. The first is that God wants them to cross into the culture, redeem wicked art forms from the pagans and use them for his glory. As Mark Alan Powell has said, 'There is a widespread feeling in the world of contemporary Christian music that there is a need to embrace culture in general.'[63] Perhaps they thought this is what Kevin Miller meant when he wrote, 'A major trend sweeping through the Evangelical subculture today is a move toward redeeming popular culture. Where you once found books decrying the evils of Hollywood, television, rock and roll or fantasy literature, you now find numerous books, web sites, and articles that seek to unearth the Christian images, parallels, messages, and characters buried throughout these mediums.'[64] Yet nowhere in the Bible does God command us to 'redeem' music, nor does Scripture give any examples of God's people redeeming the evil music of a secular or pagan culture.

The second assumption made by Christians who do not associate rock music with immorality and worldliness is that their form of rock music is sufficiently 'separated' by time, distance or source from older, cruder forms of rock. As a twenty-one-year-old put it in an e-mail to Dan Lucarini, 'I'm not sure the claim that rock music is always associated with drugs, sex and rebellion is exactly concrete. When I think about the origin of rock 'n' roll, the wholesome groups that played on American Bandstand and stuff come to mind.' She obviously did not know the real history of rock 'n' roll and what was happening behind the scenes. Personal ignorance notwithstanding, we have already demonstrated the bad reputation of rock, past and present, by using many examples from secular sources. Sadly, many of today's Christian rock bands, in mimicking the latest secular music styles, freely admit to being influenced by the very bands whose motives and methods are dubious at best and degraded at worst.

The editor of worshipmusic.com once asked this important question: 'Is it OK to be influenced by musicians from arenas other than Contemporary Christian worship circles? That's a great discussion that needs to take place in the Church today.'[65] We could not agree more. Christian musicians who write worship music for the church openly admit that their music is inspired by secular rock musicians, including some of the ones already mentioned in this book.[66] According to Billboard.com and *All Music Guide*, Third Day (the top Christian rock group in America according to the TV programme *60 Minutes*[67]) is influenced by the Southern rock of Lynyrd Skynyrd. Members of the worship band MercyMe list on their web site The Beatles, Coldplay and Electric Light Orchestra as musical influences. Gabe of the Rock and Roll Worship Circus thinks, 'The Stones are huge, and, um, Donovan and of course I think a huge influence on just the power and the driving force side of the music is [Pink] Floyd and Zeppelin, you know.'[68]

In an e-mail interview with Steve Mason, guitarist for Jars of Clay, he was asked what he would consider as some of the major musical influences that help to get the creative juices flowing? His answer: 'We've always considered ourselves fans of Rock and Roll, even before musicians, maybe. Ha-ha. The historical (Beatles, Rolling Stones, Fleetwood Mac) references, the alternative country and singer/songwriters (Jayhawks, Tom Petty, Alison Krause, Ryan Adams) to where we feel music is going (Interpol, Keane, Butterfly Boucher, Kanye West).'[69]

When asked in an interview for *Renown* magazine 'What kind of music do you dig?', Matt Thiessen of Relient K replied: 'I like stuff like Midtown and Starting Line [punk revival/emo bands] ... I could go on for days.'[70] Members of Five Iron Frenzy were in an industrial thrash metal band and they list among their all-time favourite concerts such bands as KISS, the Backstreet Boys, Elvis Costello and Joe Jackson.[71] One female member was quoted as saying, 'It's my dream to someday be a rocker woman with wrinkles, tight pants and a raunchy voice. Like Pat Benetar.'[72]

In an interview on 14 September 2002 with *Christian Guitar Resources*, Jeremy Camp admits that 'a lot of the alternative/

grunge era was the start of some of my influence. Like Pearl Jam, Stone Temple Pilots, those type of bands. Then I liked Dave Matthews ... amazing.' Camp also credits Matchbox Twenty and Creed in a *Christianity Today* review of his CD *Stay* that also compares his vocal style to Scott Stapp, lead singer of Creed. David Ruis is described as 'what Jim Morrison would have sounded like if he were a Christian.'[73] (Of course this begs the question, 'Why would any Christian want to be compared to the grossly immoral and occult-influenced Morrison?') David Gate, a UK-based worship leader and worship artist associated with New Wine and Soul Survivor, quotes his musical influences as being The Beatles, Jeff Buckley, David Bowie, Bjork and Radiohead. He jokes: 'As a young male worship leader I am also obliged to like U2 and Coldplay.'[74] It may surprise the fans of Sanctus Real to learn that Matt Hammitt's preferences in music include Sigur Rof, an Icelandic post-rock band with strange, nihilistic lyrics and one song called 'Mother Earth' that mocks the Lord's Prayer.[75]

Worship leaders and worship pastors also boast on their church web sites about secular musical influences such as Bon Jovi, Billy Joel, Sting, Huey Lewis and the News, Coldplay and the Dave Matthews Band. Worship band members talk on web sites of their inspiration from Led Zeppelin, Metallica, Black Sabbath, Godsmack, Lynyrd Skynyrd, Geddy Lee of RUSH, Stevie Ray Vaughn and Eric Clapton; the list goes on and on. At a large church in Arizona, the Children's Pastor loves P.O.D. and the Junior High Pastor's favourite music group is Stavesacre, a band described on their web site as post hardcore/metal and whose fans show their worship and adoration of the band by getting tattoos with the band's logo.

Senior pastors and even seminary professors are now confessing their love for rock music, apparently feeling comfortable doing so now that the old standards of modesty and propriety have been torn down. One Southern Baptist seminary student wrote us to say, 'No one is really addressing the rock music issue and the students have an "anything goes" mentality. And it might be a good idea that the issue is not addressed by the faculty because one of the deans and a New Testament professor have publicly stated that their favourite band is The Beatles. That seemed very inappropriate to me coming from two men that pastor churches.'

This all equates to one very slim degree of separation between the secular rock music that is used to glorify rebellion, pride, sexual immorality and blasphemy, and the rock music that is used for the praise and worship of a holy God. It is our earnest hope that young Christians reading this will now be sufficiently informed to see that Christian rock is not wholly immune from the ungodly influences of secular rock.

'It produces excellent evangelistic results.'

At first glance, this seems to be true. The Christian press regularly reports dozens, hundreds and sometimes thousands of 'decisions for Christ' registered at rock music events and the immediate, visible results from roadshow religion seem to relegate the effect of straightforward preaching to that of a badly beaten also-ran. But is this the whole story — or even the *real* story?

In the first place, the pragmatic argument is simply not valid. We gladly accept the sovereignty of God in salvation and cannot deny that in his gracious wisdom he has saved young people and others in rock music events, but the fact that God uses any means is not of itself any indication that the means itself is biblically valid. As Frank Schaeffer points out in his telling book *Addicted to Mediocrity*, 'The excuse that "sometimes people are saved" is no excuse at all. People have been saved in concentration camps because God can bring good from evil, but this does not justify the evil.' The point is well made. God used a pagan Egyptian Pharaoh as an instrument in releasing the entire nation of Israel from slavery — and even told him that he had raised him up 'for this purpose' (Exodus 9:16). Yet this ruler was a godless tyrant and certainly not an example for us to follow.

Secondly, in assessing 'results' the headline is not the same as the bottom line. When we conducted a census among nearly 2,000 young people, asking them to indicate the circumstances in which they were converted, or the major influence in their conversion, only some two per cent mentioned music. When we went further and tried to assess the lasting results of 'musical evangelism' the results were just as bleak. In one case, a short time after 100 'decisions' had been recorded only one of those concerned seemed to show even a mild interest in Christian things.

Christian rock is now a high-powered, multi-coloured, glossily packed, heavily promoted industry, yet it seems that when the music stops, the applause dies down, the lights go out, the cash is counted and the show moves on, what is left in the way of positive spiritual gain is only a microscopic fraction of what is claimed. When there is that kind of difference between the headline and the bottom line, something, somewhere, is seriously wrong. It is time to strip the bandwagon down and start again.

As we now try to do this, one particular biblical command springs to mind: 'Therefore, whether you eat or drink, or whatever you do, do all to the glory of God' (1 Corinthians 10:31). A respected theologian has commented that this may mean 'Do everything with God's glory in view' or 'Do everything in such a way that God may be glorified', but both interpretations really amount to the same thing. Our dominant motive in doing *anything* should not be to please ourselves, or even to please other people, but to bring glory to our holy, sovereign God and Saviour.

10.

GETTING IN TUNE WITH GOD

The world behind me, the cross before me,
No turning back, no turning back.

(A converted Indian prince)[1]

Jesus has always had more fans than followers, and many people attracted by his personality, fascinated by his power or impressed by his teaching have never truly submitted to him as the Lord of their lives. This is not surprising. The reason most people do not become Christians is not because being a follower of Jesus is too soft, but because it is too hard. There are many like the man who said, 'Lord, I will follow you, but...' (Luke 9:61) and not so many prepared to fulfil the basic conditions for discipleship: 'If anyone comes to me and does not hate ... his own life ... he cannot be my disciple' (Luke 14:26).

Those are not easy terms, but they are simple. Nominal Christianity can skate around many of its demands, but biblical Christianity implies obedience to Jesus in every part of life, whatever the cost. It means setting aside one's own tastes and preferences, likes and dislikes, and submitting every area of life to this one crucial test: *what does Jesus want me to do?* He himself put it like this: 'My sheep hear my voice, and I know them, and they follow me' (John 10:27). Nothing could be clearer. Two hallmarks of the genuine Christian are a desire to hear whatever

Jesus says and a determination to do whatever he commands, to have what someone has called 'an open ear and an obedient foot'!

With that in mind, let us turn specifically to the question of Christian music. What are some of the biblical principles that apply? Before answering that question, it goes without saying that all Christian music must submit to the same principles. Personal taste is not the issue. A classical style must keep to the same rules as a contemporary one; the organ and the guitar must be treated alike; the robed choir must be assessed in the same way as the rock group; Handel must meet the same criteria as hip-hop. So what principles should govern the music we use in God's service? Perhaps the most direct way for the authors of this book to apply this is to allow us to ask you a series of questions about the music you write, play, sing, listen to, or use in worship or evangelism.

Does it help you to hear the Word of God clearly?

The Bible says that 'Faith comes by hearing, and hearing by the word of God' (Romans 10:17) and speaks about clearly 'handling the word of God' (2 Corinthians 4:2). It says that the church is to be cleansed with it (Ephesians 5:26), sanctified through it (John 17:17; Ephesians 5:26), consecrated by it (1 Timothy 4:5, NIV), equipped for spiritual warfare in it (Ephesians 6:17), gently reproved by it (Colossians 3:16) and instructed by it (Colossians 3:16). We will have our hearts judged by it (Hebrews 4:12), our behaviour corrected by it (2 Timothy 4:2), our lives encouraged through it (2 Timothy 4:2) and will overcome by it (1 John 2:14). In addition, the written word of God leads us to Jesus Christ, who is the living Word. This all tells us that Scripture is of the utmost importance for salvation, sanctification and life itself.

The first test that Christian music faces concerns its relationship to the words that go with it. There is obviously no saving or sanctifying truth in the music alone; the words are the vehicles God uses to bring biblical truths into our hearts and minds. This means that we must do our utmost to ensure that in both worship and evangelism nothing must distort or blur or in any way push into the background 'the word of truth' (Ephesians 1:13), what is elsewhere called 'the word of the truth of the gospel' (Colossians 1:5). This principle must also be rigorously applied to the character of the composition, because if this detracts from the content or clarity of the words the whole performance is an exercise in futility.

The lyrics must face the same test. Is their content and presentation such that the truth of Scripture comes through clearly, with no distortion or unbiblical emphasis? Some of the older hymns score heavily here, as they are no more than the Psalms or other parts of Scripture set to poetry and music. The same happily applies to many modern songs that have the same basis. But what about the lyrics for other songs? Are they always Bible-based? Is it the Word of God that shines through? Is there solid doctrinal content? We need to be aware that not all hymnology (or 'songology'!) is good theology.

Pulling music and lyrics together, can we imagine playing loud or discordant music (or music of any kind) throughout a preacher's sermon in order to help in getting the message across? Why is it that Christian teens who listen to secular rock are quick to say, 'I only like the music, I don't listen to the words', but when challenged about loud Christian rock they say just the opposite and claim that the lyrics make all the difference?

John Calvin's words remain as relevant as when they were first written: 'We must beware ... lest our ears be more intent on the music than our minds on the spiritual meaning of the words ... Songs composed merely to tickle and delight the ear are unbecoming to the majesty of the church and cannot but be most displeasing to God.'[2] Strange as it may seem, it is also possible for music to be too good to use in Christian worship, because it draws attention *from* the words instead of *to* them. In his book *Worship in the Melting Pot*, Peter Masters tells us that is why Charles Spurgeon did not even allow an organ in the Metropolitan Tabernacle. Whatever we may think of that decision, we must ensure that our music must always be the servant of the Word of God, never its master. Augustine certainly recognized this. In his *Confessions* he wrote, 'I am inclined to approve the custom of singing in church. Nevertheless when it happens that I am more moved by the song than the thing which is sung, I confess that I sin in a manner deserving of punishment, and then I should rather not hear the singing.'

For an illustration of what we mean, we want to quote from *Background to the Task*, which was published in 1968 as a supplement to *On the Other Side*, a report by the Evangelical Alliance Commission on Evangelism. In a section called 'Modern Music and Evangelism' Colin Chapman wrote about some of the factors which made it difficult to use pop/rock music to communicate the gospel and at one point mentioned the difficulty of using an idiom in which 'love' plays such a large part. He then went on to say this:

> If we are using an idiom or a medium which in the majority of cases is used to speak about some aspect of love, what effect is this likely to have on the content of the gospel song and on the content of what actually comes across to the listener? Could it be that in using this idiom we have been unconsciously influenced by the associations of the idiom, with the result that when we present Christ in a gospel song we *appear* to be presenting him primarily as a kind of heavenly lover? Could it be that what some of the audience hear is not so much a challenge to come to terms with the God who had made them and to whom they are

accountable for their lives, but rather an invitation to fall in love with Jesus? ... But would we not be more faithful to the gospel if we said that it is our refusal to love God which constitutes the compelling need for us to come to terms with God?

Chapman's questions still need answering today and they point up one of the greatest dangers in the Christian music field. In an earlier chapter we quoted leading Christian singers admitting that the content of most outreach songs is doctrinally inadequate. If that is the case, they fail at the first hurdle and we have no right to use them for outreach. Nor should we carelessly use romantic music idioms or styles in church when addressing almighty God. A. W. Tozer was scathing in his denunciation of this kind of pseudo-intimacy:

Much of the singing in certain types of meetings has in it more of romance than it has of the Holy Ghost. Both words and music are designed to rouse the libidinous [lewd; full of lust]. Christ is courted with a familiarity that reveals a total ignorance of Who He is. It is not the reverent intimacy of the adoring saint but *the impudent familiarity of the carnal lover* [3] (emphasis added).

Does this music match up with the glory of God?

The first recorded song in Scripture is in Exodus 15 and was sung by Moses and the Israelites to celebrate their miraculous deliverance from the Egyptians. It includes these remarkable words: 'The LORD is my strength and song, and he has become my salvation' (Exodus 15:2). What is remarkable about this statement is that Moses refers to God as 'my song', and it would be impossible to link the nature of God and the nature of the song more closely than that. God not only caused the song, he characterized it. No wonder Matthew Henry calls it 'a holy song, consecrated to the honour of God, and intended to exalt his name and celebrate his praise, and his only'.[4]

Can the same be said of your Christian music? Accepting that its beat, rhythm and syncopations are saying things, are these things that express the purity, majesty, holiness and serenity of God? Music about God should be like God in the sense that it should reflect him, magnify him and communicate something of his character. Does it do this? Is it pure in its tone, lovely in its melody? Applying the question directly to the subject of our study, does rock music achieve any of this?

The American evangelist David Wilkerson has had a remarkable ministry among drop-outs and other under-privileged young people in New York and elsewhere, and is very familiar with today's youth scene. How does he answer the question? In his book *Get your hands off my throat* he says this:

> Christian rock groups are brought to our youth crusades by sponsoring churches. They appear on my stage with their drums and loud guitars, hand clapping their way through songs that speak of Jesus, but with the primitive beat of rock. I try not to act surprised, offended or ashamed. You see, I want so much to relate to these young people. The kids in the audience seem to love every beat. They clap, they smile, they relate, they turn on and they get excited. But something inside me, deep in my soul, does not feel right. There's a small hurt which I can't explain. I feel as though the Holy Spirit within me does not witness to the rock sounds in the middle of a salvation meeting. I also have a sense, an inner knowledge, that the gentle Holy Spirit is not comfortable in the atmosphere this music creates.

Is Wilkerson right?

Does the music divide or unify Christians?

In encouraging Christians in Rome to praise God, Paul prayed that God would grant them to be 'like-minded toward one another, according to Christ Jesus, that you may with one mind and one mouth glorify the God and Father of our Lord Jesus Christ' (Romans 15:5-6). Notice the clear connection Paul makes between like-mindedness and the effectiveness of corporate praise. As the English scholar William Burkitt wrote, 'Unity among Christians ... especially in church-communion is a very desirable mercy, and much to be prayed for by the ministers of God.'[5] Albert Barnes commented that to be like-minded meant 'to keep from divisions and strifes, according to the example and spirit of Christ; his was a spirit of peace.'[6] As we saw earlier in this book, music often prevents this from being the case in the church today.

One motive given for bringing rock into church is to reach out to unchurched people who like that kind of music. This seems worthy enough on the surface, but how can we claim that it is honouring to God when the same music violates the law of brotherly love between Christians by erecting a stumbling block in the church? The Bible teaches that 'every city or house divided against itself will not stand' (Matthew 12:25), and it is scathing in its denunciation of those who cause divisions and quarrels in the church.

Some searching questions need to be faced here. What about your music? Does it help to unite all ages within the church or does it divide the church into age groups and taste preferences? Does it promote a sense of gracious understanding or tend to produce friction?

Does this music tend to give you a repentant view of man's depravity?

In describing man's spiritual state, the Bible says, 'The heart is deceitful above all things, and desperately wicked; who can know

225

it?' (Jeremiah 17:9). One of man's most persistent follies is to imagine that whenever he chooses he can pull himself up by his spiritual bootstraps, turn to God, get cleaned up and become a member of God's family. This is emphatically not the case. Man is by nature corrupt, vile, morally and spiritually depraved, and rotten to the core. Does your music give you a *repentant* view of this? The word in italics is all-important. There is certainly a great deal of music that gives a view of man's depravity. Rock music's heavy emphasis on violence, anarchy, rebellion, sexual promiscuity, homosexuality, the drug culture, blasphemy, occultism and the like is saying something that is both loud and clear. One would certainly hope that 'Christian' rock would not glorify those things, but neutrality is not enough. Does it lead you to search your heart and not just tap your feet, swing your arms or waggle your hips? Does it get beyond the tingling to the truth? Does it make clear to you the reality of man's spiritual condition apart from God?

We have already suggested the great difficulties that any idiom aimed at bringing pleasure has in conveying the 'bad news' that it is vital for man to grasp before he can appreciate the nature of the 'good news' of the gospel. Does the music you are playing, singing or hearing honestly overcome all those difficulties and do it in such a way that it helps to bring you and others to a place of repentance, a place where you loathe sin and want to have nothing to do with it?

Does your style of music encourage you to disciplined, godly living?

Discovering the details of God's will for life is the constant concern of every serious-minded Christian, but the overall will of God could not be clearer: 'For this is the will of God, your sanctification [holiness]' (1 Thessalonians 4:3). Yet holiness does not come easily; godliness is never handed to the Christian on a plate. The Christian life is a fight, not a festival; a conflict, not a concert. It is a constant battle against the forces of evil and calls for vigilance, discipline, sacrifice and spiritual determination. Does your music tend to lead you in these directions, or does it tend to be sentimental or self-indulgent? Does it help you to focus your mind on things that are 'true ... noble ... just ... pure ... lovely ... of good report ...virtuous ... and praiseworthy' (Philippians 4:8)? Even more importantly, does the music itself and the way it is performed enable you to focus your attention on God and not on the performers?

The Christian musician Keith Green, who died in a airplane crash when he was just twenty-eight years old, once wrote, 'I repent of ever having recorded one single song, and ever having played in one concert, if my music and (more importantly) my life has not provoked you in godly jealousy (Romans 11:11) to sell out completely to Jesus!'[7] Does the music you like take you in that direction? Or does it provoke other Christians around you to head in the opposite direction?

Does this kind of music help you to separate yourself from the world?

The Bible could not be clearer on the Christian's duty here: 'Do not love the world or the things in the world. If anyone loves the world, the love of the Father is not in him' (1 John 2:15). That has always been a tall order and perhaps never taller than in this day and age. Christians are under siege, pressurized day after day to conform to philosophies, values, standards and life-styles diametrically opposed to those laid down in Scripture, where we are told that 'God did not call us to uncleanness, but in holiness' (1 Thessalonians 4:7) and that as far as these things are concerned we are to 'come out from among them and be separate' (2 Corinthians 6:17). Yet in his book *Anatomy of Pop*, Roy Connolly adds this comment to the many we have quoted concerning the rock music ethos: 'The music is more at home in the club, the pub and the brothel, in close association with other group entertainment, drinking and seduction.'

What voice are you hearing in your music? Does it appeal to the sensual or to the spiritual? Does it have its roots in this world or in heaven? Does it stimulate appetites that are pure or impure? Does it lead you to want more of the world's values, or less of them? Are godless people comfortable with it or embarrassed by it? Does it help or hinder a desire to break free from the worldly way of doing things? There is no neutrality here — the Bible makes it clear that 'Whoever therefore wants to be a friend of the world makes himself an enemy of God' (James 4:4). The question is not essentially one of what music you like, but of whom you love.

Is this the kind of music that you can imagine being part of a spiritual revival?

Revival is a time when God himself breaks through in astonishing power and glory and therefore a time when we should expect to see an emphasis on those things which have his blessing. The psalmist prayed, 'Will you not revive us again, that your people may rejoice in you?' (Psalm 85:6) — a reminder that revival is sent from God, not staged by man.

Today we hear breathless boasts that there is a great revival taking place. In February 2006 broadcaster Pat Robertson told *Good Morning America*, 'I believe we're in the middle of a great religious revival in America.'[8] Peter Drucker, the dean of American management, called Rick Warren 'the inventor of perpetual revival.'[9] These days, so-called 'revival' is often accompanied by a rock music beat, with Christian rock stars used to pull in the crowds. One person attending the Billy Graham Crusade in New York wrote, 'This promised to be a good, old-fashioned revival. The audience was immediately assaulted by the sound of Christian rock.'[10] Rock singers Jars of Clay, Michael W. Smith, MercyMe and Tree63 performed during the crusade.

This report of a 2005 Delirious? concert goes even further: 'The first thumping beats of "Grace like a river" and "Rain Down" got the crowd up on their feet and us in the standing area jumping like kangaroos on pogo sticks. A jester's hat was thrown onstage and the [lead singer] proceeded to thrust it on his head and throw himself about onstage like a madman. This had the whole crowd doubled over in hysterics, and an encore was demanded unanimously. The lyric I will always remember from that night is: "Revival, that's what we're calling this place".'[11] Chris Tomlin, the popular worship leader and rock musician from Texas who was nominated for nine Dove Awards in 2006, appeals to the classic revival passage 2 Chronicles 7:14 in his song 'America', singing 'The Lord is coming, coming to America. Can you feel the fire, can you see the wind?'[12] The words may sound as if they are talking about the real thing, but is there any evidence that this is the case? Do these modern 'revivals' match up to those recorded in the Bible and subsequent church history?

It has been suggested that music is always strongly associated with every genuine revival, but while this may have an element of truth in it, it certainly needs to be heavily qualified. For example, in genuine revival, music is never prominent as a performance. There is certainly congregational singing as God's people rejoice in the Lord, but we are not aware of any genuine revival that has centred on a musical 'star'. Surely that is significant?

Wales has experienced revival on several occasions, the last of them in 1904. Yet although there were claims of 100,000 conversions at the time, the long-term results of the 1904 revival were comparatively disappointing. For example, it is

229

said that there were 2,000 conversions on Anglesey alone, yet a generation later the island was virtually a spiritual wilderness. Writing in *Reformation Today*, Gwynne Williams suggests some of the reasons for a lack of depth in the work associated with Evan Roberts (the leading preacher during the revival) and says there came a point when he and many of his followers 'lost touch with the essential sanity of New Testament Christianity. Human techniques were used to build up an atmosphere of expectancy; repetitive prayer or the studied use of music were especially to the fore.' He then describes his own great-grandfather telling how 'hymns and solos were carefully arranged so as to provide the revivalist with an audience which had been emotionally moved' and adds, 'Incidentally these were the first real examples of entertainment evangelism in Wales, Roberts himself being almost always accompanied by musicians.'

That is a fascinating glimpse into the church's history, but it is more than that. The Spanish philosopher George Santayana famously said, 'Those who cannot remember history are condemned to repeat it'[13] and the lessons from 1904 can begin to be learned by asking ourselves some questions. Is this music God-centred or man-centred? Does it concentrate on the Lord's glory or on man's feelings? Does it draw attention to the performers or to Christ? Whenever music makes it difficult to see the Son for the stars, we can be sure that there is something wrong.

Many today are claiming revival through worship and evangelism experiences tied closely to rock music, but we have yet to see a single case in which rock music has been used in a genuine revival, one marked by widespread confession of sin, repentance and godliness. The evidence suggests otherwise, and while rock-induced 'revivals' of young people are producing extravagant claims, the outward behaviour of the 'revived' often betrays an absence of true biblical repentance and a frequent tendency toward worldliness rather than disciplined godliness.

Would you expect to find this kind of music in heaven?

Earlier in this book we quoted Martin Luther as saying that the man who did not appreciate music was 'a clod'. We can go further than that and say that the Christian who does not appreciate music is almost a contradiction in terms, because he is on his way to a place where he will be surrounded by music for all eternity! One of the things revealed by God to the apostle John during his remarkable vision on the island of Patmos was that there will be music in heaven. One of the most breathtaking passages in all Scripture records three amazing songs of praise. The first is where 'four living creatures and the twenty-four elders ... sang a new song' (Revelation 5:8-9, NIV). Then we are told that 'Many angels, numbering thousands upon thousands, and ten thousand times ten thousand ... sang' (Revelation 5:11, NIV). Finally John saw 'every creature in heaven and on earth and under the earth and on the sea, and all that is in them, singing: "To him who sits on the throne and to the Lamb be praise and honour and glory and power, for ever and ever!"' (Revelation 5:13, NIV).

The first choir had twenty-eight members — four 'living creatures' and twenty-four elders; then they were joined by at least 104 million angels (work it out!); and finally by every creature in the entire universe. No wonder the nineteenth-century English poet Christina Rossetti described heaven as the homeland of music! But what kind of music is it? Is it music as we know it, with staves and scales, chords and canons? Will there be melody, harmony and rhythm as we know them here? We have no idea. We are not given any details about the music, perhaps to enable us to concentrate on the words. It will certainly be 'a new song', but as the contemporary British preacher William Freel has said, 'No composer can estimate its value, no instrument can play its harmony, no voice can pronounce its beauty, no modulator can convey its height or its depth; this song is arranged to please the ear of God.'[14]

That immediately points us to some important and inescapable questions. Does the music you enjoy suggest that it was arranged for the same ear? Can you imagine it being enjoyed by God the Father? Does it promote a sense of awe and reverence? Can you imagine it being enjoyed by God the Son? Does it give undivided glory to 'the Lamb who was slain'? (Revelation 5:12). Can you imagine it being enjoyed by God the Holy Spirit? Does it speak of peace, purity and a spirit of worship? There are other questions to be asked, too. Can you imagine this music being played and sung by angels and archangels, cherubim and seraphim? Perhaps even more testing is this: can you imagine that when you get to heaven and stand before the indescribable majesty of the triune God of glory, this is the kind of music you will want to play and sing and he will delight to hear?

Some Christians would dare to answer those questions in the affirmative and, as we read in chapter 1, even claim that heaven will be a big rock music concert. We remind you of the story in which the leader of a ladies' group in a church showed a video that pictured heaven as a massive rock party, after which she then played some loud and chaotic rock music to show them how wonderful heaven will be. When one lady disagreed with her, the leader replied, 'You have your opinion and I have mine. Do you really think that we would just be angels with wings, flying all around, strumming on harps all the time?' 'No,' the objector answered, 'I only believe what the Bible says about heaven.' Turning to leave, the leader retorted, 'Well, if you don't like it, then don't watch it!' This is hardly a biblical response!

The apostle Paul says of Christians that 'Our citizenship is in heaven' (Philippians 3:20). That being so, every part of life here and now should be seen as a preparation for that glorious experience. Our music is no exception. It should reflect hearts that long to be in tune with God in every part of life.

11.

BACK TO SQUARE ONE

*Do right and God's recompense to you
will be the power to do more right.*
(British preacher F. W. Robertson)[1]

The story is told of a man who during an election campaign had a bumper sticker on his car reading, 'My mind is made up; don't confuse me with the facts.' The story has been around for many years, but still has a lot of mileage in it. People whose approach to contentious issues is fuelled by prejudice often shut their ears to anything that seems to contradict their position. The suitability of rock music in worship and evangelism is certainly such an issue and as its implications are so far-reaching and serious we need to do all we can to ensure that we approach it with open minds and teachable spirits.

Throughout this book we have tried to examine the whole subject carefully and courteously, listening to what the experts say and keeping subjective preferences in check. We hope we have succeeded, but we need to take one further step and address a final, critical question: how should Christians respond to the rock music issue?

By the book

One of the most unusual books in the Bible is Ecclesiastes. Written by an anonymous author known only as 'the Teacher', it is a remarkable commentary on human life and on man's relationship with God. On the last page, we read these words: 'Now all has been heard; here is the conclusion of the matter: Fear God and keep his commandments, for this is the whole duty of man' (Ecclesiastes 12:13, NIV). Of course 'the Teacher' is right. When all is said and done, man's whole duty consists in fearing (worshipping) God and being obedient to his Word. Someone has said that loving God is reading the Bible and doing what it says, and it is difficult to disagree with that. Yet as far as rock music in worship and evangelism is concerned, how to apply the statement is both clear and unclear! It is clear in the sense that obedience is the only thing needed, with cultural differences, personal preferences and human opinions firmly set aside. It is unclear in that the Bible makes no mention of rock music! So where do we go from here?

In his excellent book *Nothing but the Truth*, Brian Edwards has a chapter entitled 'The Bible, sufficient and final' in which he says this: 'All matters of doctrine and life are to be brought to the final test of Scripture. There are no subjects upon which Scripture has nothing to say either by direct command or indirect principle — this is what is meant by the sufficiency of Scripture.'[2] While we have seen ample evidence in the Bible that we are to use music for praising God when we gather to worship him, as far as types of music in church life are concerned there are no direct commands in the Bible. Specifically, as we saw in an earlier chapter, there are no directions about the use of *any* kind of music in evangelism. It is neither commanded nor commended. There is no example of its being used. It is not even hinted at. For many Christians, that draws a line under the whole subject, leaving all the arguments we have brought to bear in this book completely irrelevant. People who take this line would presumably go along with the Puritan preacher John Trapp in saying, 'Where Scripture hath no tongue, we must have no ears.' This approach has an impeccable pedigree, one which runs through many of the historic doctrinal confessions which surrounded the Reformation. The *Heidelberg Catechism* (1563) said that we were not to worship God 'in any other way than he has commanded in his Word'. The *Belgic Confession* (1566) claimed that the Scriptures 'fully contain the will of God ... The whole manner of worship God requires of us is written in them.' The *Westminster Confession of Faith* (1646) asserted that 'The acceptable way of worshipping the true God is instituted by himself' and God may not be worshipped according to 'the imaginations and devices of men ... or in any other way not prescribed in the Holy Scripture'. The *Baptist Confession of Faith* (1689) stated, 'The only acceptable way of worshipping the true God is appointed by himself in accordance with his own will ... and all other forms of worship not prescribed in Holy Scripture are expressly forbidden.' Whatever else may be thought, these statements were not drawn up by extremists or cranks, but by our fathers in the faith, those to whom, under God's sovereignty, we owe our Christian heritage today.

If this is your position, reading this book has presumably been purely academic, as the silence of Scripture on the subject had already convinced you of the line you ought to take. Yet it must be said that a rigid application of this rule (what theologians call 'the regulative principle') is not as straightforward as it might seem, as it leaves some interesting questions unanswered. There is neither space nor need to raise these here, but we need to look at another perfectly honourable way of applying the Bible's teaching.

Putting principles into practice

Brian Edwards sets us on the right track by illustrating the difference between biblical commands and biblical principles. He points out that a church which keeps a register of its members is doing something not commanded in Scripture; but as there is a biblical principle which says that things should be done 'decently and in order' (1 Corinthians 14:40) this makes a list of church members sensible and practical. On the other hand, if a church were to make a charge for membership it would be violating a biblical principle, as the Bible teaches that a Christian's giving should be 'in keeping with his income' (1 Corinthians 16:2, NIV) and not according to a scale of fees laid down by the church.[3]

How does this apply to the question of rock music? In the course of this book we have sought to bring biblical principles to bear on the subject at every stage, in both worship and evangelism, and it will be helpful if at this point we summarize our salient conclusions:

- Words are of paramount importance — nothing must detract or distract from them in any way;
- Any kind of psychological manipulation must be avoided;
- The Bible's message must be addressed directly to the mind and not merely to the emotions;
- The message must tell the 'bad news' as well as the 'good news' and it must be communicated seriously, earnestly, urgently;
- The communicator must do everything possible to be eclipsed by the message;
- Nothing must be done that will stimulate unwholesome thoughts or appetites;
- Extreme care must be taken not to introduce stumbling blocks into any area of Christian life;
- As with any other method of ministry, music choices can be judged as either appropriate or inappropriate for God's service;

- Everything must be done to avoid the worldliness that causes divisions in the body of Christ;
- Christians must take care not to mix light with darkness, all the more when it comes to ministering the gospel and worshipping the Lord;
- The worship of God must not be sold at a profit!

It is our conviction that rock music fails to meet these and other biblical principles and is therefore contrary to the teaching of Scripture.

The law of freedom

Although we have tried to present the issue fairly and positively, that list and our conclusion may come across to some readers as being harsh, cramping, negative and destructive. Yet if it is biblically sound, those objections are both irrelevant and wrong. Scripture calls itself 'the law of liberty' (James 2:12), while one of the psalmists says, 'I will walk at liberty, for I seek your precepts' (Psalm 119:45). This means that the person who is tied to Scripture is set free from everything else and this emancipation is part of what Paul calls 'the glorious liberty of the children of God' (Romans 8:21). How does this apply to our conclusions? What kind of freedom would you have if you decided to abandon rock music? The difficulty in answering the question is not in knowing where to start, but in knowing when to stop.

Freedom from compromise

In the first place, you would be free from the constant pressure of needing to keep in step with the latest musical trend, idiom or fad. You would not need to be musically 'cool'.

Turning your back on rock music would set you free from the need to wrench your church music away from its grubby associations such as rebelliousness, occultism, sexuality and the drug culture. Christian rock artists often imitate the clothing, gestures, performance and voices of secular performers. The whole style is basically worldly, but you would be set free from this and from the related danger of rock gospel presentations creating or stimulating an appetite for the same kind of music outside of a Christian framework.

Freedom from hindering the message

You would also be free from the nagging question of whether your worship or the worship of those you lead was falsely stimulated by the suggestive power of rock music. You would be free from the perils of producing an emotional response based on the beat, rhythm and pulse of the music rather than on the words. You would also be free from the serious consequences of evacuating the message in order to accommodate the music and from the trivializing of truth which results from trying to reduce great doctrines to 'pop words'. (This danger is notoriously difficult to avoid, and a certain amount of questionable doggerel has found its way into some of our best-known traditional hymns as well as modern songs that are in no way associated with rock music.) In addition, you would be free from the twin dangers associated with the quality of the music, namely that either the music is so good or so powerful that it overwhelms the words, or so poor that the words are condemned along with the performance.

Freedom from the pressure of results

You would be free from the temptation of relying on the music to 'get results' and the embarrassment of needing to explain why so soon after a large number of 'decisions' were recorded, there was so little lasting effect to be seen in the lives of many of those concerned. A youth group once pleaded with one of the authors to include a rock band in an evangelistic mission because 'if we get a band it will make it easier for people to get saved'. His answer was to say, 'That depends on who does the saving!' There was no band (rock or otherwise) on the day of Pentecost when 3,000 were converted, nor in the amazing days which followed, when 'the Lord added to the church daily those who were being saved' (Acts 2:47). You would obviously long for God to use your evangelistic efforts to bring people to himself, but you would be free to place your unqualified confidence in his Word and to avoid carnal pressure to produce immediate results.

Freedom from following the teaching of men

You would also be free from 'teaching as doctrines the commandments of men' (Mark 7:7) when it comes to worship and evangelism. No longer would you be required to defend rock music by using arguments taken out of historical or biblical context or lifted from the self-serving logic of the latest 'pop Christianity' preacher or Christian rock artist. You would be free from adherence to the contradictory 'Christian rock' faith system we covered back in chapter 3, a credo created by rock apologists that includes discredited beliefs such as 'music is amoral', 'God created rock' and 'the end justifies the means'. You could rely instead solely on the Holy Spirit to teach and guide your worship and evangelism by the Word.

Freedom from causing offence

Finally, and by no means unimportantly, you would be free from the apostle Paul's censure of those who flaunt their liberty of choice and knowingly place a stumbling block in the way of their brothers and sisters in Christ.

The other side of freedom

All the freedoms we have mentioned so far might be called 'negative freedoms' in that they refer to areas of danger and difficulty from which you would be delivered by abandoning the use of rock music in worship and evangelism. But there is another side to freedom. Immediately after the end of the Second World War the Soviet Union erected the notorious Iron Curtain to seal off itself and its dependent Eastern European allies from open contact with the West. Yet during the forty-five years in which it stood, many people risked their lives to find a way through it. When they did so, they not only escaped *out* of the repressive captivity of Eastern Europe but *into* the freedom enjoyed by the West. By abandoning rock music you would not only be set free from the negative factors we have just listed, you would be free to experience an infinitely healthier dimension of Christian life and witness.

Freedom to preach the gospel

In the first place, you would be free to concentrate much more (as speaker or listener) on the preaching of the Word of God. This would obviously be true in the contexts of worship and teaching, but in the specific area of evangelism many Christians seem to have forgotten or failed to notice the central place that God has given to preaching. John the Baptist prepared the way for the coming of Jesus by 'preaching in the wilderness of Judea' (Matthew 3:1). As soon as Jesus began his public ministry he 'began to preach' (Matthew 4:17). His final command to his disciples was

'Go into all the world and preach the gospel to every creature' (Mark 16:15). As a result, we read that 'daily in the temple, and in every house they did not cease teaching and preaching Jesus as the Christ' (Acts 5:42). When persecution drove 'ordinary' church members out of Jerusalem, 'those who were scattered went everywhere preaching the word' (Acts 8:4). Paul was crystal clear about his own commission: 'For Christ did not send me to baptize, but to preach the gospel' (1 Corinthians 1:17). He told Titus that God had 'manifested his word through preaching, which was committed to me according to the commandment of God our Saviour' (Titus 1:3). Having rejoiced that 'whoever calls upon the name of the Lord shall be saved' (Romans 10:13), he went on to ask these questions: 'How then shall they call on him in whom they have not believed? And how shall they believe in him of whom they have not heard? And how shall they hear without a preacher?' (Romans 10:14). In a very telling comment on this, Geoffrey Wilson says, 'The apostles constantly laboured to inform the minds of their hearers. They did not exercise a commission to pander to the basest instincts of the natural man.'[4]

We have lost that emphasis today. As Paul Bassett rightly notes, 'We sing of Christ, recite Christ, dramatize Christ, but less and less do we preach Christ.'[5] Straightforward preaching is slowly being sidelined and straightforward preachers are becoming an endangered species! It would not be an exaggeration to say that music has become an obsession for many of those involved in evangelism today, especially among young people. In one major event after another the band or group is the main attraction. In a very real sense, the medium has become the message. Surely it is time to turn the tide? We believe that those in positions of responsibility need to do some serious, honest, biblical rethinking in this area. The Bible tells us that when Christ ascended into heaven he made full provision for the ongoing work of the kingdom of God by bestowing various gifts on the church: 'some to be apostles, some prophets, some evangelists, and some pastors and teachers...' (Ephesians 4:11). It is surely significant that there are no musicians in the list!

Yet some people still insist that music in general, and rock music in particular, is a better medium than words for the communication of the gospel. In a letter from which he has given us permission to quote, Robert Andrews of Chapel Lane Productions says that in certain situations 'when we choose to preach to them using words only, the level of communication is minimal'. Another Christian heavily involved in contemporary Christian music went so far as to say, 'If it is "impossible to communicate the gospel of Romans in music, drama or dance" (a phrase the Welsh preacher Geoff Thomas had used) it is even more impossible for preachers, whose words can go nowhere as far to communicate the depth of the concepts involved.' We wonder what comment that might have produced from Dr Martyn Lloyd-Jones, who managed to keep going through Romans at Westminster Chapel on Friday nights for thirteen years, from 1955-1968, without needing a single note of music to communicate 'the depth of the concepts involved'!

Even more importantly, that philosophy fails to grasp the tremendous truth that preaching cannot be divorced from the gospel. The method and the message are inseparable — and non-verbal communication does not count as preaching. There is an obvious example in Paul's testimony that 'Christ did not send me to baptize, but to preach the gospel' (1 Corinthians 1:17). Baptism is obviously a valid form of communication, one that is biblical and God-ordained, but Paul's point is that it is quite distinct from the preaching of the gospel. Baptism is good, right and biblical, but it is not preaching.

The point becomes even clearer when we take a closer look at Paul's phrase, 'to preach the gospel'. In the original Greek this is just one word — *euangeliseathai*, which we sometimes transliterate 'to evangelize'. But the word Paul uses is a verbal form of the noun *euangelion* and we would be more strictly

accurate to translate his statement: 'Christ did not send me
to baptize, but to gospel.' The gospel and the preaching of the
gospel are as closely linked as that. A little further on in his
letter, Paul says that people would have preferred some other
form of communication: 'Jews request a sign, and Greeks seek
after wisdom' (1 Corinthians 1:22). What was Paul's response to
the demands of these 'seekers'? God had used him to perform
miracles before; why not ask for power to perform more? He
also had the intellectual capacity to tangle with the Greeks at a
rational and philosophical level; why not try to win them over
that way? Yet Paul's response was to satisfy neither group. He
knew of only one way to meet their need: 'We preach Christ
crucified' (1 Corinthians 1:23). As far as Paul was concerned,
nothing else could properly communicate the gospel, not even
the exciting alternatives on offer. Then if preaching cannot be
replaced by miracles, how can it possibly be replaced by music?

In saying this we are not for one moment suggesting that
there is no place for sung praise in evangelism. The words of
the psalmist, 'Let everything that has breath praise the LORD'
(Psalm 150:6), give us all the biblical warrant we need for this.
Our concern is with the characteristics of the music and the
content of the lyrics, both of which must conform to biblical
principles if they are to be glorying to God. We are also aware
that the influence of John and Charles Wesley's hymns prompted
the saying, 'Methodism was born in song' and that at one point
there was a measure of spiritual revival in Wales following the
publication of an edition of William Williams' hymns.

Freedom to worship God as he intended

Secondly, you would be free to worship God as a true New
Covenant believer in line with New Testament teaching. Your
worship can now be offered to God 'with reverence and godly

fear' (Hebrews 12:28); with your body 'holy and acceptable to God' and 'not conformed to this world' (Romans 12:1-2); and wholly free from idolatry (2 Corinthians 6:16-17). As Christians, we are no longer required to bring a sin offering to satisfy the righteous demands of a holy God because 'we have been sanctified through the offering of the body of Jesus Christ *once for all*' (Hebrews 10:10). Your worship would therefore be able to focus with delight on bringing the New Covenant sacrifices of a redeemed heart, such as the 'sacrifice of praise — the fruit of lips that confess his name', knowing that 'with *such sacrifices God is well pleased*' (Hebrews 13:15-16, NIV). Again, if you had an opportunity to bring a song to a Christian assembly you would avoid the divisive elements of rock music (and its often shallow words) and instead be able to unite the hearts and minds of Christians of all ages in worshipping God according to biblical principles. This would in turn help to promote peace through unity, exactly along the lines of Paul's prayer: 'May the God who gives encouragement and endurance give you a spirit of unity among yourselves as you follow Christ Jesus, so that *with one heart and mouth* you may glorify the God and Father of our Lord Jesus Christ' (Romans 15:5-6).

Freedom to follow New Testament precedents

Thirdly, you would be free to concentrate on what are clearly New Testament methods of evangelism. What are they? Writing in the British monthly newspaper *Evangelical Times*, Geoff Thomas suggested, 'The only New Testament precedents for spreading the gospel are godly living, praying and bold speaking.'[6] That sounds like a pretty thin agenda, but it is far from it, because the 'bold speaking' covers an almost endless variety of things. 'Bold speaking' can obviously take place in a pulpit or on a platform, but it can also take place at informal church-based functions or on neutral ground; it can take place at home or at work, at a social or sports club, at school, college or university, in a car, a coach, a train or an aircraft — in fact wherever two or more people get into conversation. When the Iron Curtain was standing church leaders in Eastern Europe told us that at one stage they had become discouraged at not being able to use many of the evangelistic methods available to us in the West. Then they had second thoughts and decided that they were wrong to feel like that, because they could use all the methods available to the church in the New Testament! As Geoff Thomas adds in his article, 'What turned the world upside down then is sufficient to do it today.'[7] Time saved in advertising, planning, organizing, supporting and attending gospel concerts, religious road shows and the like could be put to better use in activities that have clear New Testament backing.

Freedom to witness more effectively

Fourthly, you would be free to spend more time in personal evangelism. There is a case for saying that this was the most widely used method of evangelism in the New Testament — and that it is the most widely neglected in the church today. In his paperback *Evangelism — Now and Then*, Michael Green comments, 'This is the biggest difference between the New Testament church and our own. Their responsibility of bearing witness to Jesus rested fairly and squarely upon every single member ... These days evangelism is spasmodic (if it happens at all), expensive ... and is dependent upon the skills of the resident evangelist or visiting specialist. This is exceedingly foolish.' One of the reasons it is foolish is that it limits the greatest task in the world to the efforts of a tiny minority of Christians and to a very small fraction of their time. In the business world, that kind of policy would be a recipe for bankruptcy. In a report published by the Church of England in 1945 under the title *Towards the Conversion of England*, it was said, 'There will be no widespread evangelization of England unless the work is undertaken by the lay people of the church.' The same principle applies in every other country in the world.

This also helps to pinpoint another weakness of 'gospel rock', namely, that its 'target area' is so limited. It would be no exaggeration to call it juvenile, in that it appeals largely to young people, ranging from pre-teens to those in their twenties or just beyond. It has little to say to the mature and middle-aged and nothing at all to the elderly, the sick, the dying, or the millions who are turned off by its very style. What is more, it would be totally out of place in a house meeting, a funeral, a classroom, a hospital ward and countless other settings. By striking contrast, verbal communication is relevant to every person, in every place and at any time. There is no situation in which the spoken word may not be an effective vehicle for communicating the gospel, *for the simple reason that it is the method God ordained for the purpose.*

One of the most exciting things about personal evangelism is that it is something open to every Christian. Have you ever thought of the wisdom of God in this? You do not have to be musical or theatrical, gifted or extrovert, nor do you have to gather an audience or advertise your ability. Going back to Geoff Thomas's three New Testament methods, every Christian can pray, every Christian is called to live a godly life and every Christian can speak about Christ. In his infinite love and wisdom, God has put the greatest privilege in the world within the reach of every Christian believer!

Yet realistic and consistent personal evangelism takes time. It means building bridges of personal friendship, investing in people's lives as well as their souls. It means getting to grips with their personal situations, trying to think through their problems and patiently seeking to answer their questions. Personal evangelism is not a hit-and-run affair, and it is not realistically done by taking people along to a rock music event.

Freedom to deepen your knowledge of God

Fifthly, you would be set free to invest more time in personal Bible study and prayer. This is not a change of subject. The key to effective personal witnessing for Christ (and to effective Christian living as a whole) is not to be found in frantic activity, but in the Christian's personal relationship with God. Moving in exciting circles is not the same as making progress! The apostle Peter points us in the right direction: 'But sanctify the Lord God in your hearts, and always be ready to give a defence to everyone who asks you a reason for the hope that is in you' (1 Peter 3:15). But how can a Christian possibly be 'ready to give a defence' unless he or she is developing a solid grounding in Scripture? Having even the best translation of the Bible in your home is no substitute for knowing what it truly says and it would be difficult to deny that for many Christians a preoccupation with rock music (playing, listening, reading, discussing, attending and so on) has been a major factor in reducing the amount of time available to invest in deepening their own spiritual lives by determined Bible study and disciplined prayer. The loss to the church and therefore to the kingdom of God has been incalculable.

The urgent need of the hour is for a generation of Christians who are determined to live 'soberly, righteously, and godly in the present age' (Titus 2:12). Anything that tends to cool that kind of determination is not only sad but ultimately tragic.

Freedom of conscience

In writing this book we believe that we have discharged an important responsibility; now the responsibility shifts from author to reader. We have tried to work through the issue thoroughly, carefully and honestly, without at any point being destructively critical of Christians who might not agree with us. We sincerely believe that the case against the use of rock music in the life of the church is overwhelming, but we also realize that our convictions are not binding on others. Our final direction would therefore come straight from Scripture: 'Let each be fully convinced in his own mind' (Romans 14:5).

The issue with which Paul was dealing when he wrote these words (the religious observance of certain days in the Jewish calendar) was not as important as the present one, but his words are powerfully relevant to our subject and they pinpoint two vital principles. The first is indicated by his use of the word 'each', which emphasizes the element of personal *liberty*, the birthright of every Christian. You have no reason to be browbeaten by anyone, nor should you ever feel forced by peer pressure to go along with the crowd. The matter under discussion is one between you and God and you have the right and the privilege of exercising your own conscience in the light of his Word. Never let the fact that many or even most Christians take a certain line on a particular issue rob you of your own God-given prerogative.

Personal responsibility

The second principle is that of your *responsibility*: Paul says that a Christian should be 'fully convinced' in his own mind. The Greek word translated 'fully convinced' is one we would use about gathering evidence and also carries with it the sense of being filled to the brim. Bring these two strands of thought together, recognize that this is not just a suggestion but a command, and you have a picture of just how great a responsibility you have. The issue of rock music in the life of the church is tremendously important, not least because God himself is the object of Christian worship and evangelism is our God-given responsibility to seek to rescue those 'having no hope and without God in the world' (Ephesians 2:12). This means that the question of how the rescue operation should be carried out and how we should approach God in worship are not matters on which vague ideas will do, and to have a 'couldn't care less' attitude is downright carnal. Here is something about which you have a responsibility to be 'fully convinced', up to the brim! You must weigh up all the evidence and think carefully and honestly about all the arguments. At the same time, you must set aside your own emotions, tastes, likings and prejudices, because in coming to a biblical conclusion these are irrelevant.

You have a right to your own judgement on the issue, but as a Christian you have a responsibility to base that judgement utterly and entirely on the commands and principles of Scripture. Simply put, *what you think must be controlled by nothing other than what God says.*

At the beginning of the year in which he died, the missionary Spencer Walton wrote these words in his diary: 'The will of God — nothing less — nothing more — nothing else.'

We rest our case.

NOTES

Chapter 1

1. The sixth-century Roman philosopher Boethius, *De Institutione Musica*.
2. *Pop Goes the Gospel*, pp.7-8.
3. A phrase connoting the passage of a point of no return. It refers to Julius Caesar's invasion of Ancient Rome when, on 10 January 49 B.C., he led his army across the Rubicon River, making conflict inevitable.
4. The Willow Creek Association, founded in 1992, claims more than 11,000 member churches from ninety denominations in forty-five countries.
5. 'Unlocking the Key to Megachurch Success' by Pauline J. Chang, *Christian Post*, Tuesday 2 Aug. 2005.
6. 'Megachurches Today 2005, Summary of Research Findings', by Scott Thumma, Dave Travis and Warren Bird, Hartford Institute for Religion Research Leadership Network, Hartford Seminary, 2005.
7. 'Megachurches draw big crowds' by Joyce Kelly and Michael Conlon, *Yahoo Religion News*, Tues. 22 Nov. 2005.
8. Worshipleader.com interview with Gerald Sharon, pastor of Worship Venues for Saddleback Church, Dec. 2005.
9. 'Worship with an Attitude', by Carmen Greco Jr, *Daily Herald*, Arlington Heights, IL, 19 March 2000.
10. *MTV News Online*, 28 Feb. 2005.
11. In jazz, a vamp is simply a repeating musical figure or 2ccompaniment (source: Vince Corozine 2002. *Arranging Music for the Real World: Classical and Commercial Aspects*, p.124). 'Vamping' is a term that refers to extended improvisation over a repeated chord change. One of the quintessential examples of

vamping is the outro to 'Freebird' by Lynyrd Skynyrd, featuring a 5-minute epic guitar solo over some repeated chords (source: Pandora.com, created by the Music Genome Project).

12. Review in *Worship Music* newsletter, 19 Jan. 2006.
13. Evangelical Lutheran Church in America web site.
14. Valley Bible Fellowship (California) web site.
15. experiencingworship.com
16. *Ibid.*
17. rockprophets.com web site.
18. Rick Warren, *The Purpose-Driven Church*, p.285.
19. 'Megachurches Today 2005, Summary of Research Findings', by Thumma, Travis and Bird.
20. Barna.org web site. Copyright © 2006 The Barna Group, Ltd. All rights reserved.
21. Interview with Marla Reid, May 2003, from www.christianmusic.about.com
22. Interview with Bill Gaither on www.christianmusic.about.com 6 Dec. 2004.
23. 2005 interview, *Renown* magazine.
24. 'Our Love Is Loud' by Sandra Chambers, *Charisma* magazine, Feb. 2003.
25. Interviewed on the Jesus Freak Hideout web site.
26. 'Hills to Die On' chapter, *Fools Gold*, John MacArthur, editor.
27. Pastors.com web site.
28. *Rick Warren Hits Home Run* by Dan Wooding, ASSIST Ministries, 17 April 2005.
29. Warren, *The Purpose-Driven Church*, p.280.
30. Warren, *The Purpose-Driven Life*, p.65.
31. *Revolution*, p.65. Note that these artists are all rock musicians.
32. Name withheld by request, e-mail to Dan Lucarini, 6 September 2004.
33. Bill Gothard, *IBLP Daily Success* – Day 36.
34. Albert Barnes, *NT Commentary on Matthew's Gospel*.
35. Warren, *The Purpose-Driven Church*, p.279.

Chapter 2
1. *huH* magazine, Feb. 1995, p.36.
2. Malcolm Doney, *Summer in the City*.
3. As above.
4. Mickey Hart, *Drumming at the Edge of Magic*, p.91.

5. Voodoo is a religion forged by descendants of Dahomean, Kongo, Yoruba and other West African ethnic groups. Source: *Encyclopaedia Britannica*.
6. David Byrne interview, *Rolling Stone* magazine, 13 July 1989, p.78.
7. ABC News channel 7, Chicago, 7 Jan. 2006.
8. Steve Lawhead, *Rock Reconsidered*.
9. As above.
10. Van Zyl, *Reformation Today*.
11. Rod Gruver, *Down Beat*.
12. Doney, *Summer in the City*.
13. B. Larson, *Rock*.
14. Doney, *Summer in the City*.
15. As above.
16. Doney, *Summer in the City*.
17. Nik Cohn, 'WopBopaLooBopLopBamBam'.
18. Derek Jewell, *The Popular Voice*.
19. Doney, *Summer in the City*.
20. Jewell, *The Popular Voice*.
21. As above.
22. David Wilkerson, *Set the Trumpet to thy Mouth*.
23. Steve Lawhead, *Rock Reconsidered*.

Chapter 3

1. 'It's Only Rock 'N' Roll', The Rolling Stones, © 1974.
2. Jewell, *The Popular Voice*.
3. *All Music Guide* web site.
4. As above.
5. Mickey Hart, *Drumming at the Edge of Magic*.
6. W. Shafer, *Rock Music*.
7. A. Salter, *What is Hypnosis?*
8. *Life* magazine, 3 Oct. 1969.
9. Hart, *Drumming at the Edge of Magic*, p.185.
10. 'Moving to a spiritual beat: Drumming grows in worship services', *Milwaukee Journal Sentinel*, 7 Aug. 2005.
11. Hart, *Drumming at the Edge of Magic*.
12. As with any secular music trend, there are Christian copycats. Psalm Drummers plays at numerous worship events. On its web site, the band acknowledges drumming as a powerful tool for effecting change. The band's founder claims he had a dream

where God told him 'to gather the drummers'; he believes that God is restoring the drum to the church.

13. Barb Wilson, 'Can't Beat Drumming', *Complete Health* magazine, Winter 2004.
14. Igor Stravinsky and R. Craft, *Horizon*, Sept. 1958.
15. Tom McSloy, *National Review*, 30 June 1970.
16. Hart, *Drumming at the Edge of Magic*, p.140.
17. D. M. Lloyd-Jones, *Preaching and Preachers*.
18. David Winter, *New Singer, New Song*.
19. Lloyd-Jones, *Preaching and Preachers*.
20. Jewell, *The Popular Voice*.
21. 'Pete Townshend Warns iPod Users About Hearing Loss', *Information Week*, 4 Jan. 2006.
22. Doney, *Summer in the City*.
23. *Hit Parader*, Feb. 1982.
24. Doney, *Summer in the City*.
25. *Merriam-Webster Online Dictionary*.
26. As above.
27. D. Hanson and R. Fearn, *The Lancet*, 2 Aug. 1975.
28. W. Burns and D. Robinson, *Hearing and Noise in Industry*.
29. Hanson and Fearn, *The Lancet*, 2 Aug. 1975.
30. As above.
31. As above.
32. Rick Warren, *The Purpose-Driven Church*, p.281.
33. As above.
34. Warren, *The Purpose-Driven Life*, p.65.
35. H. Rookmaaker, *The Creative Gift*.
36. Liner notes from '25th Anniversary Edition: Liberation Suite' by Paul Baker.
37. Jewhoo.com blog.
38. artreynoldsmusic.com/bio
39. March 2001 interview on Classicrockrevisited.com
40. 'From Folk to Flyte: An Interview With Roger McGuinn' by Dan Harmon, Oct. 1996.
41. 'Age to Age' by Steve Rabey, *CCM* magazine web site.
42. As above.
43. As above.
44. *All Music Guide* web site.
45. As above.
46. 'Pastor rocks religion with U2' by Kyle Munson, *The Des Moines*

Register, 5 Oct. 2004.

47. *All Music Guide* web site.
48. Review of U2's 'How to Dismantle an Atomic Bomb' by Jude Adam, *CCM* magazine, Nov. 2004.
49. 'How To Dismantle An Idolized Bono' by Tara Leigh Cobble, *Relevant* magazine, 19 Dec. 2005.
50. *CCM* magazine, 4 Feb. 2006.
51. Rick Warren, *The Purpose-Driven Church*, p.281.
52. 'Christian rock is on a mission' by Marc Weingarten, *Los Angeles Times*, 14 April 2005.
53. *All Music Guide* web site.
54. 'Upon This Rock' by John Jeremiah Sullivan, *GQ Online* magazine, Feb. 2005.
55. Rolling Stone.com
56. 'Christian rock is on a mission' by Marc Weingarten, *Los Angeles Times*, 14 April 2005.
57. As above.
58. 'Rocking For Christ' by Bob Simon, *60 Minutes*, CBS News, 8 Dec. 2004.

Chapter 4

1. 'We sold our soul for rock 'n' roll' by Black Sabbath, NEMS, 1975.
2. L. Morris, *New Bible Dictionary*.
3. 'The Dark Side: How Rock 'n' Roll really did dance with the devil', *Mojo*, Sept. 1999, p.79.
4. 'Churches struggling for very existence' by Mark Ellis, *Challenge Weekly Online*, 25 July 2005.
5. Peter Anderson, *Talk about the Devil*, Word Books.
6. *Buzz*, April 1982.
7. *All Music Guide* web site.
8. 'Our Love Is Loud' by Sandra Chambers, *Charisma* magazine, February 2003.
9. *Option*, March/April 1995, p.82.
10. Liner notes from the *ET* soundtrack CD, MCA Records.
11. Mickey Hart, *Spirit into Sound: The Magic of Music*, pp.184, 179.
12. As above, p.33.
13. Robert Jourdain, *Music, The Brain and Ecstasy*, p.328.
14. Grace Slick, *Somebody to Love*, p.140.
15. *Axcess*, Volume 2, Issue 2, p.49.

16. Mickey Hart, *Spirit into Sound: The Magic of Music*, p.134.
17. Eric Holmberg, *Hells Bells 2*.
18. Stephen Davis, *Hammer of the Gods*, p.164.
19. Eric Holmberg, *Hells Bells 2*.
20. *Hit Parader*, Feb. 1976.
21. *Rolling Stone* magazine, 16 March 2000, p.41.
22. Steve Turner, *Hungry for Heaven*, p.114.
23. *The Dick Cavett Show*, 21 July 1969.
24. Charles Murray, *Crosstown Traffic*, p.161.
25. *Guitar Player*, Nov. 1974.
26. Eric Holmberg, *Hells Bells 2*.
27. *Break On Through – The Life and Death of Jim Morrison*, p.190.
28. Gary Greenberg, *Not Fade Away: The Online World Remembers Jerry Garcia*, pp.42-3.
29. *The Guardian*, 22 July 1995.
30. *Rolling Stone*, 14 July 2005.
31. www.bbc.co.uk/history/programmes/greatbritons.shtml
32. RockstarPix.TV interview by Michael Giambra.
33. *Led Zeppelin in Their Own Words*, p.103.
34. Peter R. Koenig, *The Laughing Gnostic: David Bowie and the Occult*.
35. *Ordo Templi Orientis* web site.
36. Lyrics to '*Tenebrarum Oratorium*'.
37. Lyrics to 'Red Rose'.
38. Lyrics to 'RUOK'.
39. *All Music Guide* web site.
40. *Rolling Stone*, 2 Oct. 1997.
41. 'Jars of Clay Rides Rising Tide of Success' by Steve Rabey of Religion News Service, *The Harrisburg PA Patriot-News*, 22 Nov. 1997.
42. Quoted in a 2002 interview on Crosswalk.com
43. *CCM* magazine, April 1999, p.55.
44. Review of concert at University of Wisconsin-Eau Claire, 22 Feb. 2003, Phantom Tollbooth web site.
45. 'True Believer', *CCM* magazine online feature #173.
46. 'Lennon on Elections', *Disc Weekly*, 2 April 1966.
47. 'Grave New World', *The Guardian*, 15 June 1994.
48. Timothy Leary, *Flashbacks*, p.44.
49. 'Thank God for the Beatles' by Geoffrey Giuliano, *The Lost Beatle Interviews*, p.379.

50. A mandala is any of various ritualistic geometric designs symbolic of the universe, used in Hinduism and Buddhism as an aid to meditation (source: *American Heritage Dictionary*, 4th edition). Loosely translated to mean 'circle', it is far more than a simple shape. It represents wholeness, and can be seen as a model for the organizational structure of life itself — a cosmic diagram that reminds us of our relation to the infinite (source: The Mandala Project.org).

51. Giuliano, *Beatles*, pp.378, 375.

52. THE BHAKTIVEDANTA BOOK TRUST, *Chant and Be Happy*.

53. A conversation with his long-time personal friend Mukunda Goswami, taped at George Harrison's home in England on 4 September 1982, and later published in the book *Chant and Be Happy*, from THE BHAKTIVEDANTA BOOK TRUST. Both Lennon and Harrison's photos appear on the book cover.

54. 'Get Back and Other Setbacks', *The Guardian*, 22 November 2003.

55. *Rolling Stone* magazine, 27 August 1987.

56. *The Doors in Their Own Words*, p.13.

57. Words and music by John Lennon. Copyright © 1971 Lenono Music. All rights reserved.

58. Associated Press, 10 Feb. 2006.

59. J. Whitehead, *Lennon's Legacy*, Gadfly Online, 19 November 2001.

60. *Rolling Stone* magazine, 13 July 1989, p.78.

61. David Henderson, *'Scuse Me While I Kiss the Sky*, p.251.

62. Mickey Hart, *Drumming at the Edge of Magic*, p.91.

63. Robert Palmer, *Rock & Roll: An Unruly History*, p.53.

64. *Spin*, March 1996, p.46.

65. *Axcess*, Volume 2, Issue 2, p.49.

66. *Rolling Stone*, 10 Dec. 1987, p.48.

67. Robert Rosen, *Nowhere Man*, p.18.

68. Gary Patterson, *Hellhounds on Their Trail*, p.181.

69. *Song* magazine, Feb. 1984, p.16.

70. *Circus*, Dec. 1981.

71. *Rolling Stone*, 28 Oct. 1971.

72. *Circus*, 26 Aug. 1980.

73. *Rolling Stone*, 12 Feb. 1976.

74. As above.

75. *Hit Parader*, July 1975.

76. Peter R. Koenig, *The Laughing Gnostic: David Bowie and the Occult.*

77. *Break On Through – The Life and Death of Jim Morrison*, p.188.

78. James Douglas Morrison, 'An American Prayer: Poems, Lyrics and Stories'.

79. Lyrics from 'Soft Parade'.

80. Lyrics from 'The End'.

81. *Time*, 15 Aug. 1975.

82. *Circus*, 19 Jan. 1977.

83. *Newsweek*, 10 May 1976.

84. *Rolling Stone*, 26 Oct. 1972.

85. *Circus*, 31 July 1983.

86. *Newsweek*, 10 Jan. 1983.

87. *Spin*, Aug. 1996, p.34.

88. *huH*, Oct. 1996, p.34.

89. As above, p.37.

90. Eric Holmberg, *Hells Bells 2.*

91. *Time*, 11 Sept. 1978.

92. *Circus*, 22 Dec. 1977.

93. *Circus*, 31 Jan. 1984, p.70.

94. *People* magazine, 6 Feb. 1995.

95. *Newsweek*, 4 Jan. 1971.

96. *Rolling Stone*, 19 Aug. 1971.

97. *Guitar Player* magazine, Nov. 1974.

98. T. Palmer, *Born Under a Bad Sign.*

99. *Buzz*, Feb. 1983.

100. As above.

101. *Renown* magazine, 12 Jan. 2004.

102. Review of the *Worship Together Live 2001* CD on worshipmusic.com

103. *Music Recommendation Guide*, Family Christian Stores web site.

104. Jamieson-Fausset-Brown, commentary on Leviticus.

105. Jeremiah Burroughs, *Gospel Worship.*

106. *Buzz*, April 1982.

Chapter 5

1. Cultural critic Martha Bayles, *Hole in Our Soul: The Loss of Beauty and Meaning in American Popular Music*, p.388.

2. Jerry Rubin, *Do It*, p.19.

3. *US News and World Report*, 31 Oct. 1977.

4. B. Larson, *Rock.*
5. *Newsweek*, 4 Jan. 1971.
6. *Rolling Stone*, 17 July 1975.
7. *USA Today*, 6 Feb. 2006.
8. Steve Lawhead, *Rock Reconsidered.*
9. *Venus*, March 2004.
10. *All Music Guide* web site.
11. *Planet*, Oct. 1981.
12. L. Roxon, *Rock Encyclopedia.*
13. *Rolling Stone*, 25 March 1976.
14. From the inside flap of *Hammer of the Gods* by Stephen Davis.
15. From the 1992 *Publishers Weekly* review of *Stairway to Heaven: Led Zeppelin Uncensored.*
16. 'That Old Devil Music', *National Review*, 24 Feb. 1989.
17. *Rolling Stone*, 16 Feb. 1984.
18. *Circus*, April 1984.
19. *All Music Guide* web site.
20. B. Larson, *Rock.*
21. Review from the *All Music Guide.*
22. *Hit Parader*, Feb. 1982.
23. Tony Palmer, *Born Under a Bad Sign.*
24. Steve Lawhead, *Rock Reconsidered.*
25. As above.
26. Doney, *Summer in the City.*
27. As above.
28. *Rolling Stone*, 7 Oct. 1976.
29. *Rolling Stone*, 9 Feb. 1978.
30. *From Rock to Rock*, p.93.
31. *USA Today*, 22 Dec. 1983.
32. Holmberg, *Hells Bells 2.*
33. Robert Palmer, *Rock & Roll: An Unruly History*, p.15.
34. *Daily Express*, 19 Dec. 1983.
35. *People*, 30 June 1975.
36. *Newsweek*, 4 Jan. 1971.
37. *Queen: A Salute.*
38. *Fort Lauderdale News*, 6 March 1969.
39. *Circus*, 31 Jan. 1976.
40. *Rolling Stone*, 7 Jan. 1971.
41. *Circus*, 23 June 1977.
42. *Entertainment Tonight*, ABC, 10 Dec. 1987.

43. *Life*, 28 June 1968.
44. *Time*, 3 Jan. 1969.
45. *Daily Mail*, 18 March 1983.
46. *Daily Mirror*, 18 Nov. 1981.
47. *Daily Mail*, 21 Jan. 1983.
48. *Daily Telegraph*, 23 Sept. 1981.
49. D.A. Noebel, *The Legacy of John Lennon*.
50. Steve Lawhead, *Rock Reconsidered*.
51. *San Francisco Chronicle*, 26 March 2006.
52. As above.
53. Steve Bonta, 'Is It "Only Rock 'N' Roll"?', *New American*, 8 April 2002.
54. As above.
55. Martin Luther, Preface to the *Wittenberg Gesangbuch*.

Chapter 6
1. 1 Corinthians 15:33 (NASB).
2. *Hells Bells 2: The Dangers of Rock 'n' Roll*, Reel 2 Real Ministries, 2001.
3. As above.
4. *Time*, 22 Sept. 1967.
5. D. Pichaske, *A Generation in Motion*.
6. *Toronto Daily Star*, 20 June 1970.
7. "Recording Industry's Marketing Practices: A Check Up", testimony before the United States House of Representatives Energy and Commerce Committee, Telecommunications and the Internet Subcommittee, by Michael Rich, MD, MPH, FAAP, American Academy of Paediatrics, 1 Oct. 2002.
8. CBS News story, 4 Sept. 2002.
9. *Circus*, 17 April 1979.
10. As above.
11. *Rolling Stone*, 2 Oct. 1997.
12. *The Guardian*, 16 Feb. 2005.
13. *Reader's Digest*, Dec. 1969.
14. *Young Life*, Volume 56, No. 2.
15. *Rock Beat*, Spring 1987.
16. Doney, *Summer in the City*.
17. *Circus*, 13 May 1976.
18. *Melody Maker*, 22 Oct. 1988.
19. *Super Rock*, June 1978.

20. *Guitar World*, June 2000.
21. *Spin*, Aug. 1991.
22. *Newsweek*, 14 Nov. 1983.
23. *USA Today*, 16 Jan. 1984.
24. Melly, *Revolt Into Style*.
25. *The Listener*, 11 Feb. 1982.
26. IMdb.com, the Internet Movie Database web site.
27. *Pretty Vacant*, broadcast on the BBC, May 2005.
28. *Body Modification E'zine* web site.
29. 'Rocking For Christ', *60 Minutes*, CBS News, 8 December 2004.
30. *Saturday Evening Post*, 15 Aug. 1964.
31. *Hit Parader*, 19 June 1975.
32. Quoted in *Dallas Morning News*, 29 Oct. 1978.
33. www.musicalschwartz.com/godspell
34. Stephen Schwartz from www.stephenschwartz.com
35. Mae West was best known as an early Hollywood sex symbol, said to be 'way ahead of her time with her sexual innuendoes and how she made fun of a puritanical society' (IMdb.com, the Internet Movie Database web site).
36. Stephen Schwartz from www.stephenschwartz.com
37. As above.
38. *Time*, 9 Nov. 1970.
39. Peter T. Chattaway, *BC Christian News*, March 2000.
40. As above.
41. *Newsweek*, 9 July 1973.
42. Appendix to J. & M. Prince, *Time to Listen, Time to Talk*.
43. Holmberg, *Hells Bells 2*.
44. Frank Zappa, *The Real Frank Zappa Book*.
45. *SPIN* magazine, Oct. 1998.
46. *Leicester Mercury*, 4 Jan. 1982.
47. D. Beaumont, *New Life* (Australia).
48. *Leicester Mercury*, 4 Jan. 1982.
49. *Buzz*, April 1982.
50. 'The Devil's Music', Salon.com, 24 Nov. 2005.
51. As above.
52. D. Porter, *Media*.
53. Quoted in J. & M. Prince, *Time to Listen, Time to Talk*.
54. *Reader's Digest*, Feb. 1970.
55. As above.
56. Quoted in *CCM* magazine, Aug.-Sept. 1981.

57. As above.
58. C. Scott, *Music: Its secret influence through the ages.*
59. *Daily Mirror*, 2 Jan. 1982.
60. *Reading Chronicle*, 5 Nov. 1982.
61. *Circus*, 13 May 1976.
62. W. Shafer, *Rock Music.*
63. S. Ostrander and L. Schroeder, *Super Learning.*
64. Timothy Leary, *Politics of Ecstasy.*
65. *Hit Parader Yearbook*, No. 6, 1967.
66. *Star Weekly Magazine*, 26 Aug. 1967.
67. *Life*, 30 Oct. 1969.
68. *Hit Parader*, Jan. 1968.
69. *Melody Maker*, 7 Oct. 1967.
70. *The Guardian*, 28 Dec. 1982.

Chapter 7
1. *Tozer on Worship and Entertainment* by James L. Snyder, comp. (Christian Publications 1997, p.95).
2. Relient K concert in Fargo ND, Nov. 2005, Phantom Tollbooth web site.
3. Relient K Live at St Paul, Minnesota, 16 Oct. 2003, Phantom Tollbooth web site.
4. *Charisma* magazine, Feb. 2003.
5. Audio Adrenaline, 6 June 2005 concert in Vaughn, Ontario, Canada, Phantom Tollbooth web site.
6. Elms in concert, Minneapolis, Minnesota, 8 Feb. 2003, Phantom Tollbooth web site.
7. Creation 2005 festival web site.
8. *Time*, 18 April 2005.
9. *Rick Warren Hits Home Run*, ASSIST Ministries, 17 April 2005.
10. Adam Clarke, *Commentary on Romans.*
11. Albert Barnes, *Commentary on Romans.*
12. James L. Snyder, comp., *Tozer on Worship and Entertainment.*
13. Steven John Camp, 'A Call for Reformation in the Contemporary Christian Music Industry: 107 Theses'.
14. K. Green, *Can God Use Rock Music?*
15. *CCM* magazine, May 2001.
16. As above.
17. Audio Adrenaline concert review, Phantom Tollbooth web site.

18. Worship Leader web site.
19. 'Nixed from American Idol', *Baptist Press*, 11 Feb. 2005.
20. 'On "Idol", image is everything, and nothing', MSNBC, 27 Jan. 2005.
21. 'Nixed from American Idol', *Baptist Press*, 11 Feb. 2005.
22. 'American Idol: Three Lessons for Worship Leaders', Integrity Music web site, May 2005.
23. Camp, 'A Call for Reformation in the Contemporary Christian Music Industry: 107 Theses'.
24. Quoted in *Solid Rock?*
25. James L. Snyder, comp., *Tozer on Worship and Entertainment.*
26. *Cassell's 20th Century Dictionary.*
27. As above.
28. P. Bassett, *God's Way.*
29. Quoted in *D. Martyn Lloyd-Jones: The First Forty Years.*
30. *Buzz*, May 1981.
31. As above.
32. D. Porter, *Media.*
33. E. Routley, *Church Music and the Christian Faith.*
34. S. Henderson, *Whose Idea of Fun is a Nightmare?*
35. Quoted in *Time*, 25 April 1969.
36. *Tampa Tribune*, 4 Sept. 1981.
37. *Melody Maker*, 10 Feb. 1968.
38. Quoted by B. Larson, *Rock and the Church.*
39. G. Lees, *High Fidelity*, Feb. 1970.
40. I. Gitler, *Bell Telephone* magazine, Jan.-Feb. 1970.
41. *Christian Herald*, 9 Jan. 1988.
42. James L. Snyder, comp., *Tozer on Worship and Entertainment.*
43. *Detroit Free Press*, 23 Oct. 2002.
44. As above.
45. As above.
46. As above.
47. As above.
48. As above.
49. As above.
50. As above.
51. As above.
52. 'Chevrolet Presents: Come Together and Worship'. An open letter to the CCM industry by Steve Camp.
53. As above.

54. Michael Coleman, President, Integrity Media, *Glory to glory,* April 2003.
55. EMI CMG extends long-term publishing agreement with major Praise & Worship publishing houses, 23 Dec. 2005, as seen at emicmg.com
56. CCLI web site.

Chapter 8
1. Nineteenth-century American poet Henry Wadsworth Longfellow, *Draper's Book of Quotations for the Christian World.*
2. Quoted in *Banner of Truth*, Jan. 1977.
3. As above.
4. Quoted by R. Bainton, *Here I Stand.*
5. Quoted in *Banner of Truth*, Jan. 1977.
6. E. Routley, *Church Music and the Christian Faith.*
7. D. Kidner, *Christian Graduate*, March 1981.
8. A. Barnes, *Barnes' Notes on the New Testament.*
9. S. Zodhiates, *The Complete Word Study Dictionary, New Testament.*
10. Adam Clarke, *Commentary on Hebrews.*

Chapter 9
1. The celebrated German composer George Friedrich Handel (1685-1759), *Draper's Book of Quotations for the Christian World.*
2. Tom Morton, *Christian Graduate*, March 1981.
3. As above.
4. Tozer, *Man: the Dwelling Place of God.*
5. Bassett, *God's Way.*
6. D. Hesselgrave, *Communicating Christ Cross-Culturally.*
7. G. Cray, Appendix to J. & M. Prince, *Time to Listen, Time to Talk.*
8. Larry Norman, *Solid Rock?*
9. As above.
10. J. Fischer, *Solid Rock?*
11. *Chambers 20th Century Dictionary.*
12. As above.
13. Plato, *Fourth Book of the Republic.*
14. Boethius, *De Institutione Musica.*
15. Oliver Strunk, *Source Readings in Music History.*
16. Grout and Palisca, *A History of Western Music*, 5th edition.

17. David Tame, *The Secret Power of Music.*
18. As above.
19. G. Stevenson, *Music and Your Emotions.*
20. H. Hanson, *American Journal of Psychiatry.*
21. Eric Holmberg, *Hells Bells 2.*
22. MuchMusic TV, Toronto, Canada, 25 May 2001.
23. *George* magazine, April/May 1996.
24. Eric Holmberg, *Hells Bells 2.*
25. As above.
26. As above.
27. *Seeing with the Eyes of Music*, 9 Aug. 2002, Christianity.com
28. *Pop Talk*, 11 Sept. 1996.
29. Jerry Rubin, *Do It.*
30. *Life* magazine, 28 June 1968.
31. *Christian Radio & Retail Weekly 2005.*
32. Grout and Palisca, *A History of Western Music*, 5th edition.
33. Theodore Gerold, *Les Peres de l'eglise et la musique, Paris.*
34. Grout and Palisca, *A History of Western Music*, 5th edition.
35. As above.
36. As above.
37. M. Johann Mathesius, *Dr Martin Luther's Leben.*
38. Charles K. Moss, *The Musical Reforms of Luther.*
39. Karl Anton, *Luther und die Musik.*
40. Erik Routley, *The Church and Music.*
41. Robert M. Stevenson, *Patterns of Protestant Church Music.*
42. *United Methodist News Service*, 13 Aug. 2002.
43. The Rev. Mike Macdonald, article published at Church Central. com, 4 Oct. 2002.
44. Luther's *Works* 53:319-20, 54:129-30.
45. 'Christian rock is on a mission', *Los Angeles Times*, 14 April 2005.
46. C. Girard, *Solid Rock?*
47. Quoted in *Solid Rock?*
48. V. Wright, *Evangelism Today*, Dec. 1981.
49. Shafer, *Rock Music.*
50. F. Garlock, *The Big Beat.*
51. J. Fischer, *Solid Solid Rock?* Quoted in *Solid Rock?*
52. As above.
53. R. Taylor, *A Return to Christian Culture.*
54. James L. Snyder, comp., *Tozer on Worship and Entertainment.*
55. *Charisma* magazine, Aug. 2003.

56. *Christianity Today*, 'Worship Albums of 2003'.
57. From the CD liner notes of the iWorship double CD set.
58. Michael Coleman, President, Integrity Media, *Glory to Glory*, April 2003.
59. From the CD liner notes of the iWorship double CD set.
60. *Life* magazine, 28 June 1968.
61. James L. Snyder, comp., *Tozer on Worship and Entertainment*.
62. As above.
63. *Christianity Today*, 'Don't Knock Rock', 19 Aug. 2002.
64. *www.christianity.ca*/entertainment/books, March 2005. This was actually a review of Christian comic books but the principle remains clear.
65. Review of the Worship Together Live 2001 CD on worshipmusic.com
66. Any Christian musician listed here who would like to publicly renounce these influences is welcome to contact the publisher of this book in writing and we will make every effort to reflect this in any future editions.
67. *60 Minutes*, CBS News, 8 Dec. 2004.
68. *National Arts Review*, 5 April 2003.
69. Interview on wisemenpromotions.com, 21 Feb. 2005.
70. *Renown* magazine, 13 Sept. 2002.
71. *Renown* magazine, 2001.
72. As above.
73. Review of the Worship Together Live 2001 CD on worshipmusic.com
74. Review of the CD *Redemption*, from Survivor.co.uk
75. *Renown* magazine, 10 June 2004.

Chapter 10

1. From the gospel song 'I have decided to follow Jesus'. The author of the lyrics is unknown but legend attributes it to an Indian prince who gave up his kingdom to follow Christ.
2. J. Calvin, *Institutes*, Vol. 2.
3. Tozer, *Born after Midnight*.
4. *Matthew Henry's Commentary*.
5. W. Burkitt, *Notes on the New Testament*.
6. A. Barnes, *New Testament Commentary*.
7. K. Green, *Music of Missions*.
8. *Good Morning America*, 2 Feb. 2006.

9. Pastors.com web site.
10. *The Nassau Weekly,* 10 Nov. 2005.
11. *Thread,* Nov. 2005.
12. Chris Tomlin, sixsteprecords/Sparrow.
13. G. Santayana, *The Life of Reason,* Vol.1.
14. W. Freel, *Survival.*

Chapter 11
1. Eighteenth-century British preacher F. W. Robertson, *Draper's Book of Quotations for the Christian World.*
2. Brian Edwards, *Nothing but the Truth,* Evangelical Press.
3. As above.
4. Geoffrey Wilson, *Romans.*
5. Bassett, *God's Way.*
6. *Evangelical Times,* May 1979.
7. As above.

Why I left the Contemporary Christian Music Movement

'Dan Lucarini invites us to wrestle with a major issue perplexing churches all over the world today. His diagnosis and prescription is going to anger some, not because of his tone (he is charitable, but firm throughout) but because he is touching a very sensitive nerve in the modern evangelical church. The matters he raises are all real and the cautions he brings are surely timely. If you consider yourself "traditional" in your approach to worship and music in the church, Lucarini provides you with an outline of almost all the key matters that must be addressed in the church's assessment of the usefulness of new musical forms. If you consider yourself "contemporary" in your perspective on worship, Lucarini raises the questions that you need to provide a sound biblical answer to before committing the church to a new direction in its corporate praise.'

J. Ligon Duncan III, PhD
Minister, First Presbyterian Church, Jackson, Mississippi, USA
Adjunct Professor, Reformed Theological Seminary
Council, Alliance of Confessing Evangelicals

'The author's honest sharing of his own spiritual and musical journey prepares the way for his assessment of what he sees to be a major problem in today's church... Lucarini's direct and uncompromising style is harnessed to a gracious spirit concerned with nothing else but God's glory. This is nowhere more evident than in his warm and wise treatment of the subject of worship and ministry.'

John Blanchard

Evangelical Press, 144 pages, ISBN 0-85234-517-8
ISBN-13 978-0-85234-517-7